GHOSTED

CREATED BY
JOSHUA WILLIAMSON

GHOSTED

JOSHUA WILLIAMSON
WRITER

GORAN SUDZUKA
ARTIST

MIROSLAV MRVA
COLORIST

RUS WOOTON
LETTERER

SEAN MACKIEWICZ
EDITOR

SERIES COVERS BY
SEAN PHILLIPS

COLLECTION COVER BY
MATTEO SCALERA

IMAGE COMICS, INC.
Robert Kirkman - Chief Operating Officer
Erik Larsen - Chief Financial Officer
Todd McFarlane - President
Marc Silvestri - Chief Executive Officer
Jim Valentino - Vice-President

Eric Stephenson - Publisher
Ron Richards - Director of Business Development
Jennifer de Guzman - Director of Trade Book Sales
Kat Salazar - PR & Marketing Coordinator
Jeremy Sullivan - Digital Marketing Coordinator
Jamie Parreno - Online Marketing Coordinator
Emilio Bautista - Sales Assistant
Branwyn Bigglestone - Senior Accounts Manager
Emily Miller - Accounts Manager
Jaemie Dudas - Administrative Assistant
Tyler Shainline - Events Coordinator
David Brothers - Content Manager
Jonathan Chan - Production Manager
Drew Gill - Art Director
Meredith Wallace - Print Manager
Monica Garcia - Senior Production Artist
Vincent Kukua - Production Artist
Jenna Savage - Production Artist
Addison Duke - Production Artist
IMAGECOMICS.COM

SKYBOUND

For SKYBOUND ENTERTAINMENT

Robert Kirkman - CEO
J.J. Didde - President
Sean Mackiewicz - Editorial Director
Shawn Kirkham - Director of Business Development
Brian Huntington - Online Editorial Director
Helen Leigh - Office Manager
Lizzy Iverson - Administrative Assistant

For international rights inquiries,
please contact: foreign@skybound.com
WWW.SKYBOUND.COM

CHAPTER ONE

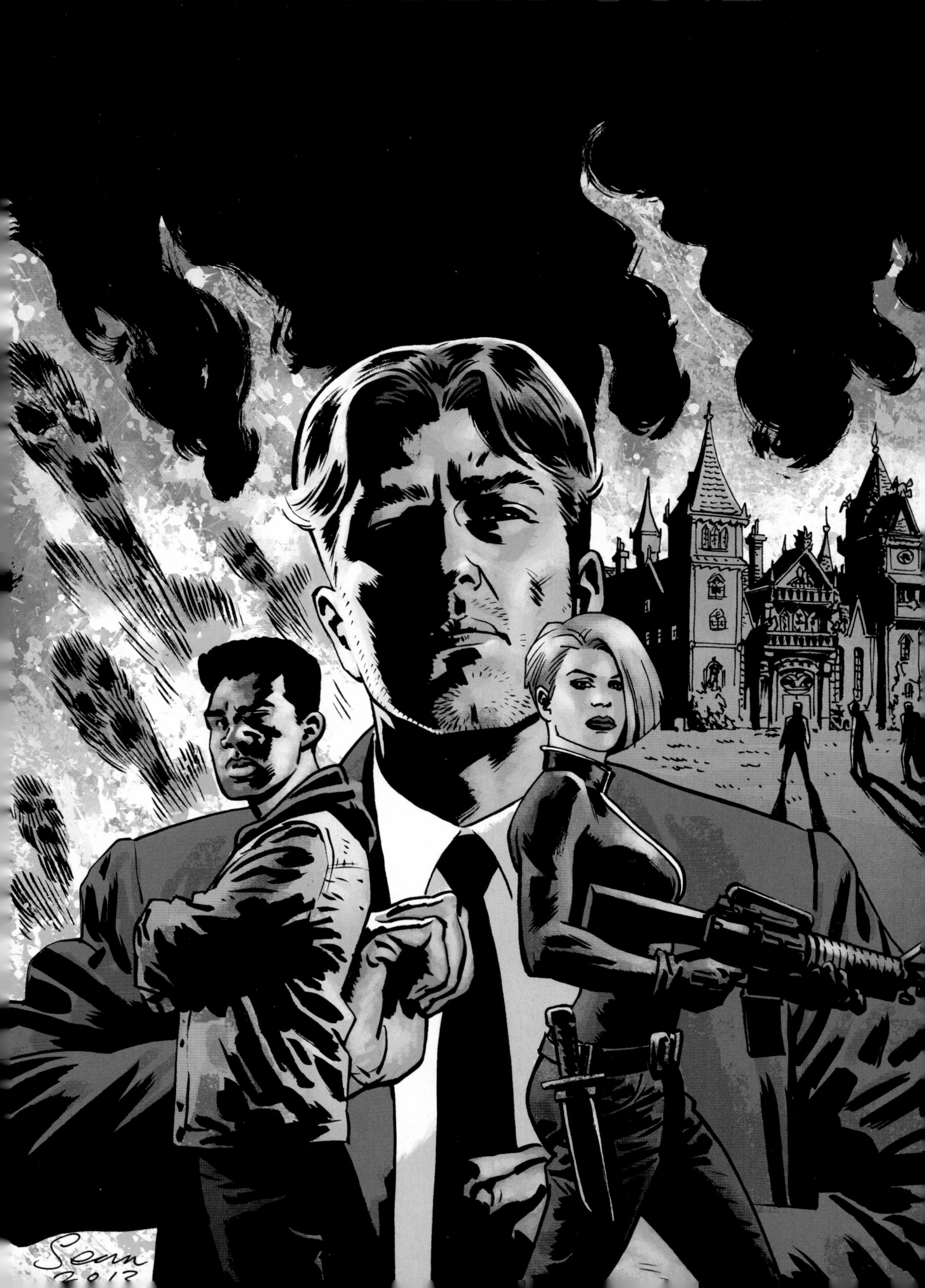

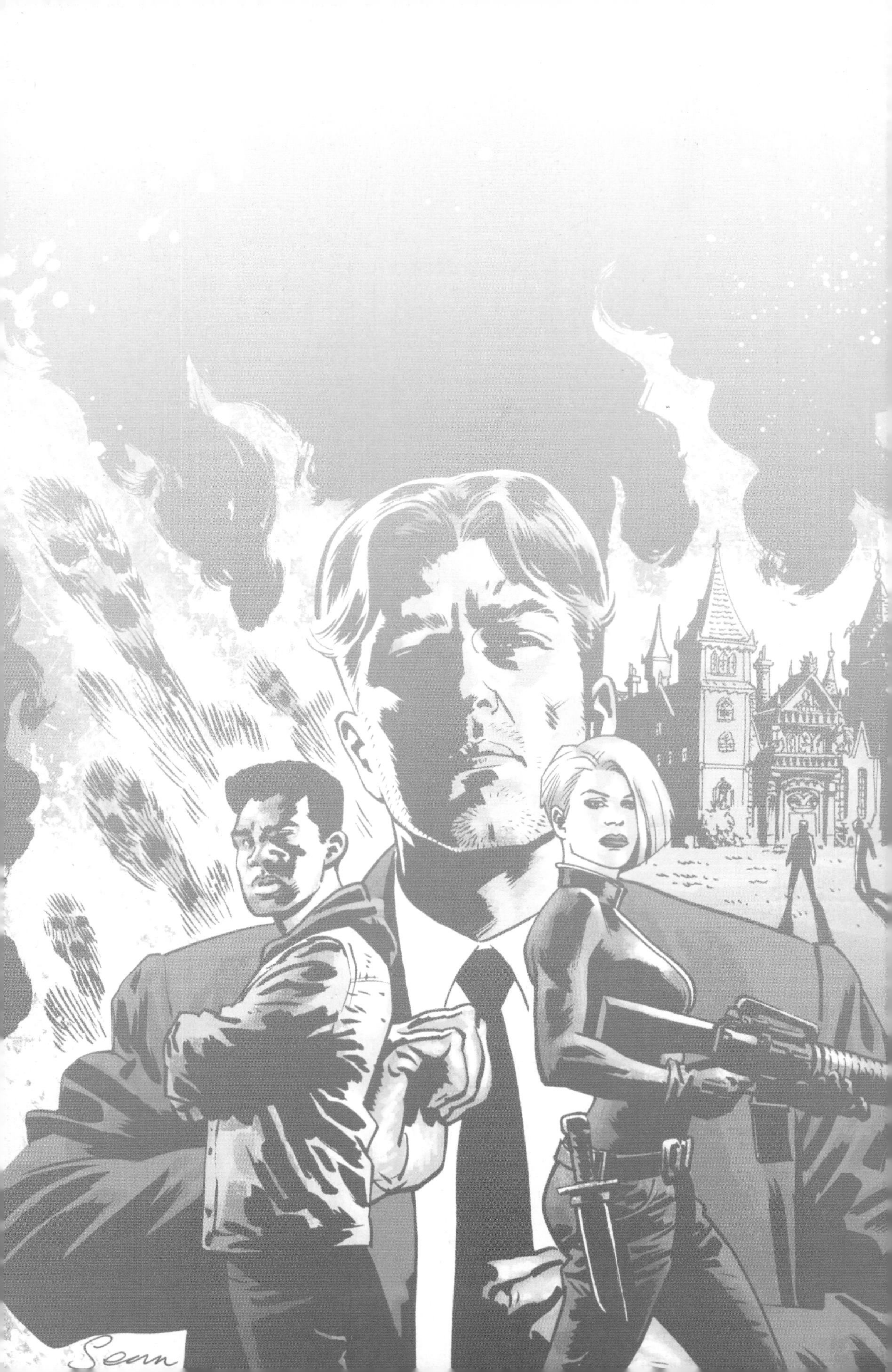

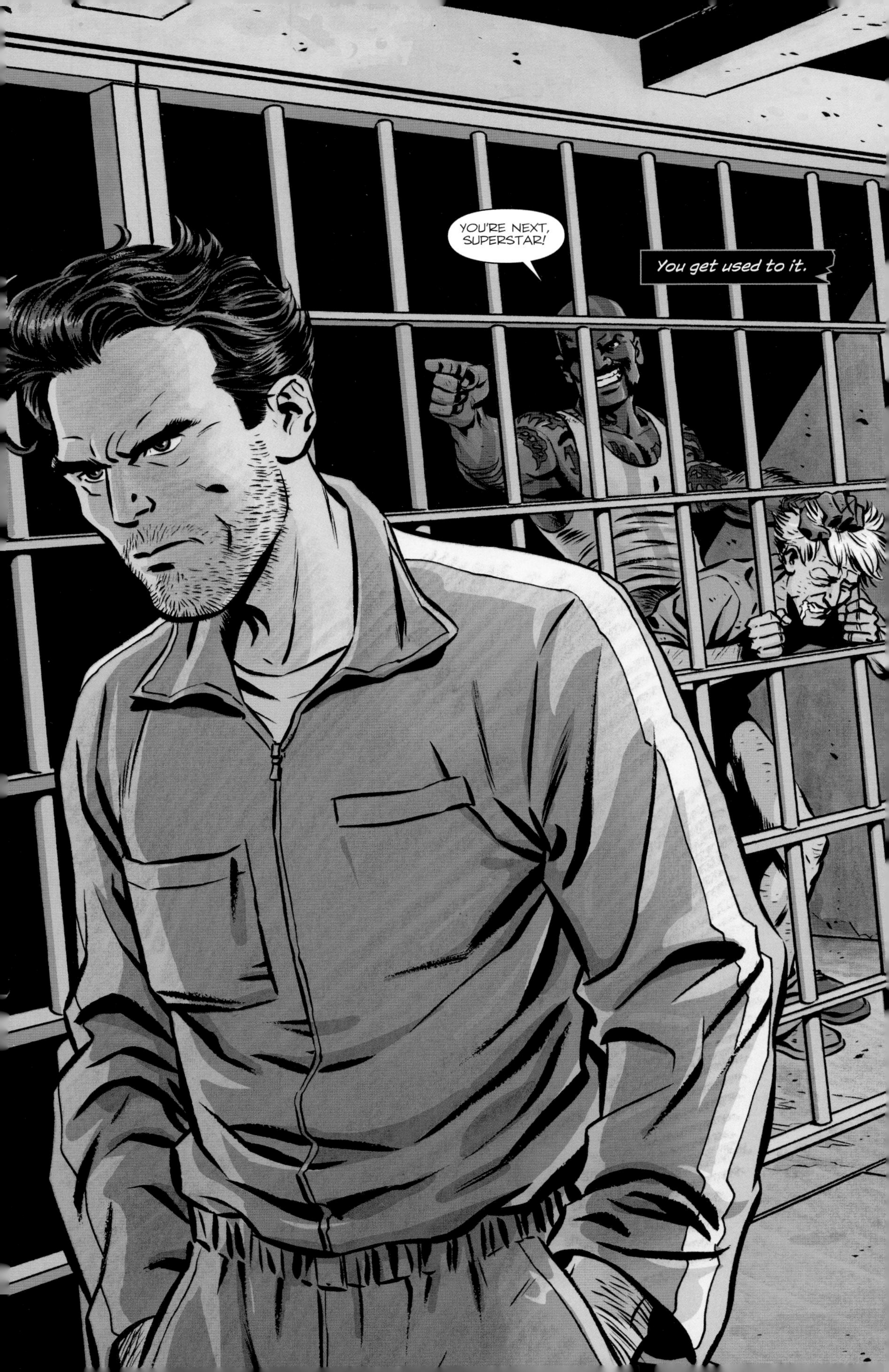
YOU'RE NEXT, SUPERSTAR!
You get used to it.

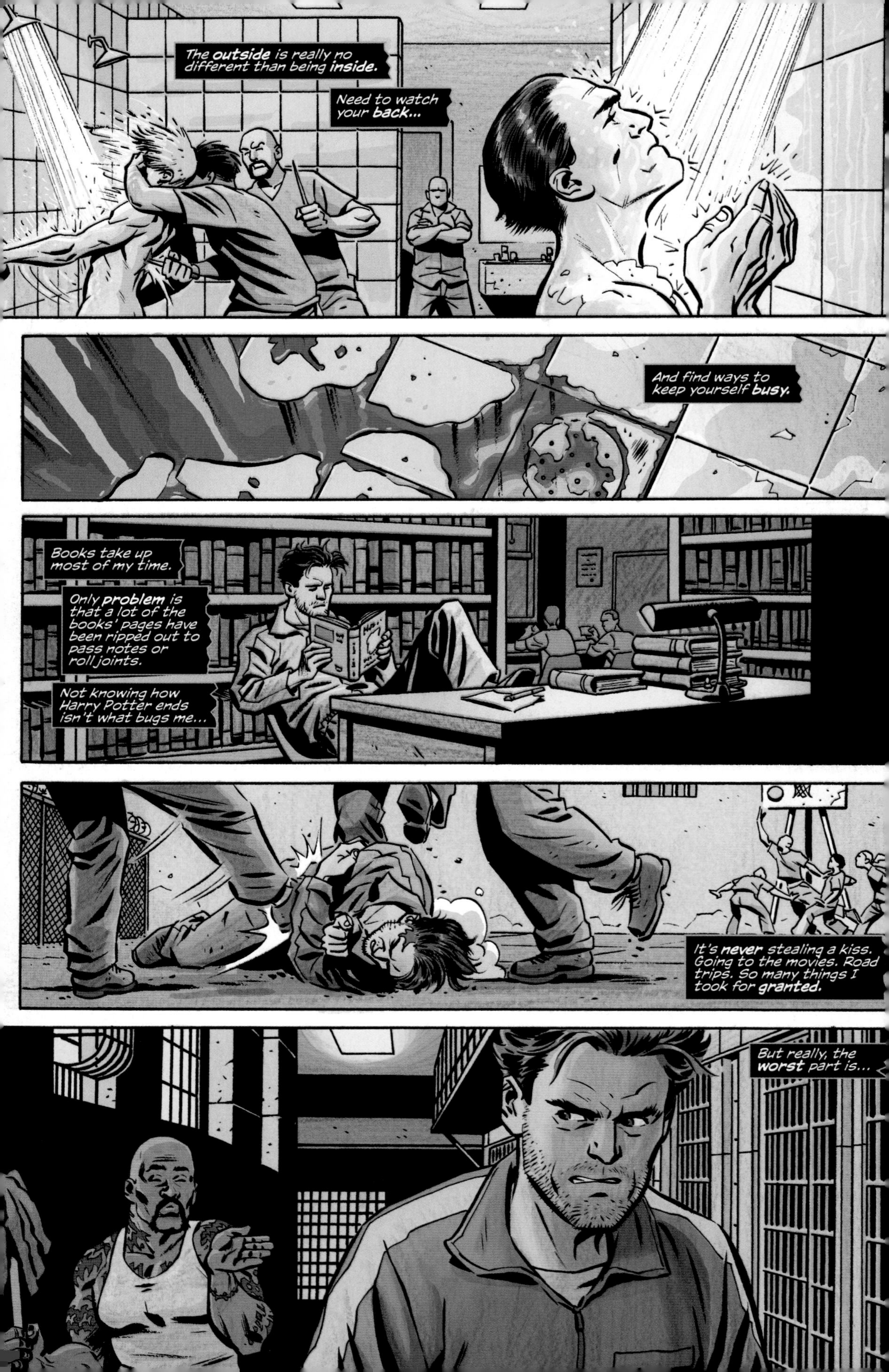
The outside is really no different than being inside.
Need to watch your back...
And find ways to keep yourself busy.
Books take up most of my time.
Only problem is that a lot of the books' pages have been ripped out to pass notes or roll joints.
Not knowing how Harry Potter ends isn't what bugs me...
It's never stealing a kiss. Going to the movies. Road trips. So many things I took for granted.
But really, the worst part is...

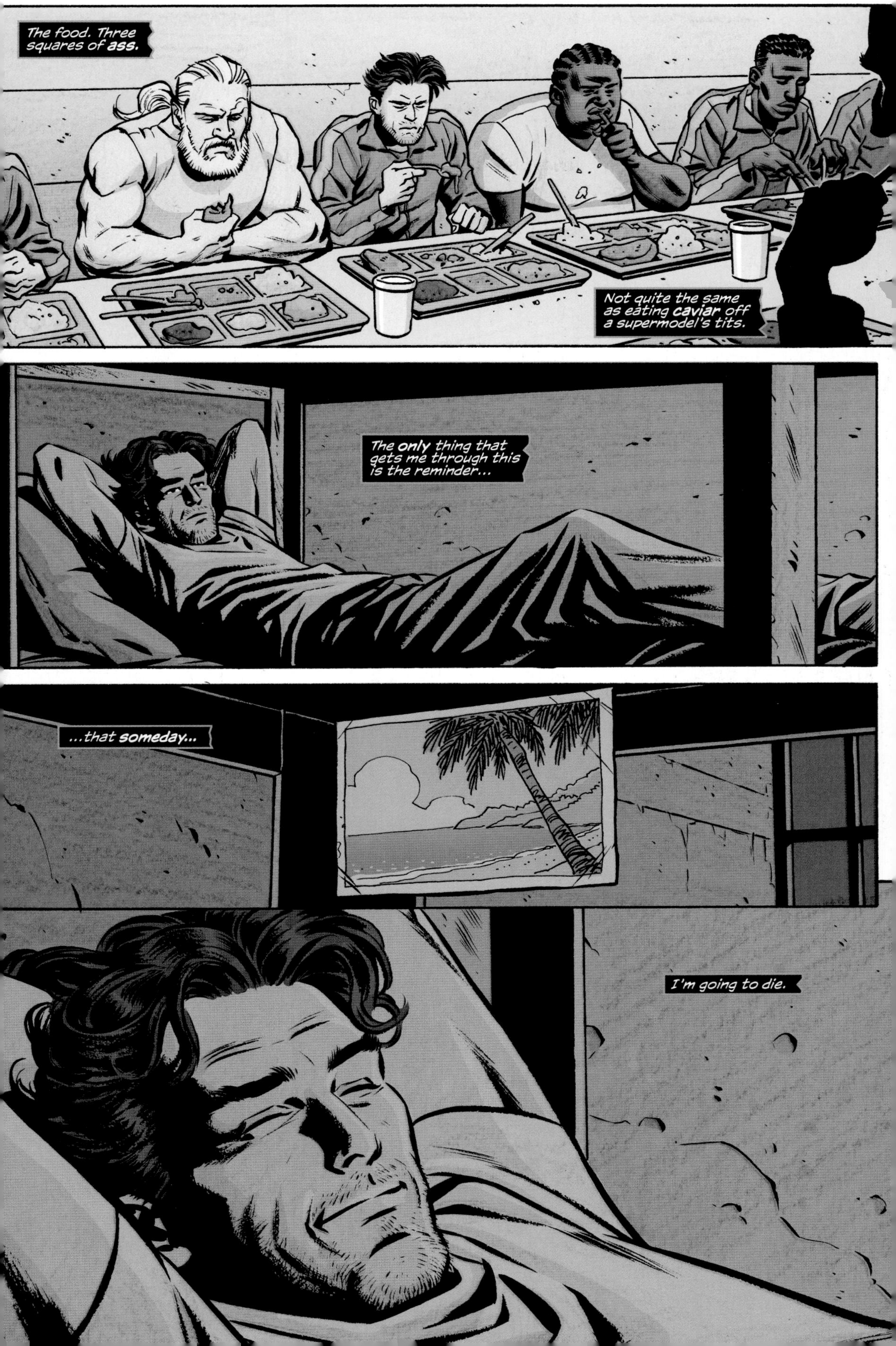
The food. Three squares of ass.
Not quite the same as eating caviar off a supermodel's tits.
The only thing that gets me through this is the reminder...
...that someday...
I'm going to die.

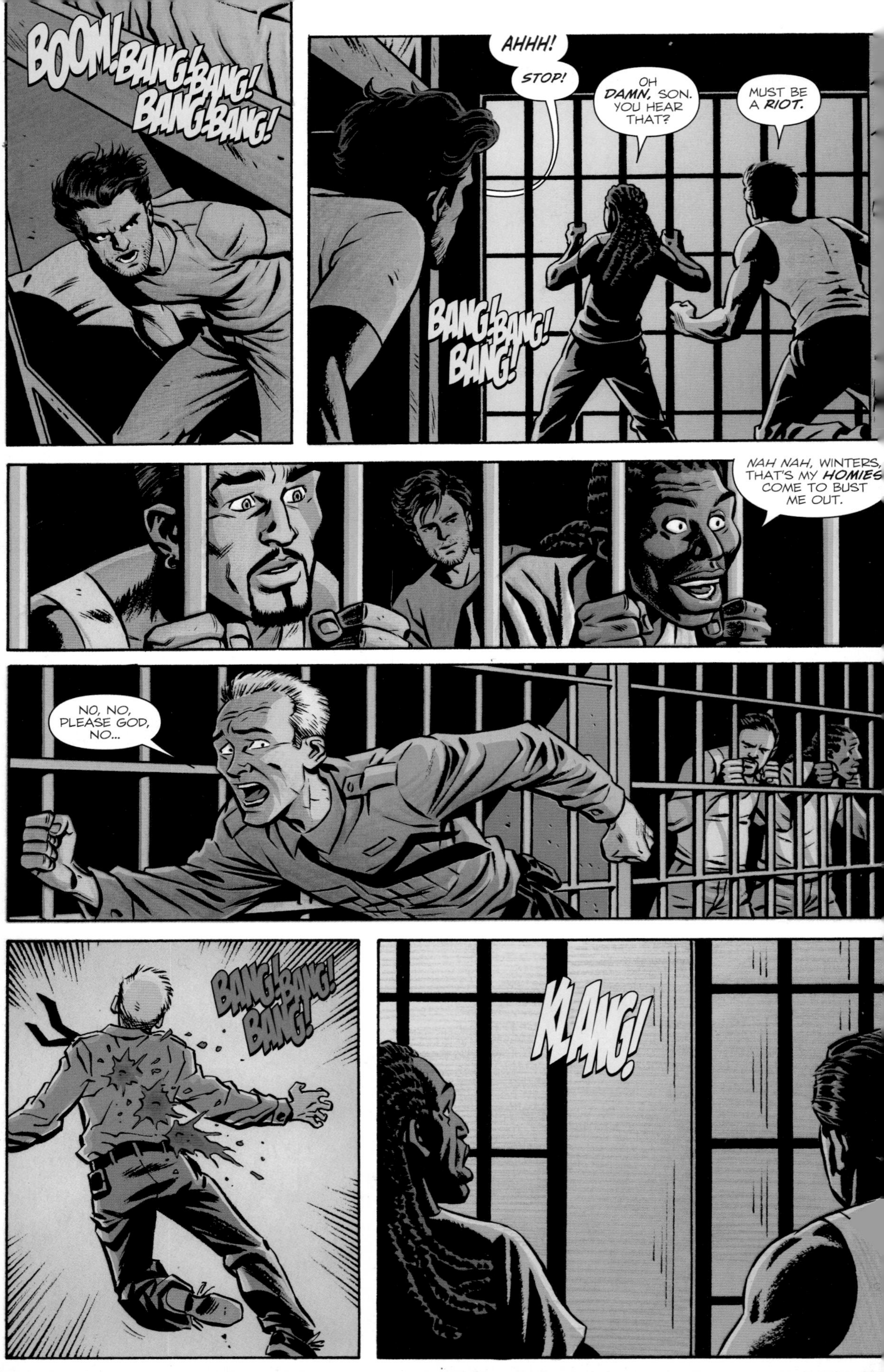
BOOM! BANG-BANG! BANG-BANG!
AHHH!
STOP!
OH DAMN, SON. YOU HEAR THAT?
MUST BE A RIOT.
BANG-BANG! BANG!
NAH NAH, WINTERS, THAT'S MY HOMIES COME TO BUST ME OUT.
NO, NO, PLEASE GOD, NO...
BANG-BANG! BANG!
KLANG!

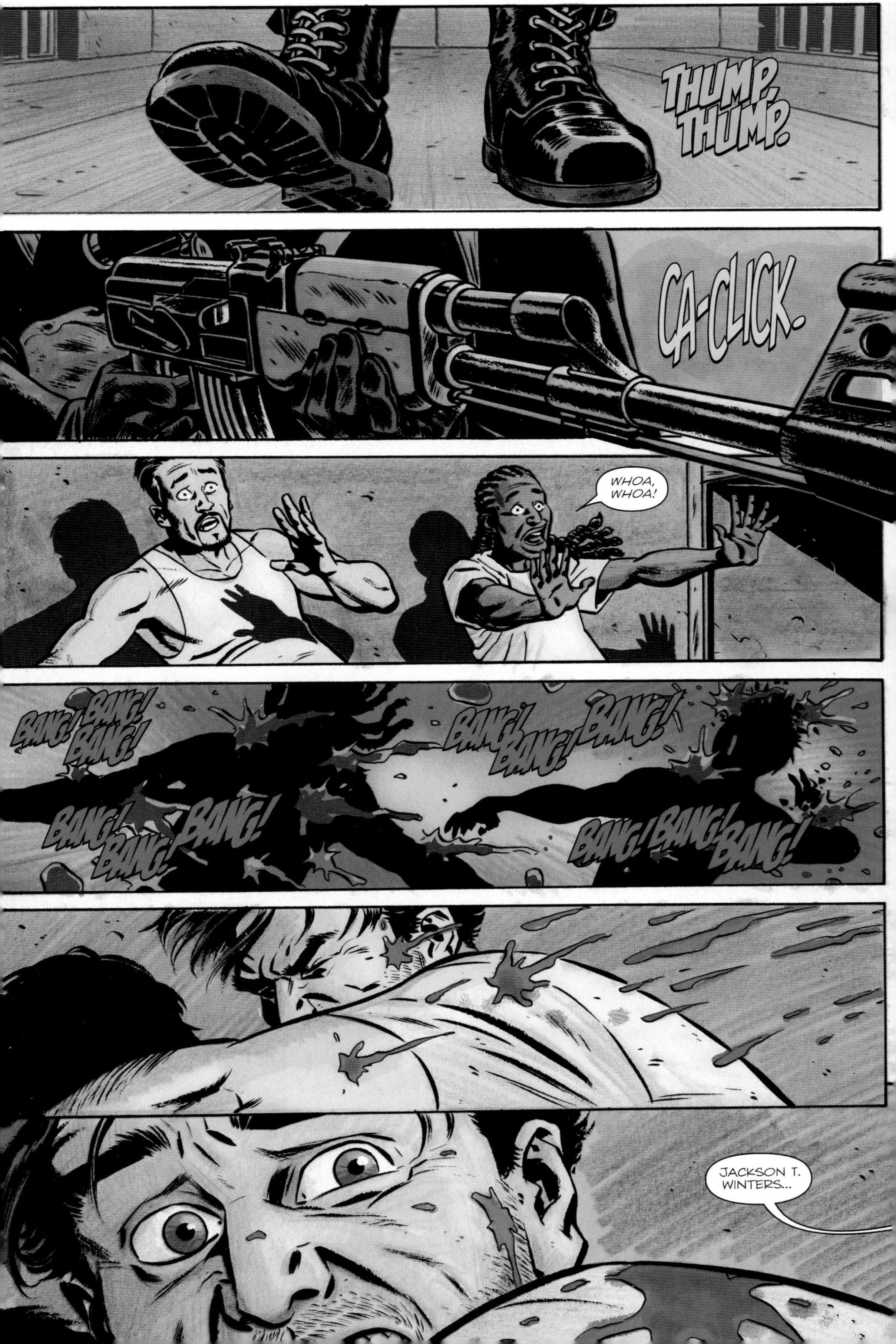
THUMP, THUMP.
CA-CLICK.
WHOA, WHOA!
BANG! BANG! BANG!
BANG! BANG! BANG!
BANG! BANG! BANG!
BANG! BANG! BANG!
JACKSON T. WINTERS...

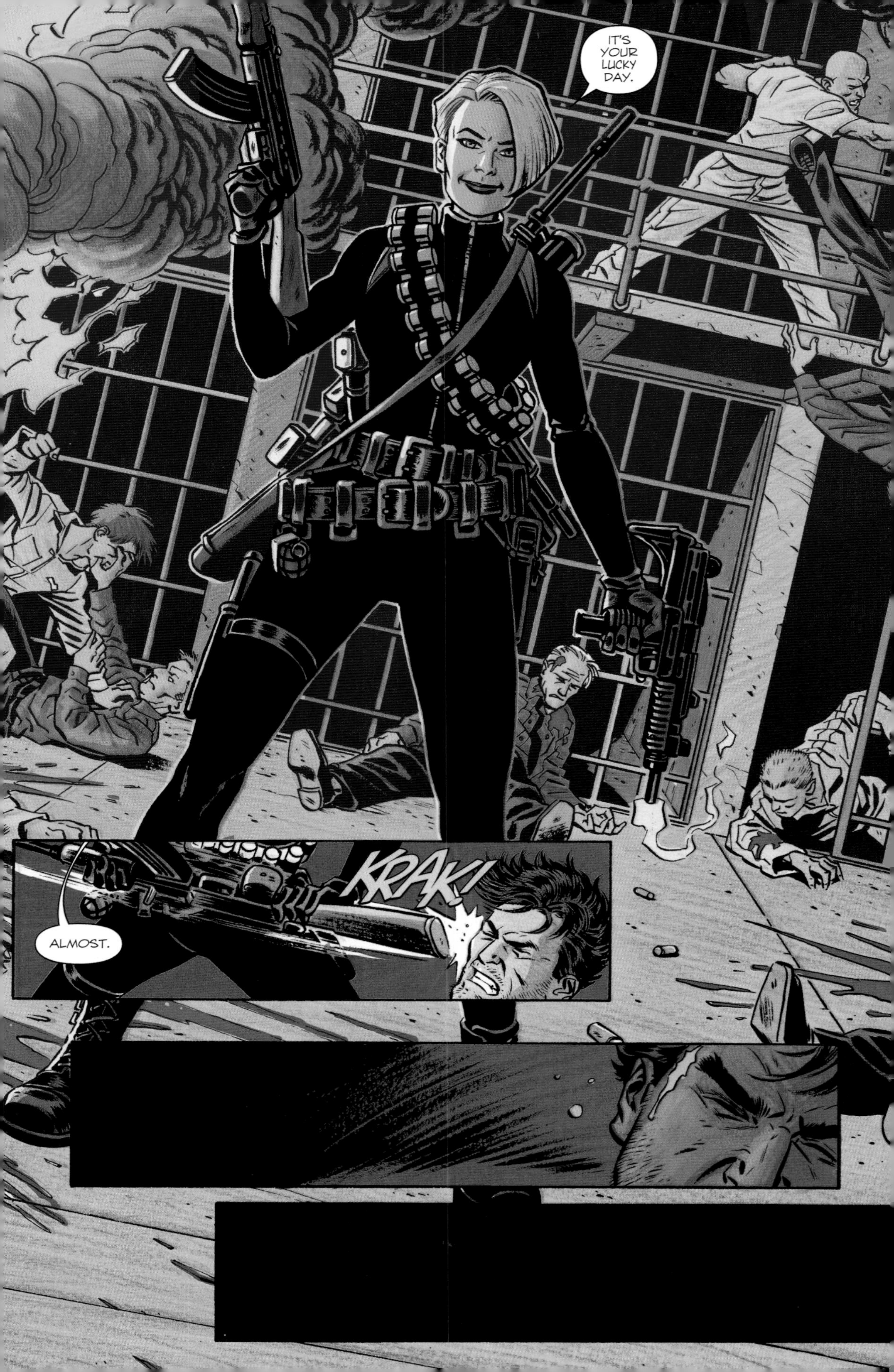
IT'S YOUR LUCKY DAY.
KRAK!
ALMOST.

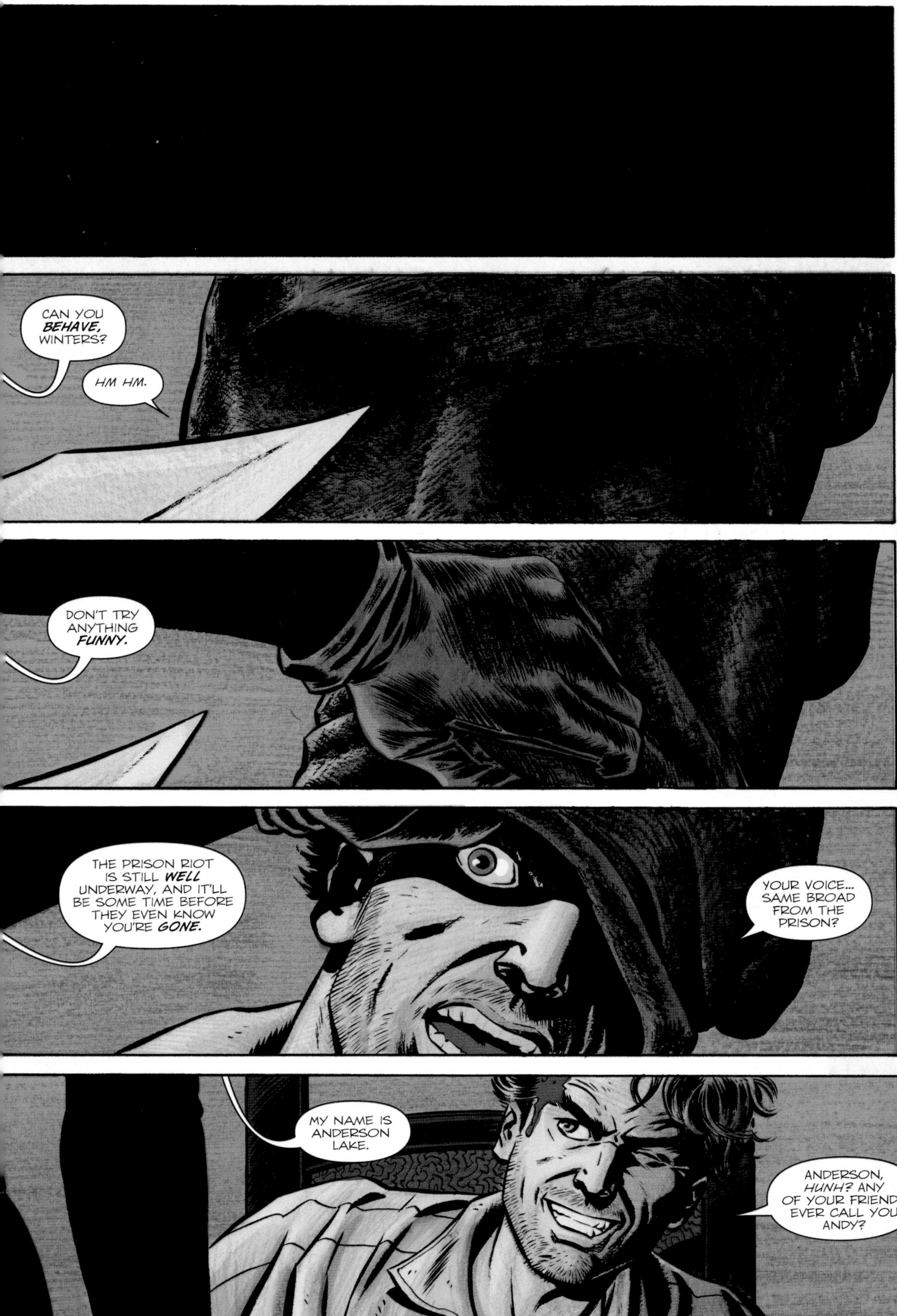
CAN YOU BEHAVE, WINTERS?
HM HM.
DON'T TRY ANYTHING FUNNY.
THE PRISON RIOT IS STILL WELL UNDERWAY, AND IT'LL BE SOME TIME BEFORE THEY EVEN KNOW YOU'RE GONE.
YOUR VOICE... SAME BROAD FROM THE PRISON?
MY NAME IS ANDERSON LAKE.
ANDERSON, HUNH? ANY OF YOUR FRIENDS EVER CALL YOU ANDY?

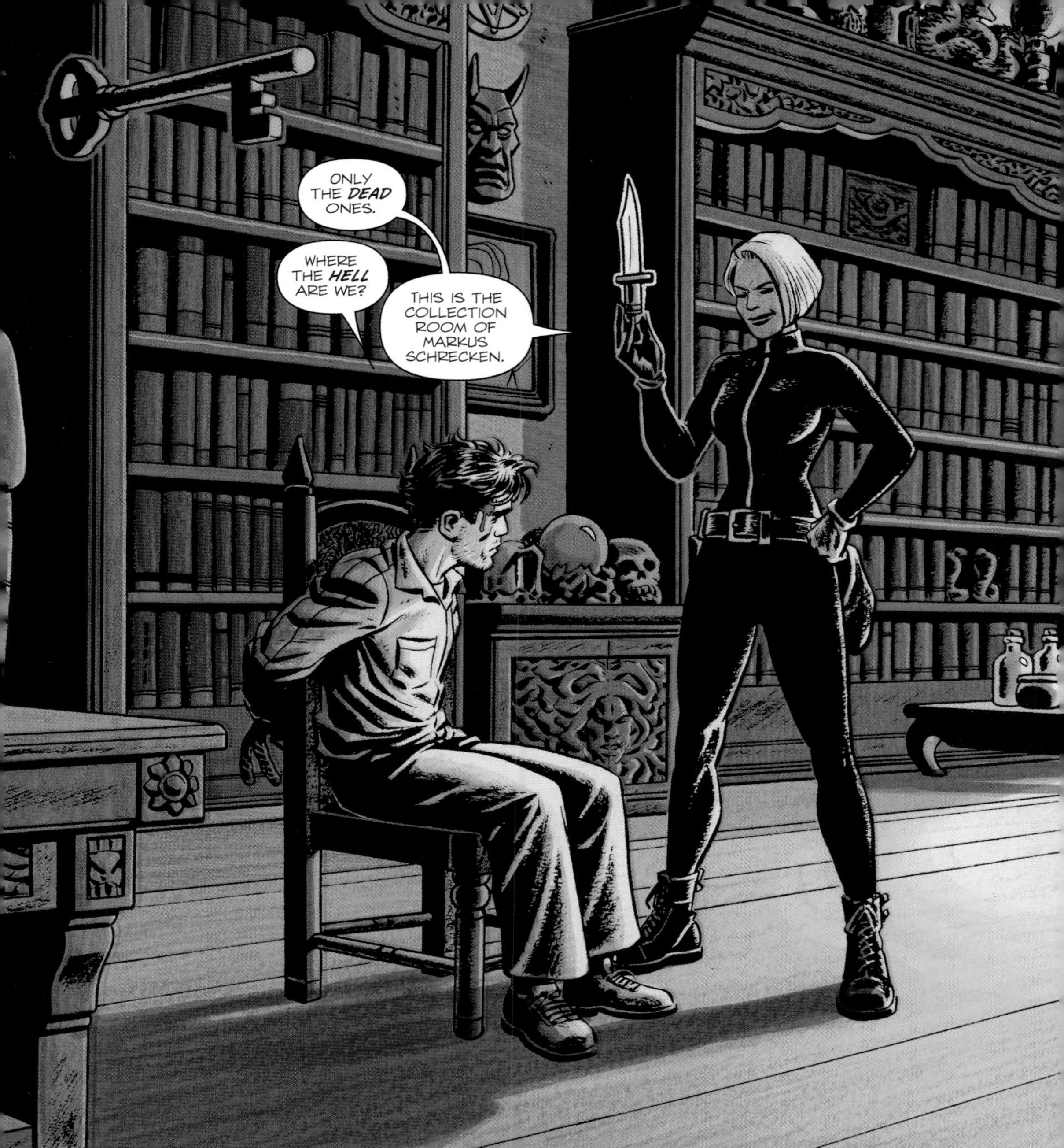
WHERE THE *HELL* ARE WE?
ONLY THE *DEAD* ONES.
THIS IS THE COLLECTION ROOM OF MARKUS SCHRECKEN.

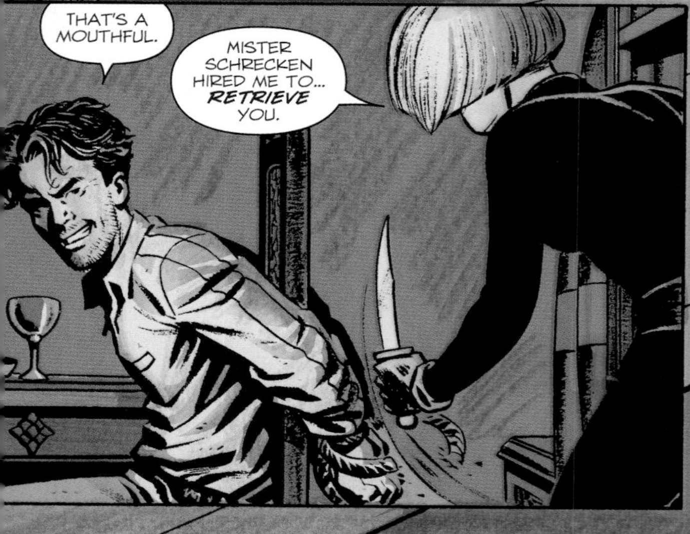
THAT'S A MOUTHFUL.
MISTER SCHRECKEN HIRED ME TO... ***RETRIEVE*** YOU.

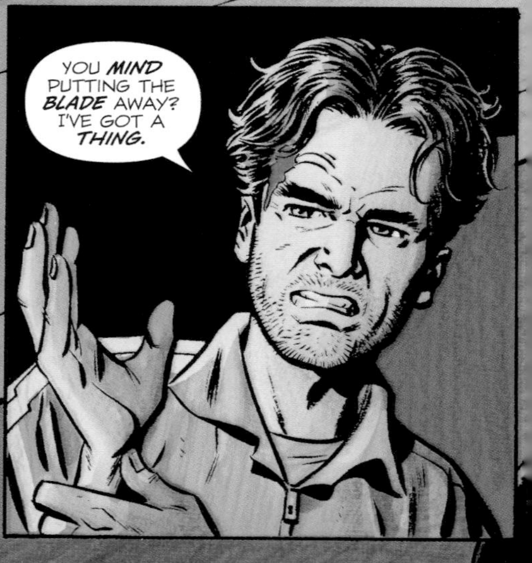
YOU ***MIND*** PUTTING THE ***BLADE*** AWAY? I'VE GOT A ***THING.***

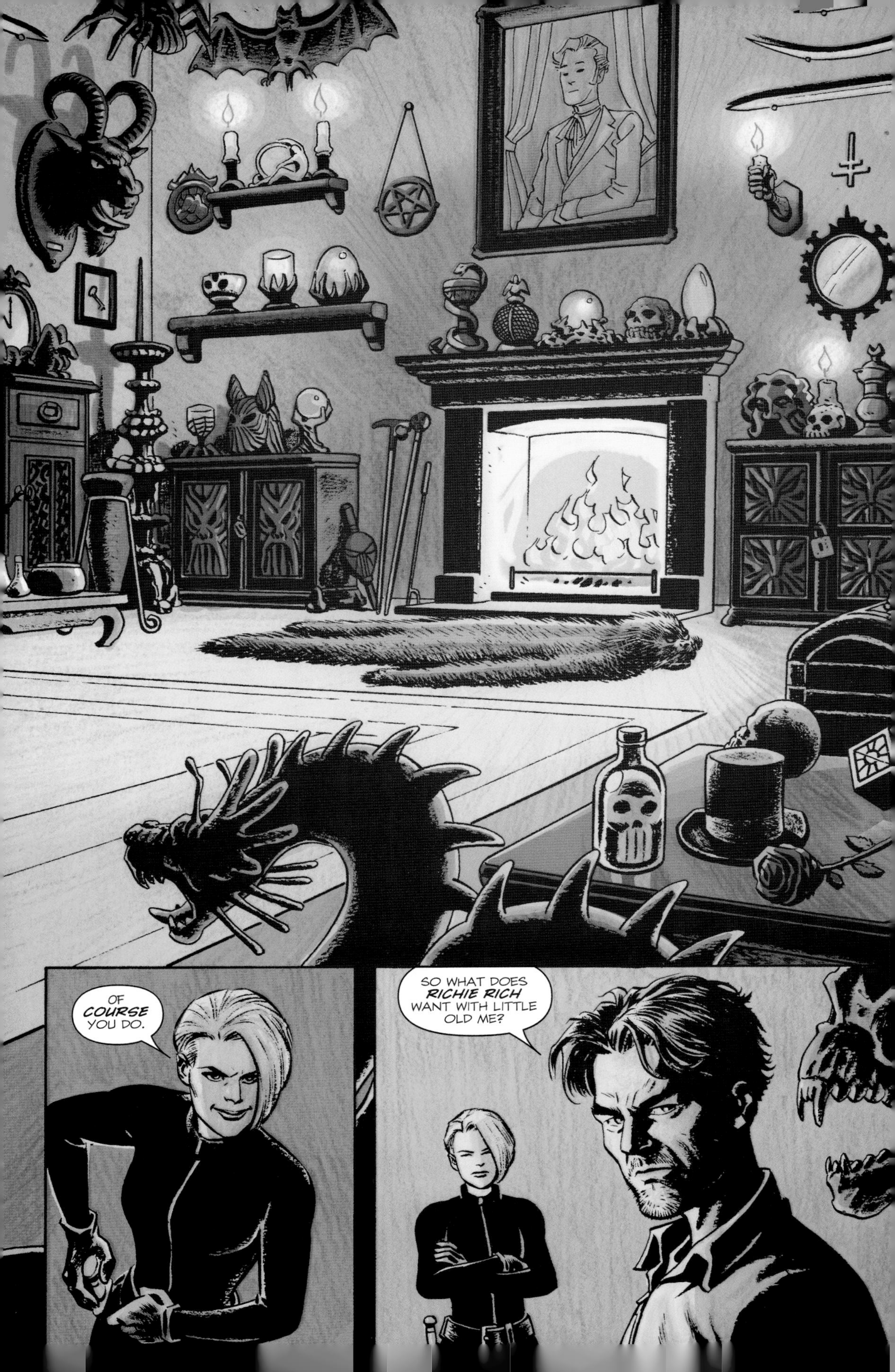
OF COURSE YOU DO.
SO WHAT DOES RICHIE RICH WANT WITH LITTLE OLD ME?

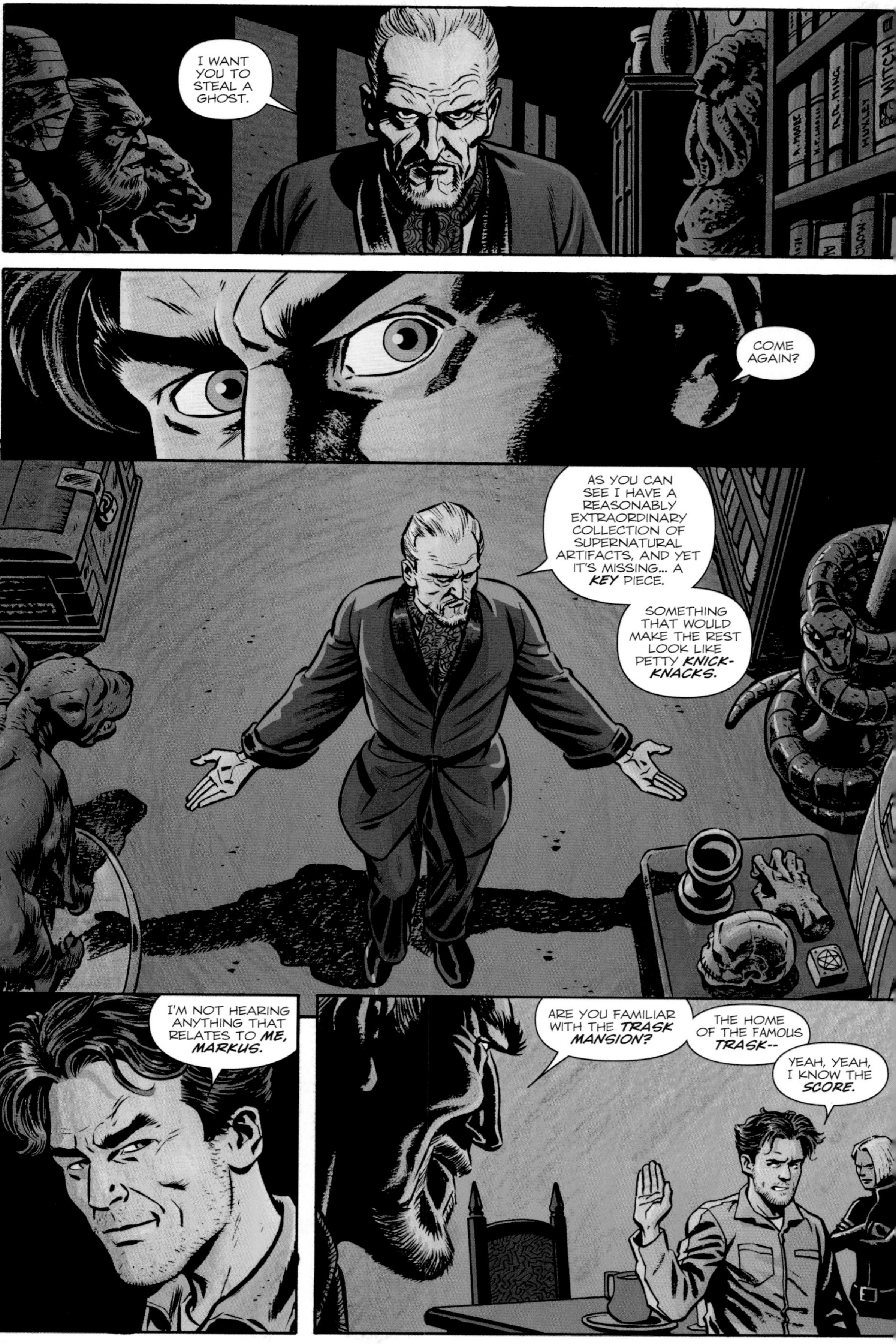
I WANT YOU TO STEAL A GHOST.
COME AGAIN?
AS YOU CAN SEE I HAVE A REASONABLY EXTRAORDINARY COLLECTION OF SUPERNATURAL ARTIFACTS, AND YET IT'S MISSING... A ***KEY*** PIECE.
SOMETHING THAT WOULD MAKE THE REST LOOK LIKE PETTY ***KNICK-KNACKS.***
I'M NOT HEARING ANYTHING THAT RELATES TO ***ME, MARKUS.***
ARE YOU FAMILIAR WITH THE ***TRASK MANSION?***
THE HOME OF THE FAMOUS ***TRASK--***
YEAH, YEAH, I KNOW THE ***SCORE.***

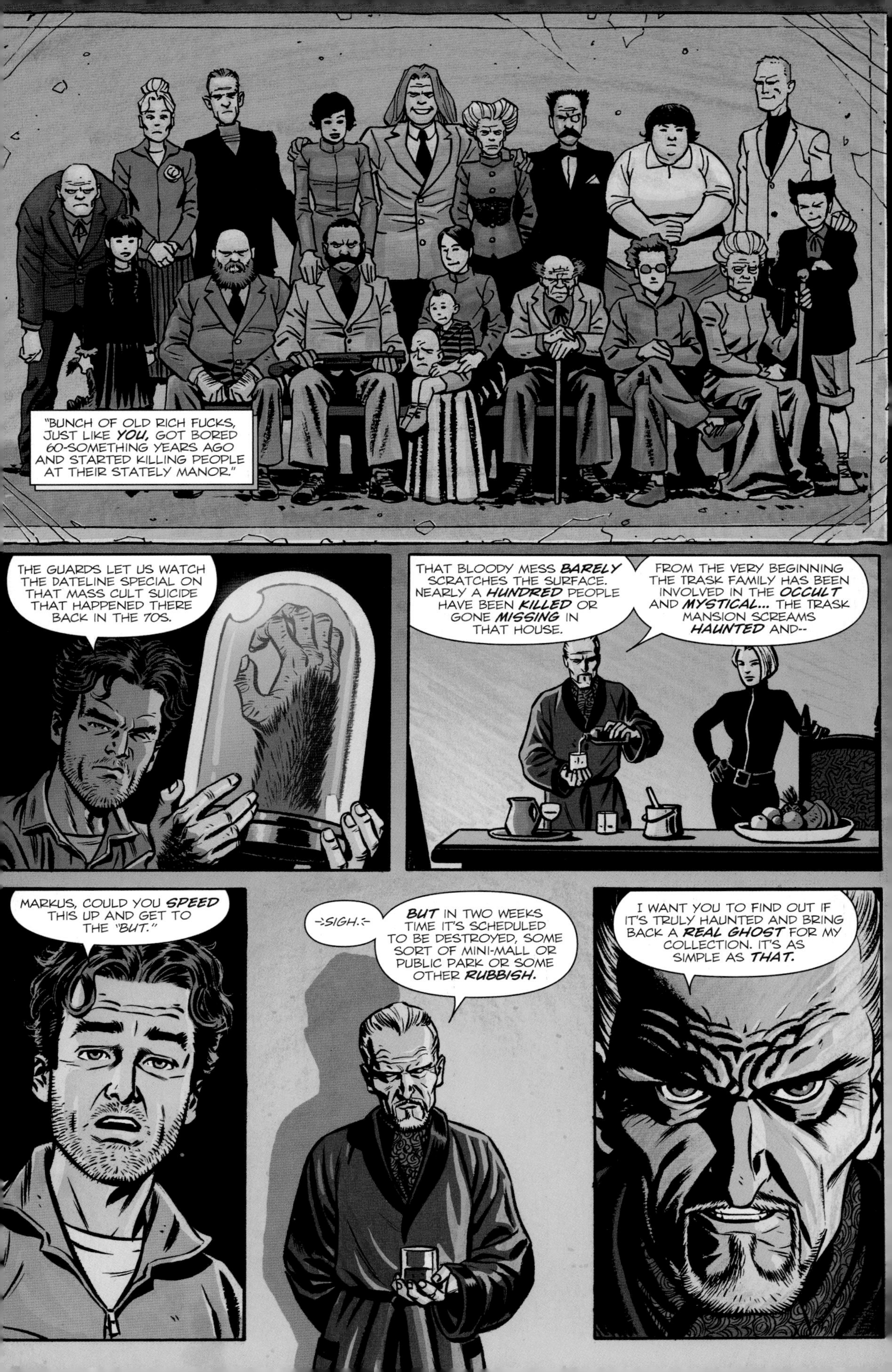
"BUNCH OF OLD RICH FUCKS, JUST LIKE YOU, GOT BORED 60-SOMETHING YEARS AGO AND STARTED KILLING PEOPLE AT THEIR STATELY MANOR."
THE GUARDS LET US WATCH THE DATELINE SPECIAL ON THAT MASS CULT SUICIDE THAT HAPPENED THERE BACK IN THE 70S.
THAT BLOODY MESS BARELY SCRATCHES THE SURFACE. NEARLY A HUNDRED PEOPLE HAVE BEEN KILLED OR GONE MISSING IN THAT HOUSE.
FROM THE VERY BEGINNING THE TRASK FAMILY HAS BEEN INVOLVED IN THE OCCULT AND MYSTICAL... THE TRASK MANSION SCREAMS HAUNTED AND--
MARKUS, COULD YOU SPEED THIS UP AND GET TO THE "BUT."
-SIGH.-
BUT IN TWO WEEKS TIME IT'S SCHEDULED TO BE DESTROYED, SOME SORT OF MINI-MALL OR PUBLIC PARK OR SOME OTHER RUBBISH.
I WANT YOU TO FIND OUT IF IT'S TRULY HAUNTED AND BRING BACK A REAL GHOST FOR MY COLLECTION. IT'S AS SIMPLE AS THAT.

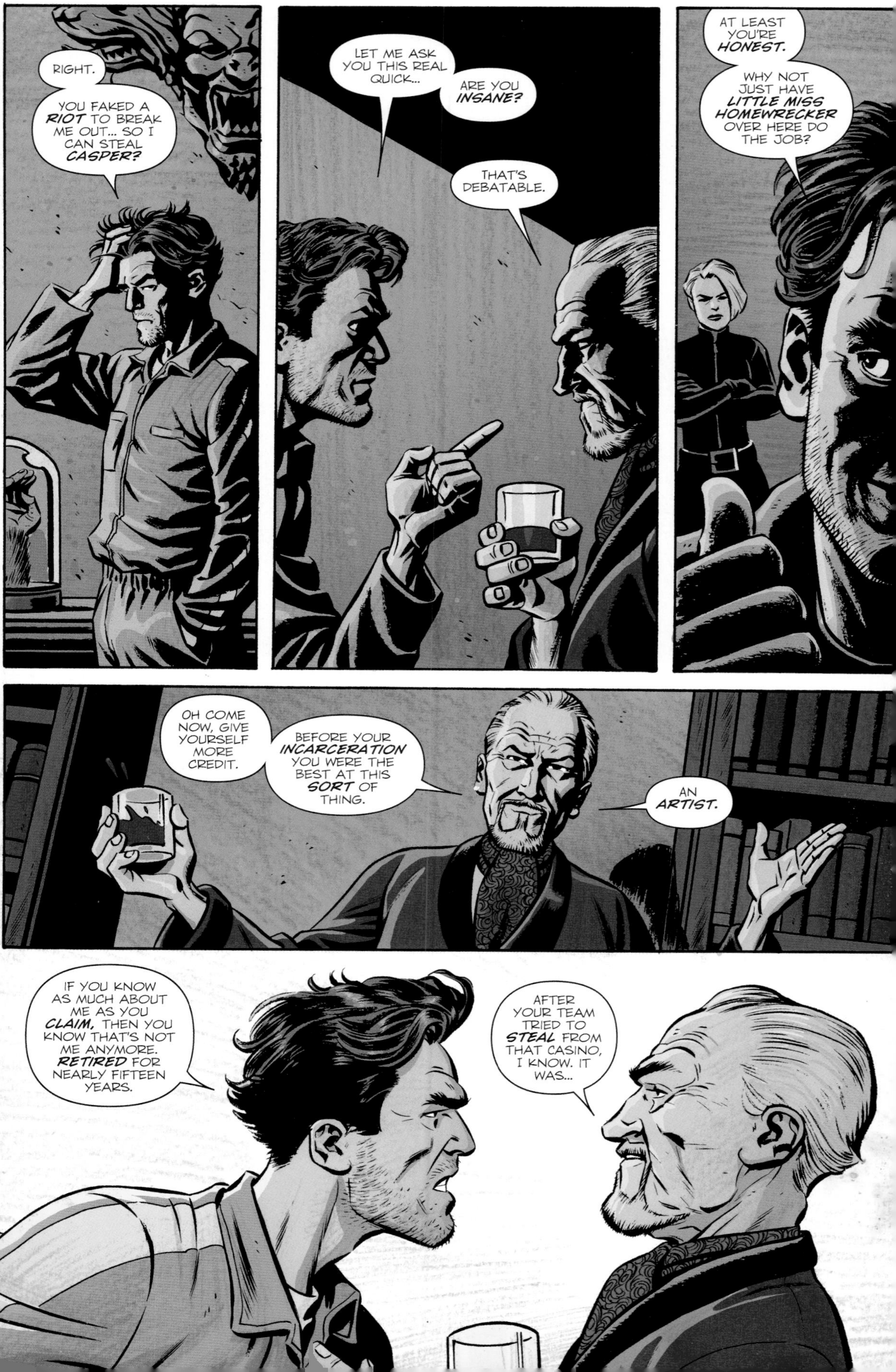
RIGHT.
YOU FAKED A RIOT TO BREAK ME OUT... SO I CAN STEAL CASPER?
LET ME ASK YOU THIS REAL QUICK...
ARE YOU INSANE?
THAT'S DEBATABLE.
AT LEAST YOU'RE HONEST.
WHY NOT JUST HAVE LITTLE MISS HOMEWRECKER OVER HERE DO THE JOB?
OH COME NOW, GIVE YOURSELF MORE CREDIT.
BEFORE YOUR INCARCERATION YOU WERE THE BEST AT THIS SORT OF THING.
AN ARTIST.
IF YOU KNOW AS MUCH ABOUT ME AS YOU CLAIM, THEN YOU KNOW THAT'S NOT ME ANYMORE. RETIRED FOR NEARLY FIFTEEN YEARS.
AFTER YOUR TEAM TRIED TO STEAL FROM THAT CASINO, I KNOW. IT WAS...

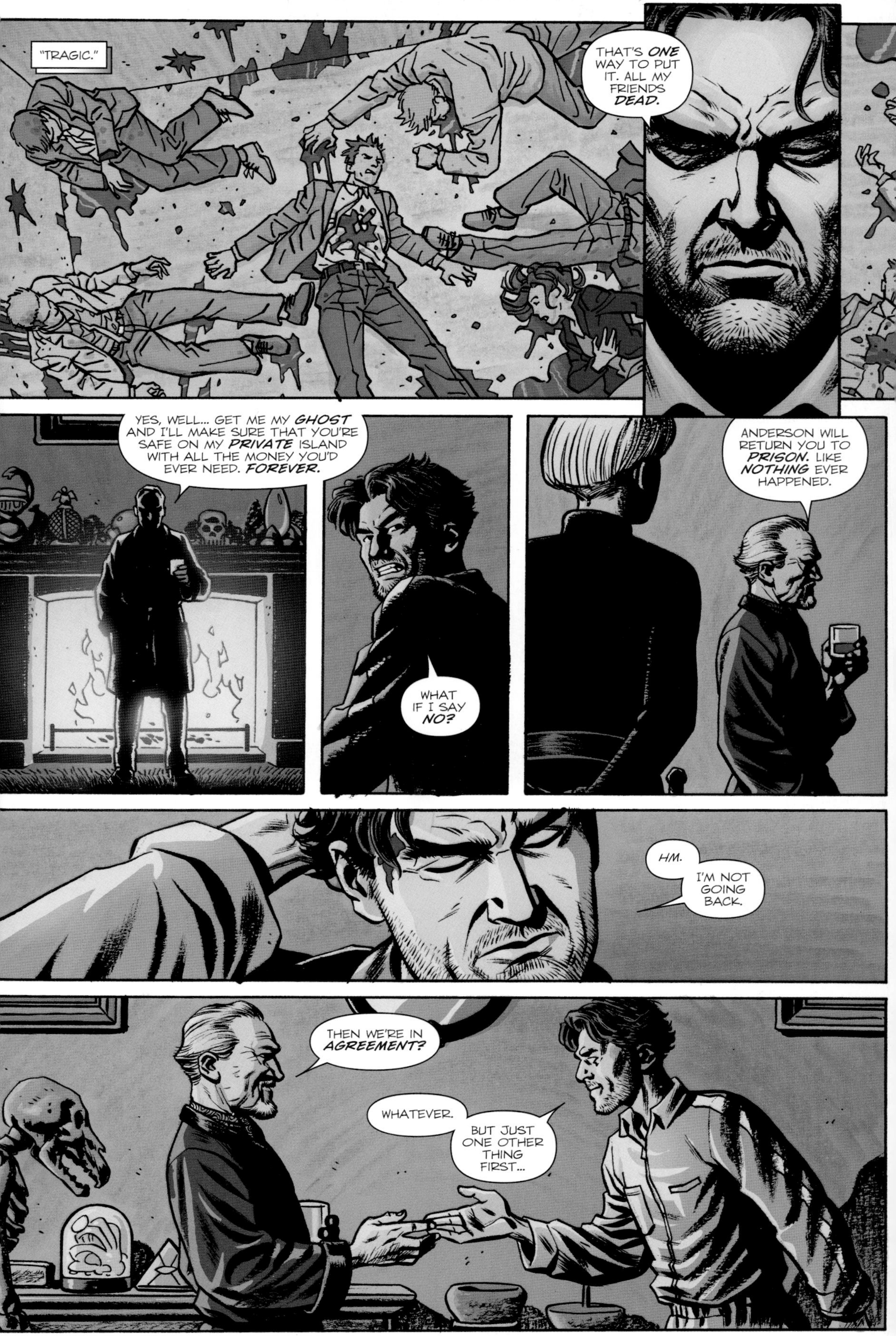
"TRAGIC."
THAT'S ONE WAY TO PUT IT. ALL MY FRIENDS DEAD.
YES, WELL... GET ME MY GHOST AND I'LL MAKE SURE THAT YOU'RE SAFE ON MY PRIVATE ISLAND WITH ALL THE MONEY YOU'D EVER NEED. FOREVER.
WHAT IF I SAY NO?
ANDERSON WILL RETURN YOU TO PRISON. LIKE NOTHING EVER HAPPENED.
HM.
I'M NOT GOING BACK.
THEN WE'RE IN AGREEMENT?
WHATEVER.
BUT JUST ONE OTHER THING FIRST...

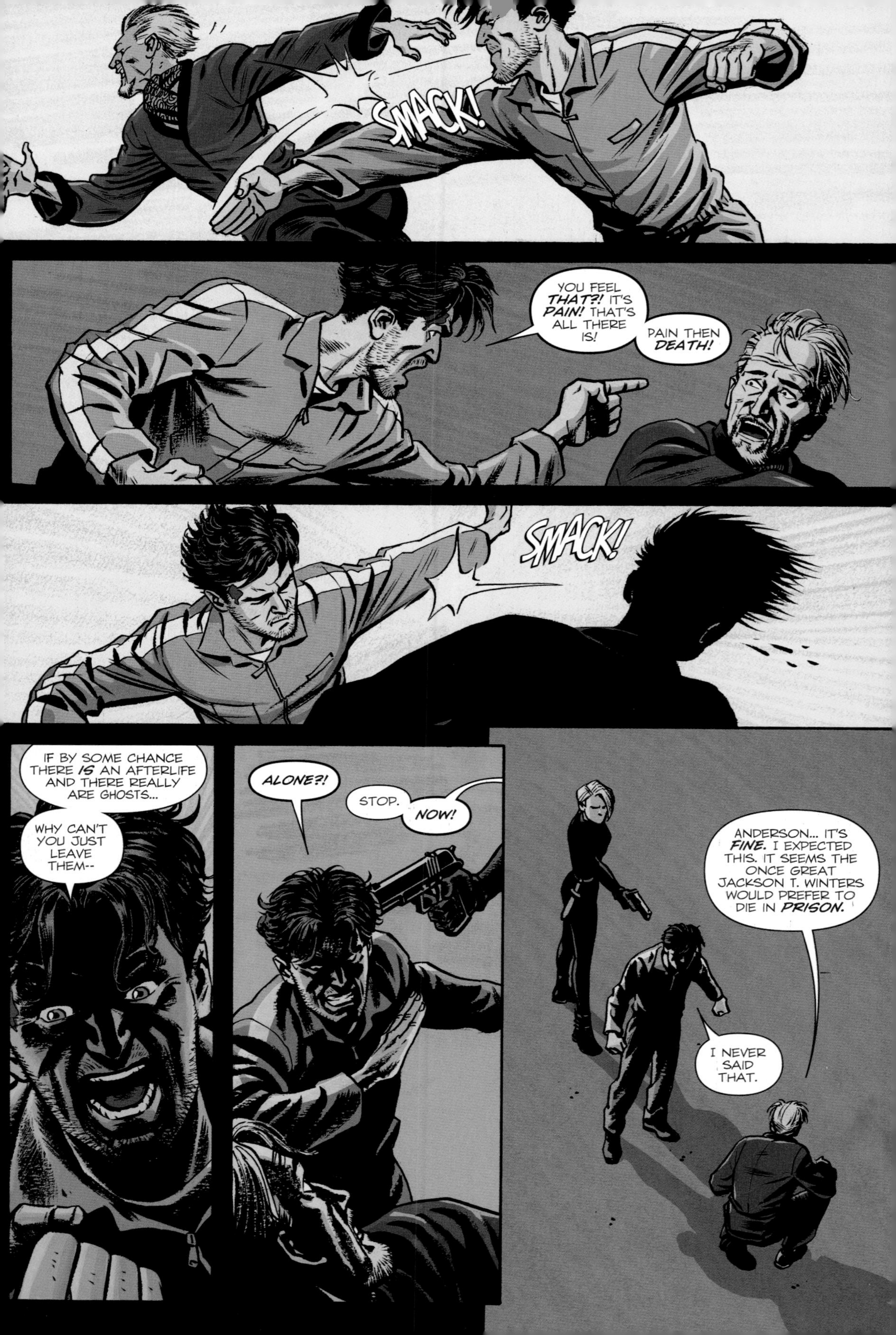
SMACK!
YOU FEEL THAT?! IT'S PAIN! THAT'S ALL THERE IS!
PAIN THEN DEATH!
SMACK!
IF BY SOME CHANCE THERE IS AN AFTERLIFE AND THERE REALLY ARE GHOSTS...
WHY CAN'T YOU JUST LEAVE THEM--
ALONE?!
STOP.
NOW!
ANDERSON... IT'S FINE. I EXPECTED THIS. IT SEEMS THE ONCE GREAT JACKSON T. WINTERS WOULD PREFER TO DIE IN PRISON.
I NEVER SAID THAT.

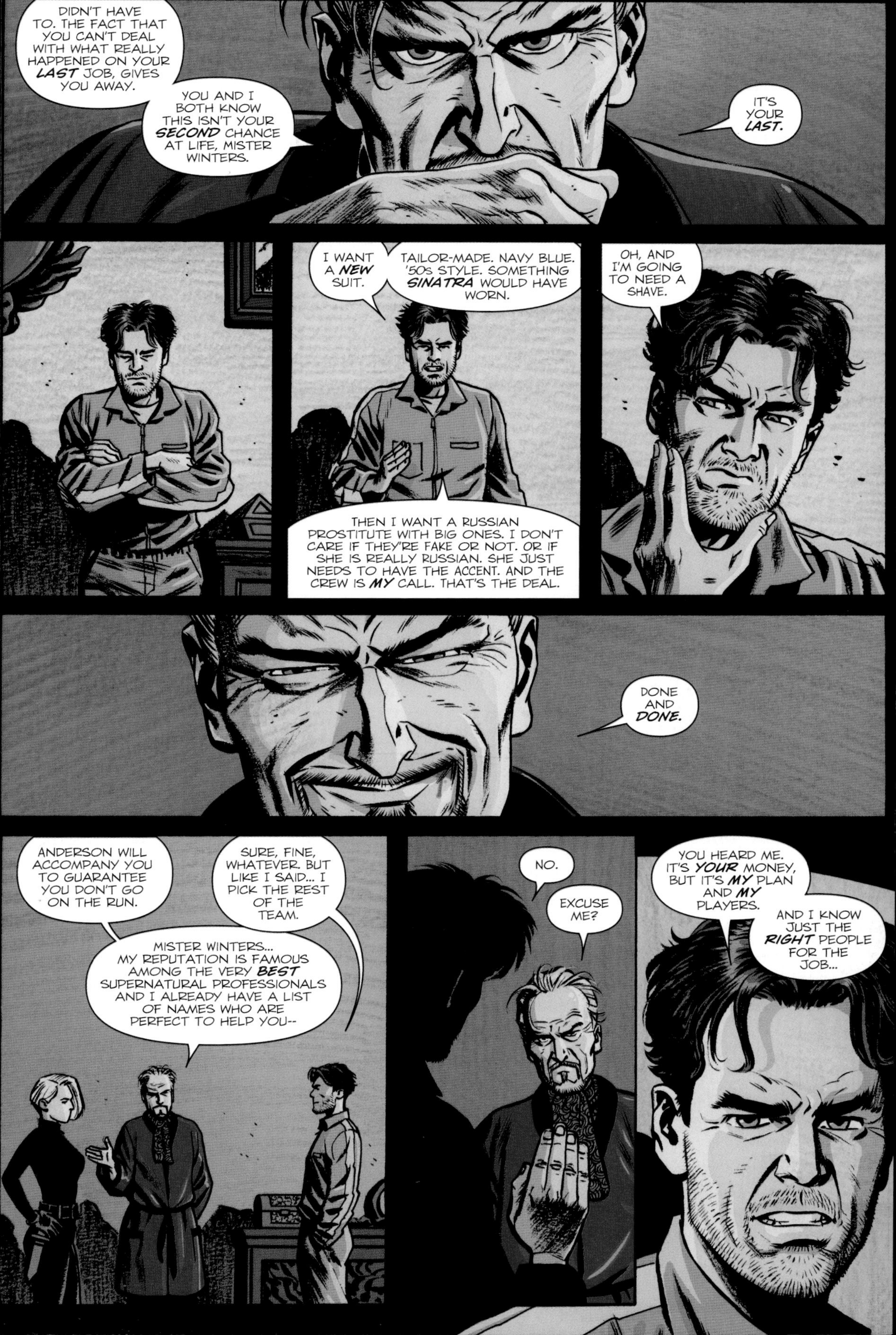
DIDN'T HAVE TO. THE FACT THAT YOU CAN'T DEAL WITH WHAT REALLY HAPPENED ON YOUR LAST JOB, GIVES YOU AWAY.
YOU AND I BOTH KNOW THIS ISN'T YOUR SECOND CHANCE AT LIFE, MISTER WINTERS.
IT'S YOUR LAST.
I WANT A NEW SUIT.
TAILOR-MADE. NAVY BLUE. '50s STYLE. SOMETHING SINATRA WOULD HAVE WORN.
THEN I WANT A RUSSIAN PROSTITUTE WITH BIG ONES. I DON'T CARE IF THEY'RE FAKE OR NOT. OR IF SHE IS REALLY RUSSIAN. SHE JUST NEEDS TO HAVE THE ACCENT. AND THE CREW IS MY CALL. THAT'S THE DEAL.
OH, AND I'M GOING TO NEED A SHAVE.
DONE AND DONE.
ANDERSON WILL ACCOMPANY YOU TO GUARANTEE YOU DON'T GO ON THE RUN.
SURE, FINE, WHATEVER. BUT LIKE I SAID... I PICK THE REST OF THE TEAM.
MISTER WINTERS... MY REPUTATION IS FAMOUS AMONG THE VERY BEST SUPERNATURAL PROFESSIONALS AND I ALREADY HAVE A LIST OF NAMES WHO ARE PERFECT TO HELP YOU--
NO.
EXCUSE ME?
YOU HEARD ME. IT'S YOUR MONEY, BUT IT'S MY PLAN AND MY PLAYERS.
AND I KNOW JUST THE RIGHT PEOPLE FOR THE JOB...

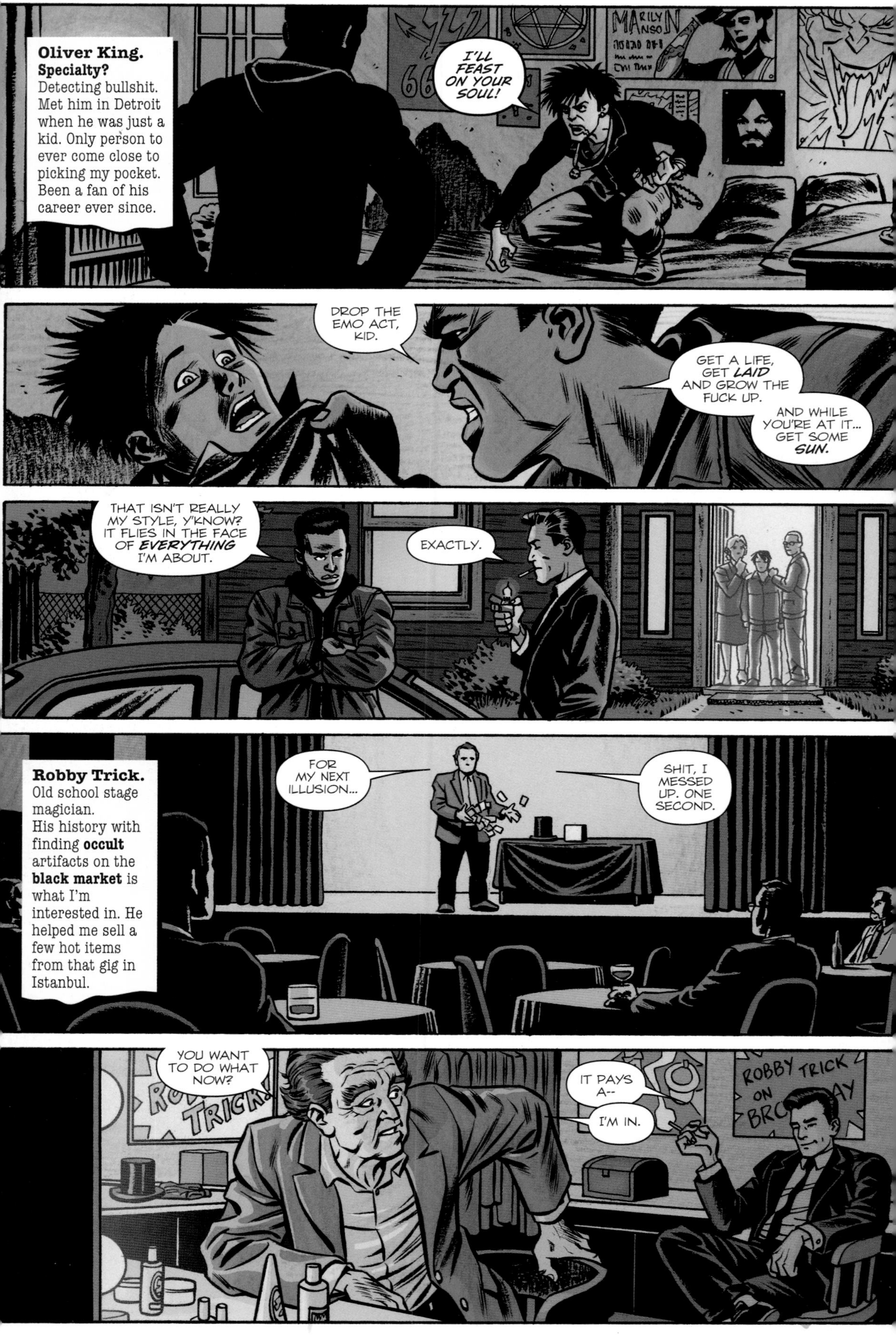
Oliver King.
Specialty?
Detecting bullshit. Met him in Detroit when he was just a kid. Only person to ever come close to picking my pocket. Been a fan of his career ever since.
I'LL FEAST ON YOUR SOUL!
DROP THE EMO ACT, KID.
GET A LIFE, GET *LAID* AND GROW THE FUCK UP.
AND WHILE YOU'RE AT IT... GET SOME ***SUN.***
THAT ISN'T REALLY MY STYLE, Y'KNOW? IT FLIES IN THE FACE OF ***EVERYTHING*** I'M ABOUT.
EXACTLY.
Robby Trick.
Old school stage magician.
His history with finding **occult** artifacts on the **black market** is what I'm interested in. He helped me sell a few hot items from that gig in Istanbul.
FOR MY NEXT ILLUSION...
SHIT, I MESSED UP. ONE SECOND.
YOU WANT TO DO WHAT NOW?
IT PAYS A--
I'M IN.

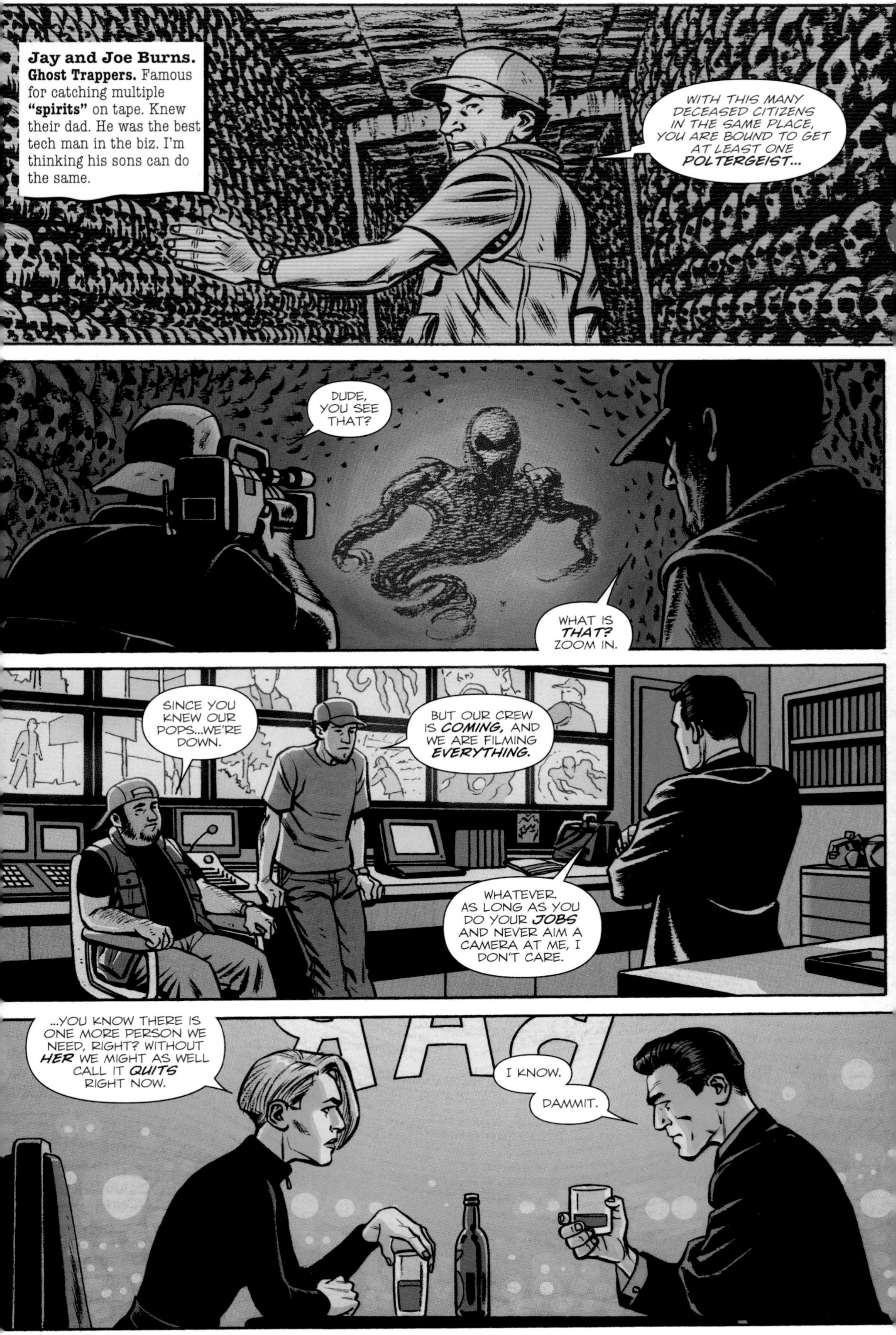

Jay and Joe Burns. Ghost Trappers. Famous for catching multiple "spirits" on tape. Knew their dad. He was the best tech man in the biz. I'm thinking his sons can do the same.
WITH THIS MANY DECEASED CITIZENS IN THE SAME PLACE, YOU ARE BOUND TO GET AT LEAST ONE POLTERGEIST...
DUDE, YOU SEE THAT?
WHAT IS THAT? ZOOM IN.
SINCE YOU KNEW OUR POPS...WE'RE DOWN.
BUT OUR CREW IS COMING, AND WE ARE FILMING EVERYTHING.
WHATEVER. AS LONG AS YOU DO YOUR JOBS AND NEVER AIM A CAMERA AT ME, I DON'T CARE.
...YOU KNOW THERE IS ONE MORE PERSON WE NEED, RIGHT? WITHOUT HER WE MIGHT AS WELL CALL IT QUITS RIGHT NOW.
I KNOW.
DAMMIT.

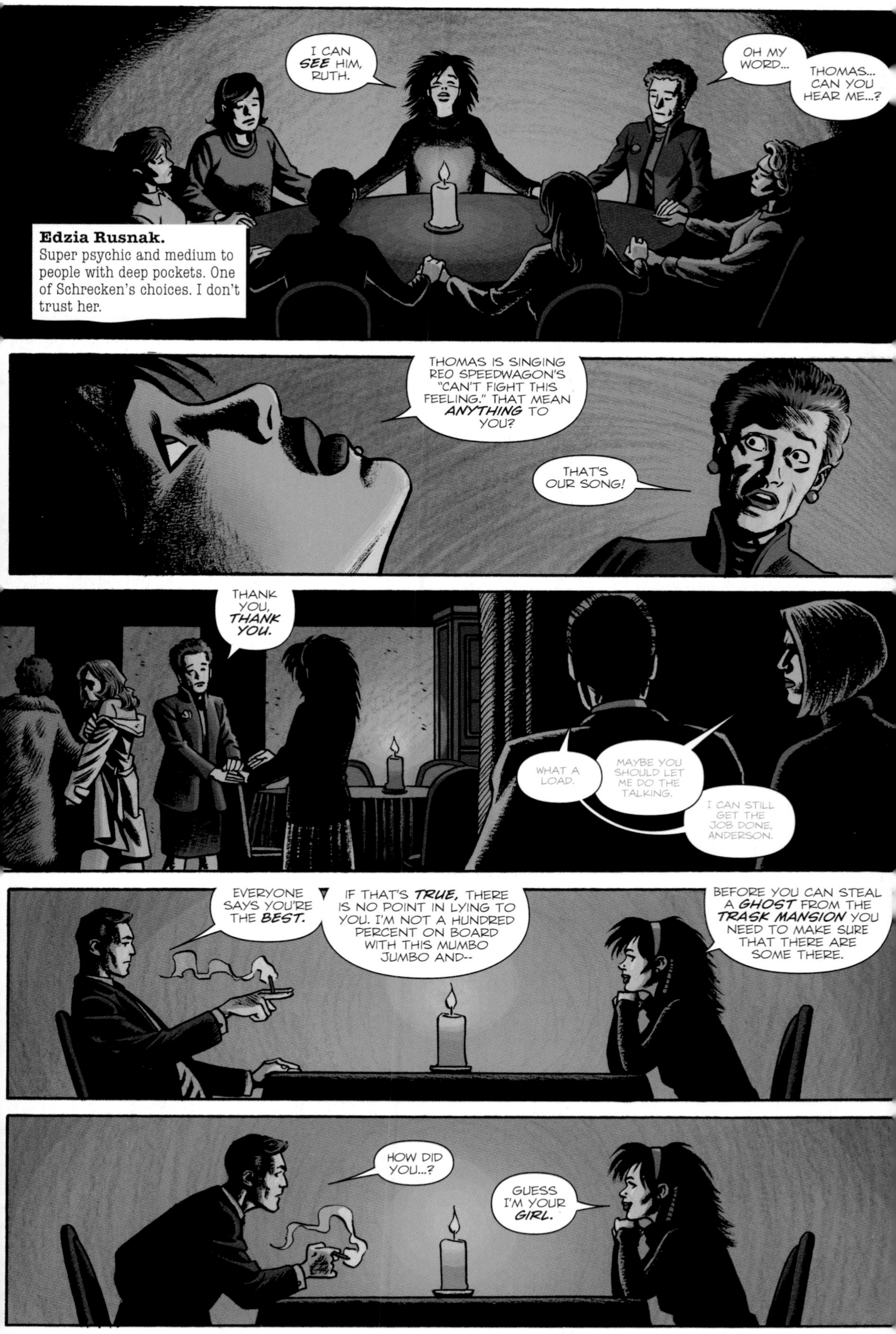
I CAN SEE HIM, RUTH.
OH MY WORD...
THOMAS... CAN YOU HEAR ME...?
Edzia Rusnak.
Super psychic and medium to people with deep pockets. One of Schrecken's choices. I don't trust her.
THOMAS IS SINGING REO SPEEDWAGON'S "CAN'T FIGHT THIS FEELING." THAT MEAN ANYTHING TO YOU?
THAT'S OUR SONG!
THANK YOU, THANK YOU.
WHAT A LOAD.
MAYBE YOU SHOULD LET ME DO THE TALKING.
I CAN STILL GET THE JOB DONE, ANDERSON.
EVERYONE SAYS YOU'RE THE BEST.
IF THAT'S TRUE, THERE IS NO POINT IN LYING TO YOU. I'M NOT A HUNDRED PERCENT ON BOARD WITH THIS MUMBO JUMBO AND--
BEFORE YOU CAN STEAL A GHOST FROM THE TRASK MANSION YOU NEED TO MAKE SURE THAT THERE ARE SOME THERE.
HOW DID YOU...?
GUESS I'M YOUR GIRL.

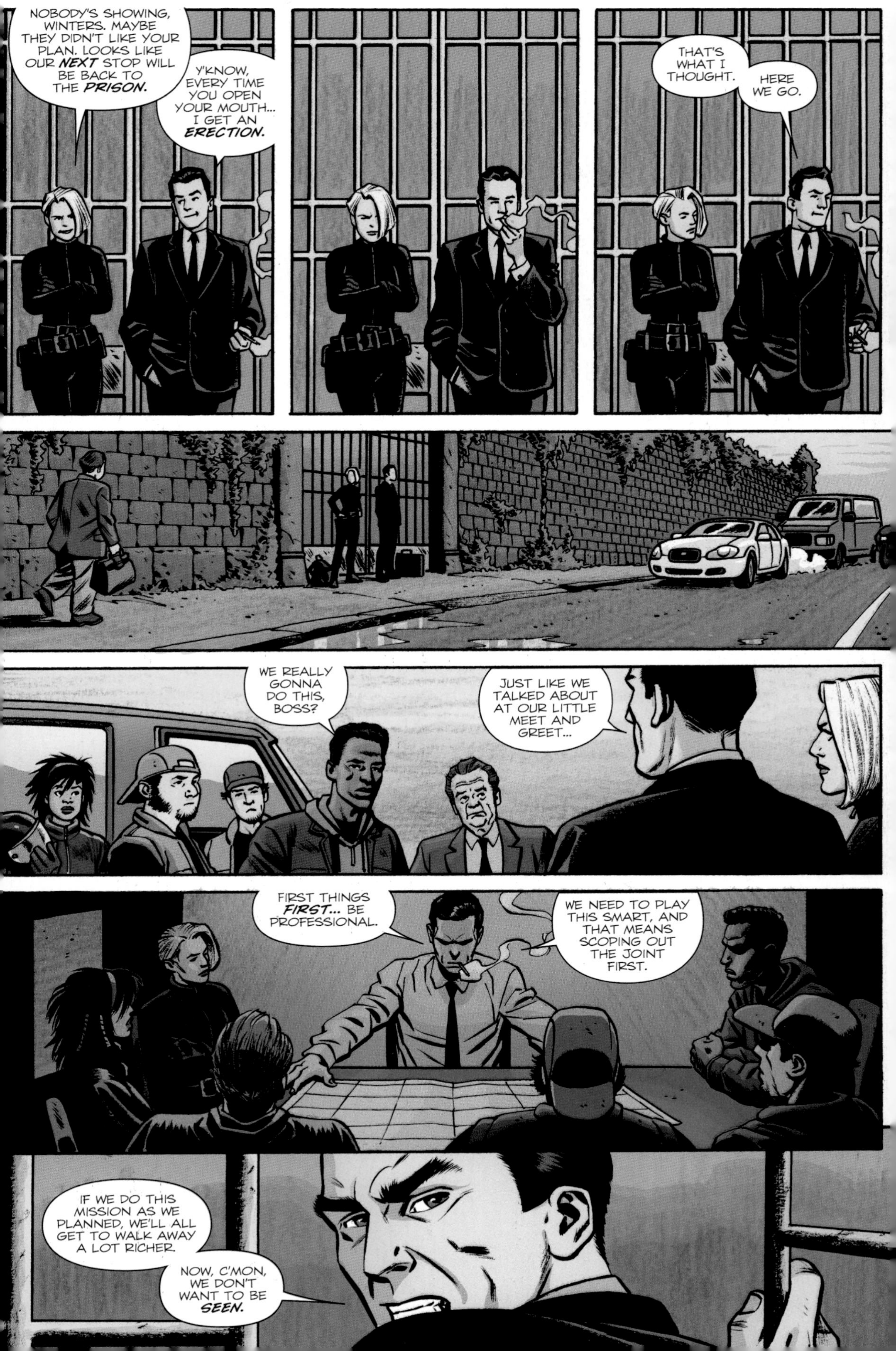
NOBODY'S SHOWING, WINTERS. MAYBE THEY DIDN'T LIKE YOUR PLAN. LOOKS LIKE OUR *NEXT* STOP WILL BE BACK TO THE *PRISON*.
Y'KNOW, EVERY TIME YOU OPEN YOUR MOUTH... I GET AN *ERECTION*.
THAT'S WHAT I THOUGHT.
HERE WE GO.
WE REALLY GONNA DO THIS, BOSS?
JUST LIKE WE TALKED ABOUT AT OUR LITTLE MEET AND GREET...
FIRST THINGS *FIRST*... BE PROFESSIONAL.
WE NEED TO PLAY THIS SMART, AND THAT MEANS SCOPING OUT THE JOINT FIRST.
IF WE DO THIS MISSION AS WE PLANNED, WE'LL ALL GET TO WALK AWAY A LOT RICHER.
NOW, C'MON, WE DON'T WANT TO BE *SEEN*.

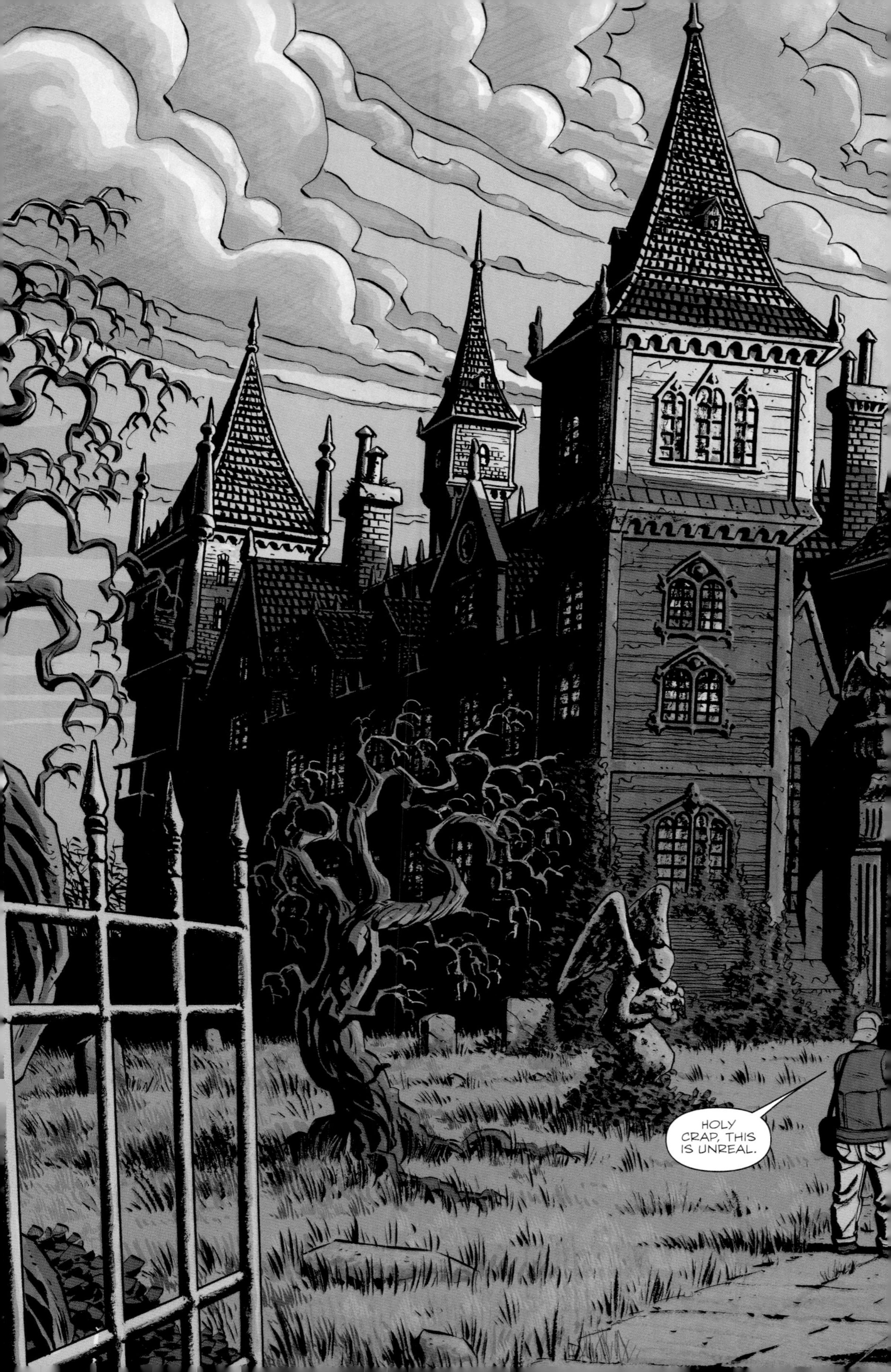
HOLY CRAP, THIS IS UNREAL.

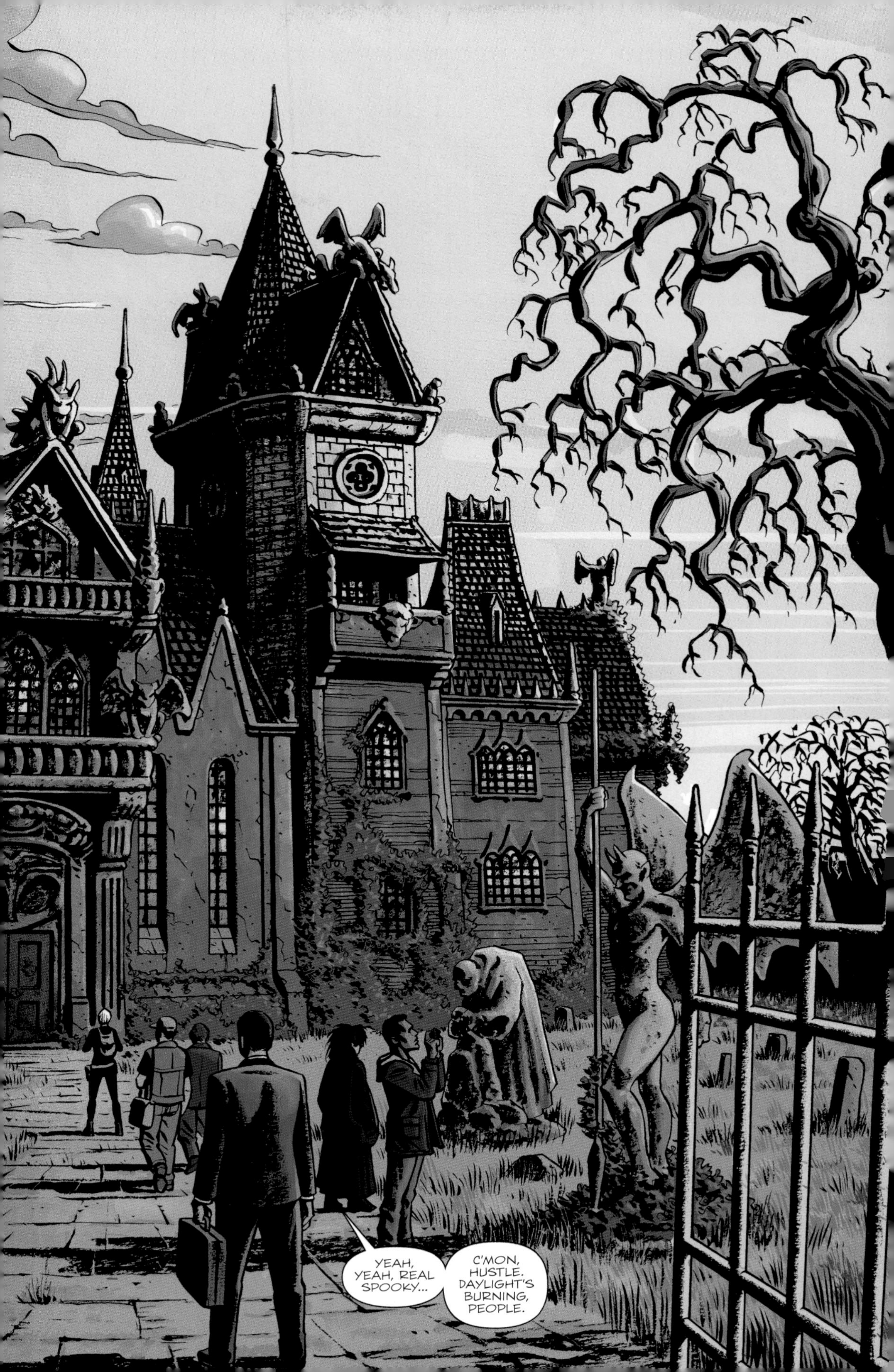
YEAH, YEAH, REAL SPOOKY...
C'MON, HUSTLE. DAYLIGHT'S BURNING, PEOPLE.

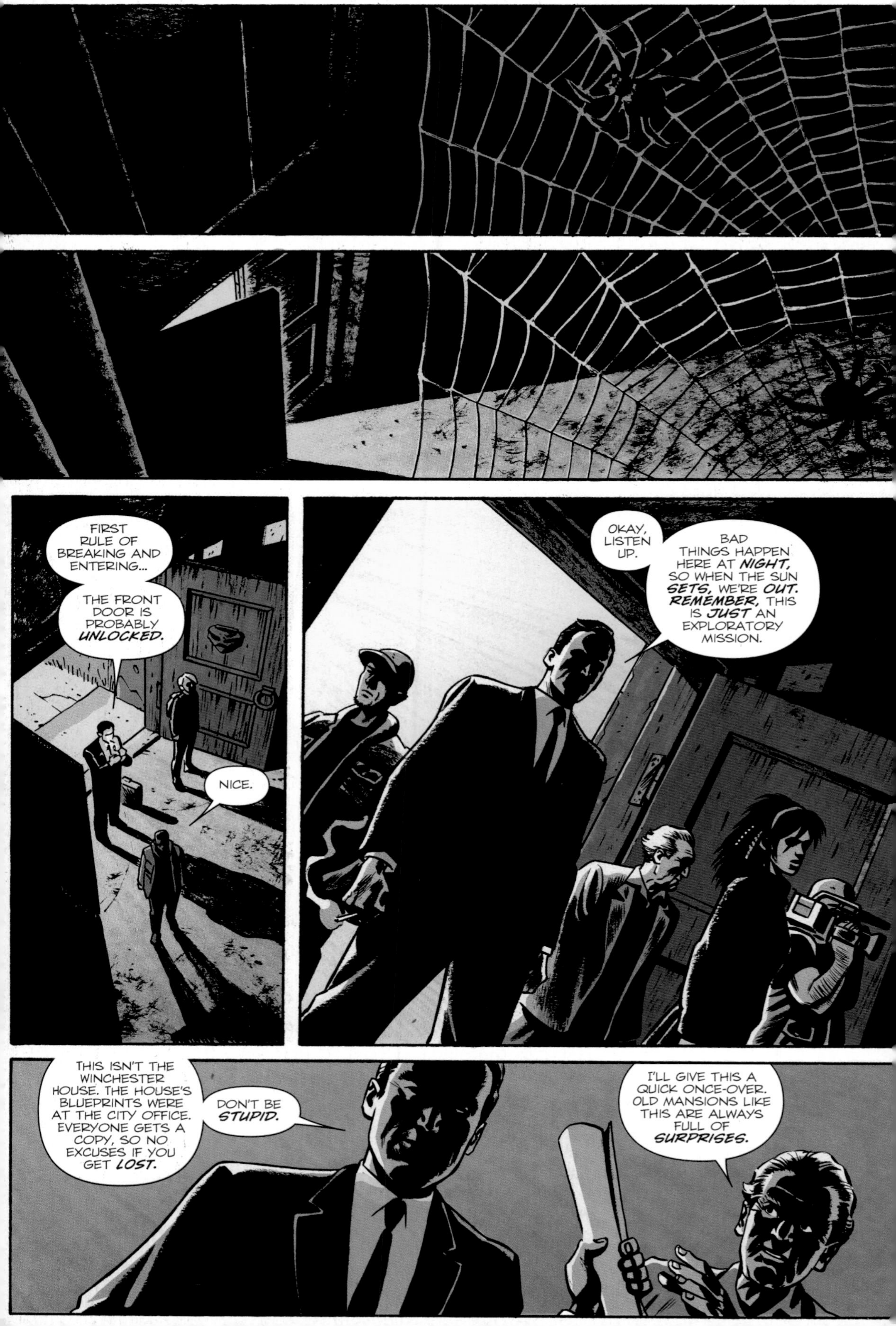
FIRST RULE OF BREAKING AND ENTERING...
THE FRONT DOOR IS PROBABLY UNLOCKED.
NICE.
OKAY, LISTEN UP.
BAD THINGS HAPPEN HERE AT NIGHT, SO WHEN THE SUN SETS, WE'RE OUT. REMEMBER, THIS IS JUST AN EXPLORATORY MISSION.
THIS ISN'T THE WINCHESTER HOUSE. THE HOUSE'S BLUEPRINTS WERE AT THE CITY OFFICE. EVERYONE GETS A COPY, SO NO EXCUSES IF YOU GET LOST.
DON'T BE STUPID.
I'LL GIVE THIS A QUICK ONCE-OVER. OLD MANSIONS LIKE THIS ARE ALWAYS FULL OF SURPRISES.

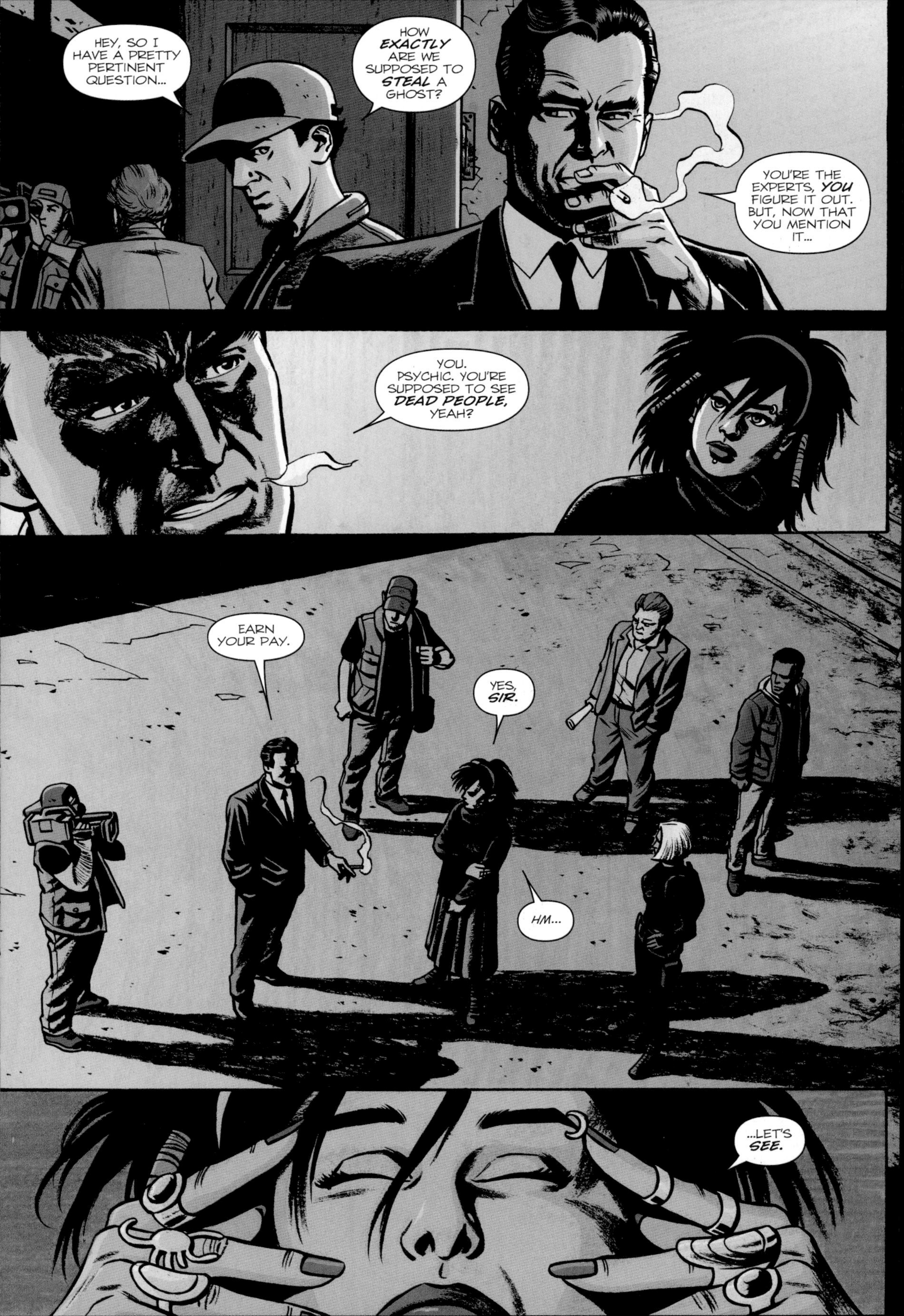
HEY, SO I HAVE A PRETTY PERTINENT QUESTION...
HOW *EXACTLY* ARE WE SUPPOSED TO *STEAL* A GHOST?
YOU'RE THE EXPERTS, *YOU* FIGURE IT OUT. BUT, NOW THAT YOU MENTION IT...
YOU. PSYCHIC. YOU'RE SUPPOSED TO SEE *DEAD PEOPLE,* YEAH?
EARN YOUR PAY.
YES, *SIR.*
HM...
...LET'S *SEE.*

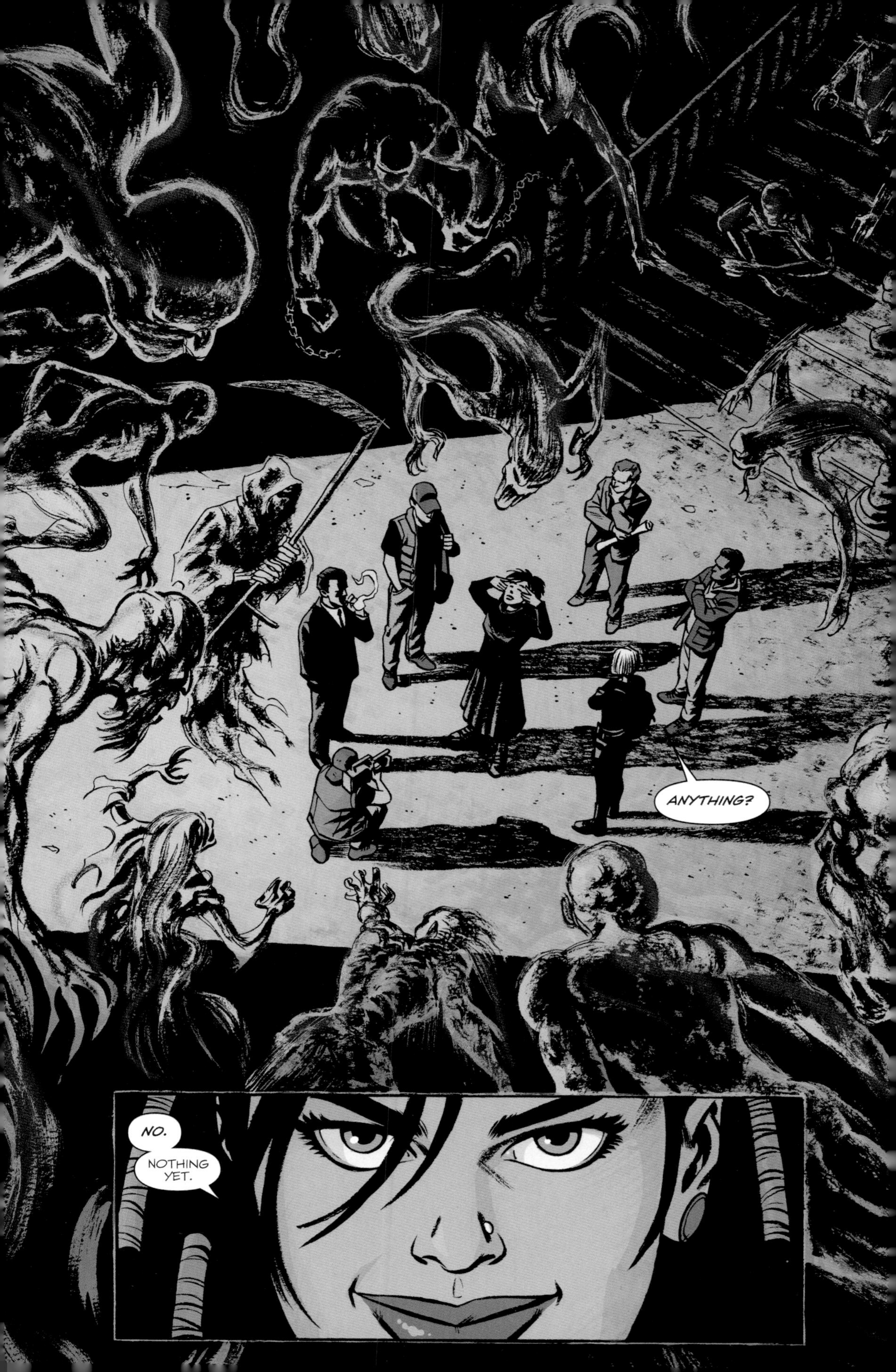
ANYTHING?
NO.
NOTHING YET.

CHAPTER TWO

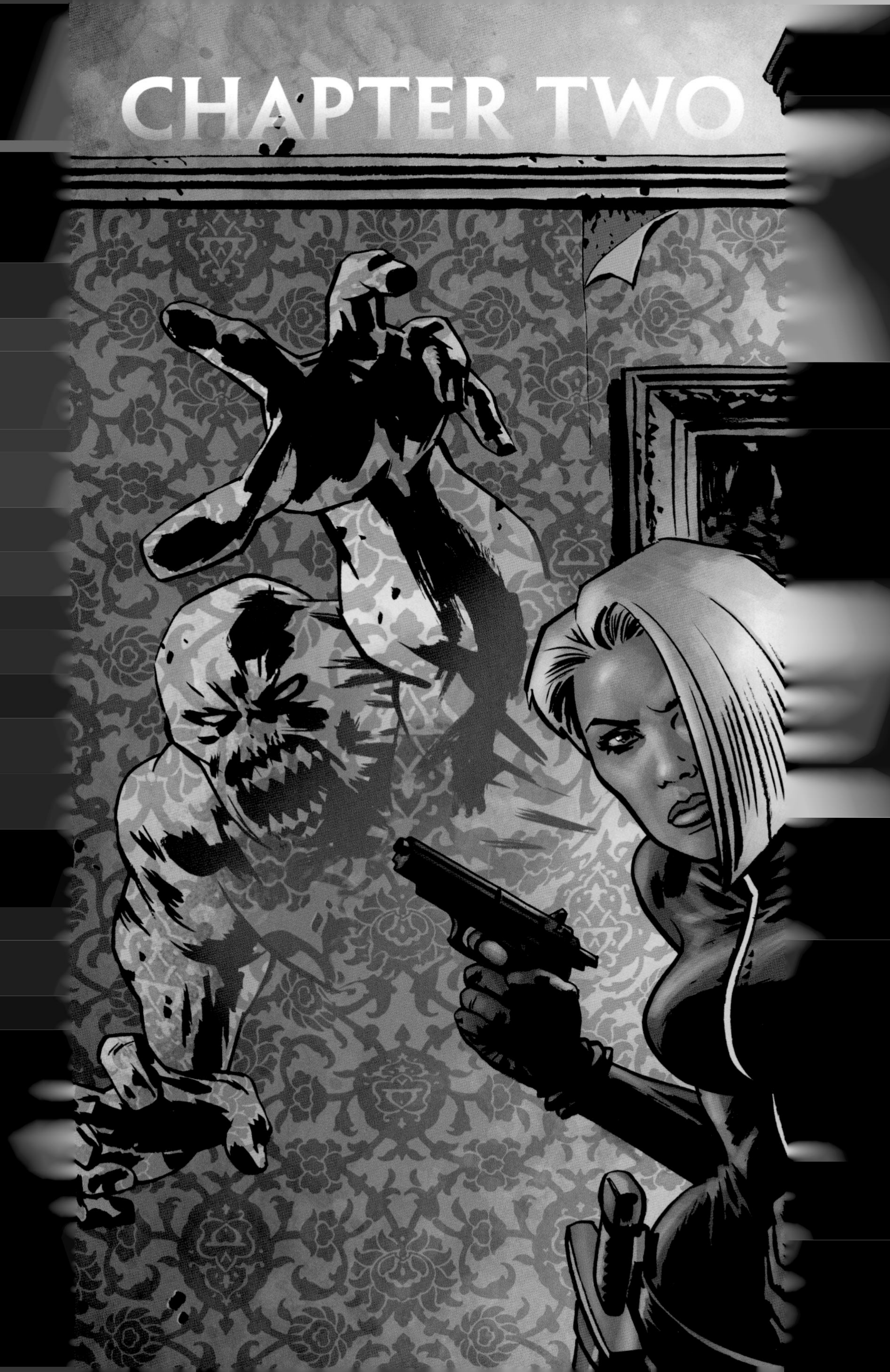

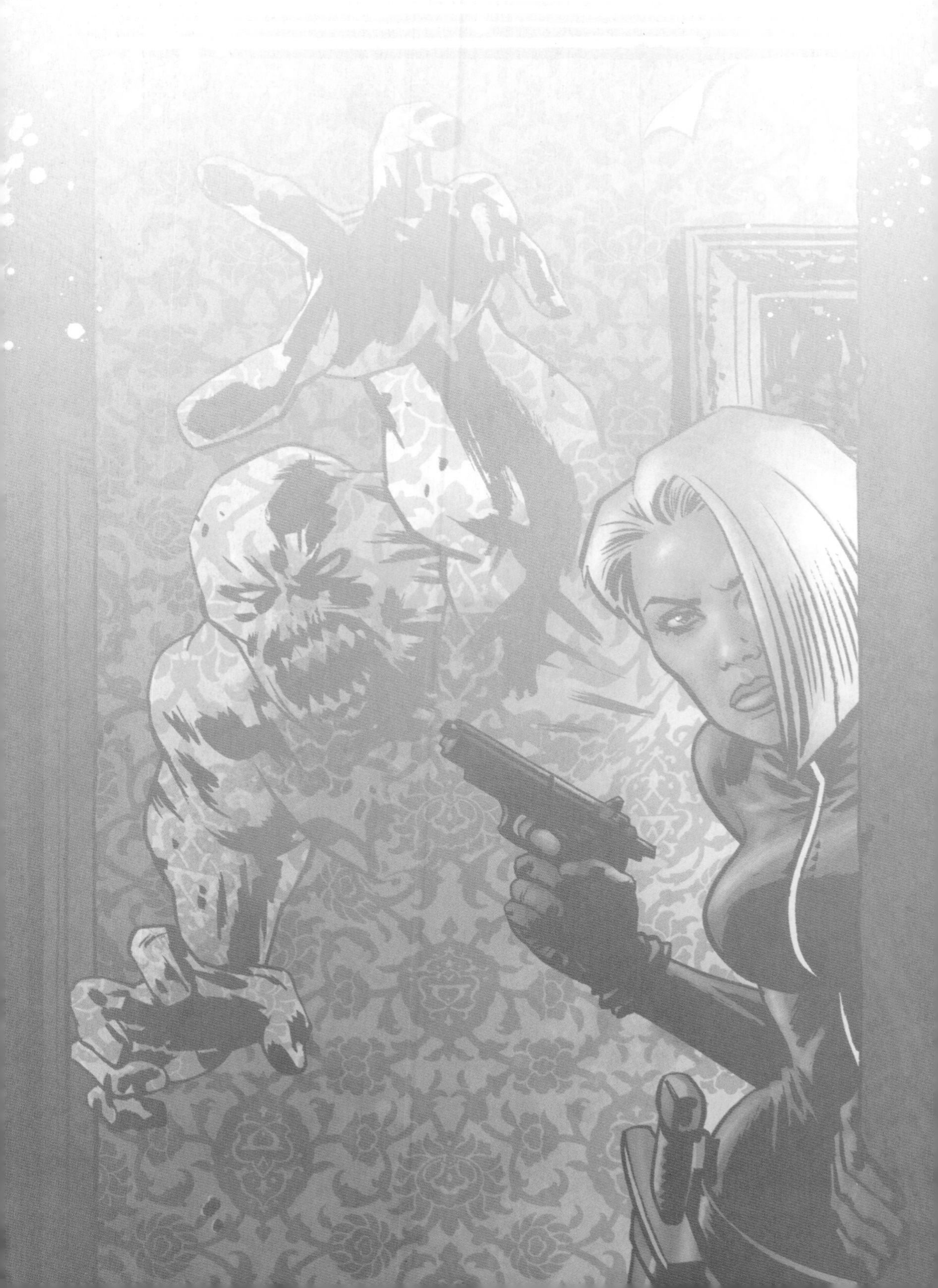

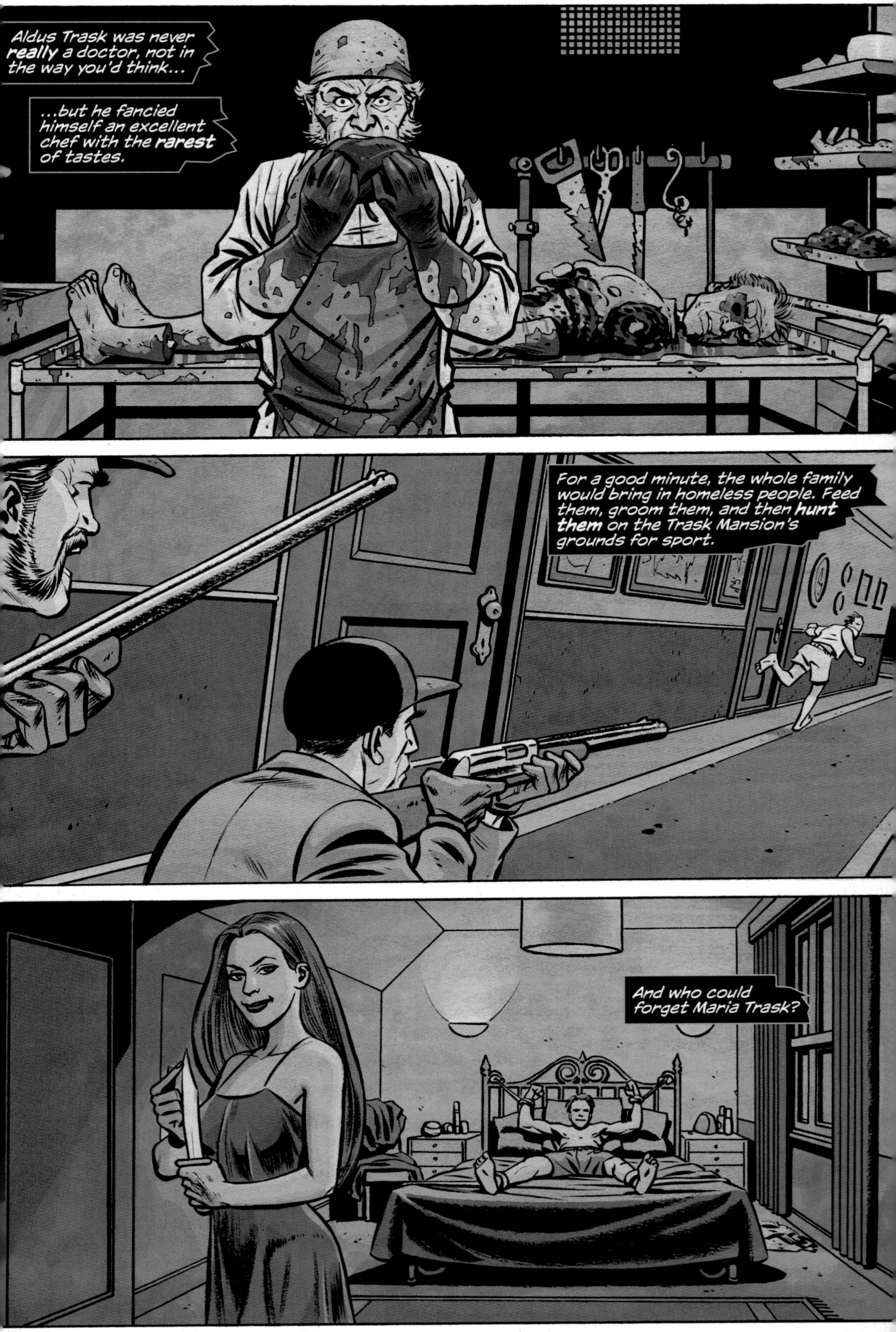
Aldus Trask was never **really** a doctor, not in the way you'd think...
...but he fancied himself an excellent chef with the **rarest** of tastes.
For a good minute, the whole family would bring in homeless people. Feed them, groom them, and then **hunt them** on the Trask Mansion's grounds for sport.
And who could forget Maria Trask?

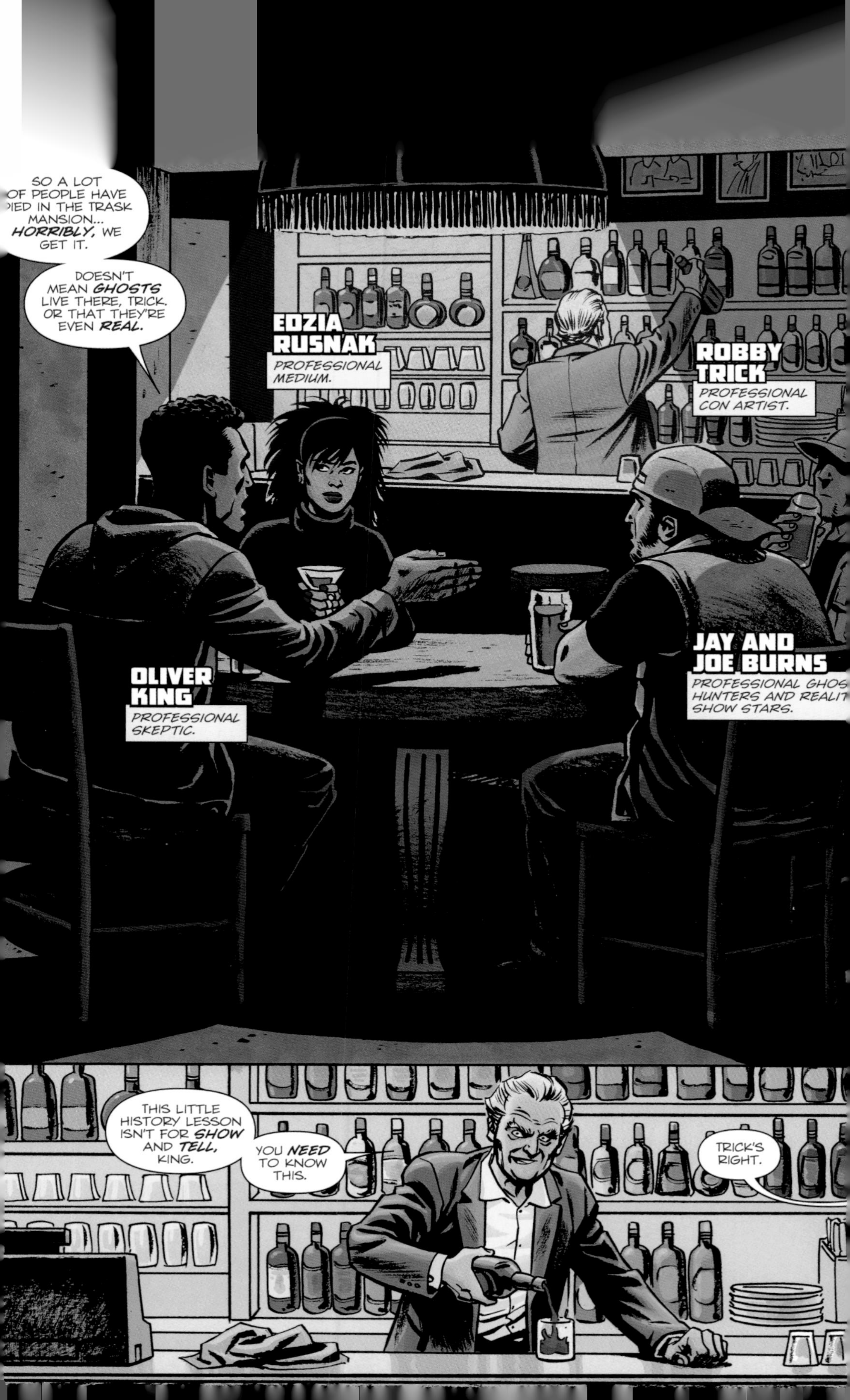
SO A LOT OF PEOPLE HAVE DIED IN THE TRASK MANSION... HORRIBLY, WE GET IT.
DOESN'T MEAN GHOSTS LIVE THERE, TRICK. OR THAT THEY'RE EVEN REAL.
EDZIA RUSNAK
PROFESSIONAL MEDIUM.
ROBBY TRICK
PROFESSIONAL CON ARTIST.
OLIVER KING
PROFESSIONAL SKEPTIC.
JAY AND JOE BURNS
PROFESSIONAL GHOST HUNTERS AND REALITY SHOW STARS.
THIS LITTLE HISTORY LESSON ISN'T FOR SHOW AND TELL, KING.
YOU NEED TO KNOW THIS.
TRICK'S RIGHT.

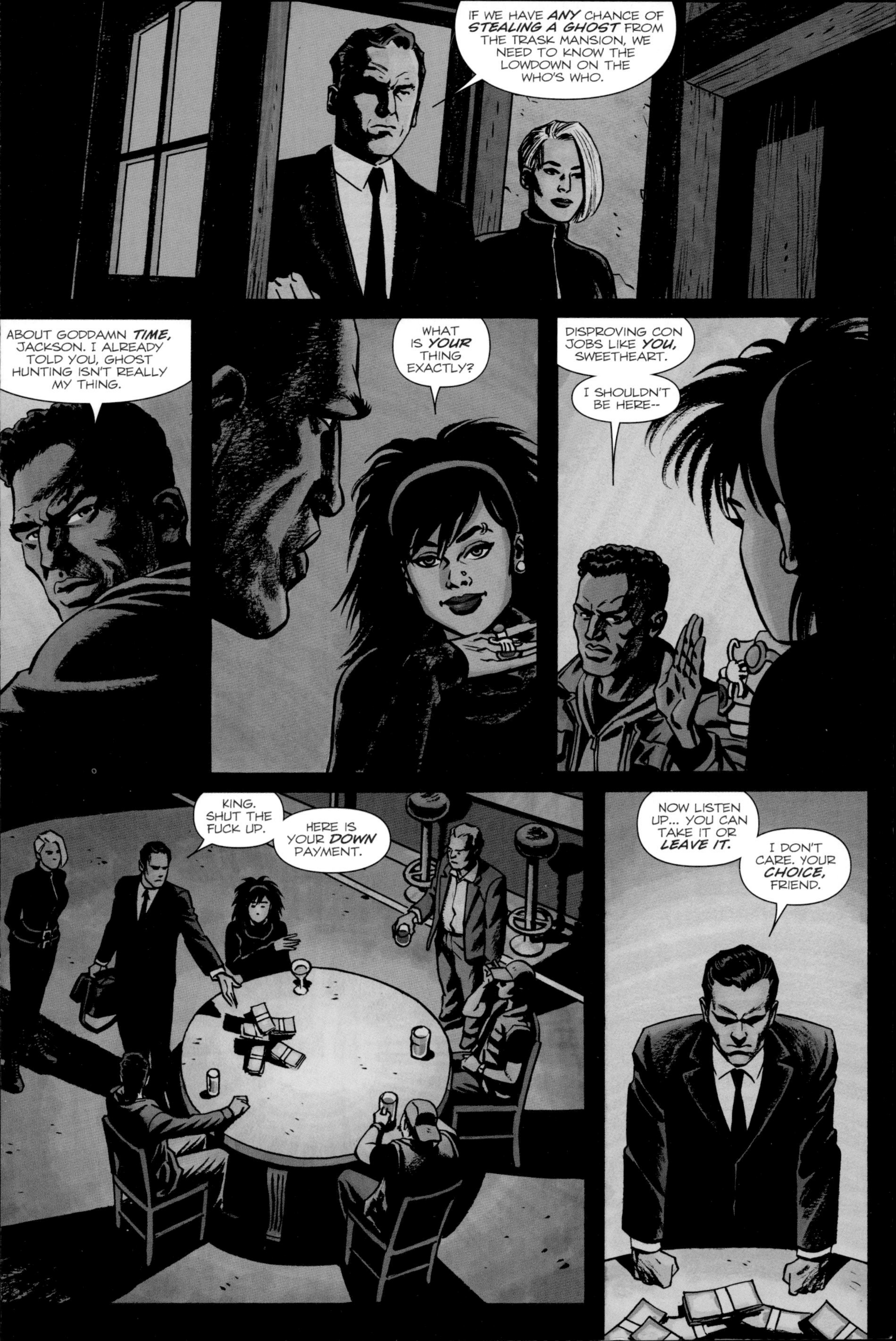
IF WE HAVE ANY CHANCE OF STEALING A GHOST FROM THE TRASK MANSION, WE NEED TO KNOW THE LOWDOWN ON THE WHO'S WHO.
ABOUT GODDAMN TIME, JACKSON. I ALREADY TOLD YOU, GHOST HUNTING ISN'T REALLY MY THING.
WHAT IS YOUR THING EXACTLY?
DISPROVING CON JOBS LIKE YOU, SWEETHEART.
I SHOULDN'T BE HERE--
KING. SHUT THE FUCK UP.
HERE IS YOUR DOWN PAYMENT.
NOW LISTEN UP... YOU CAN TAKE IT OR LEAVE IT.
I DON'T CARE. YOUR CHOICE, FRIEND.

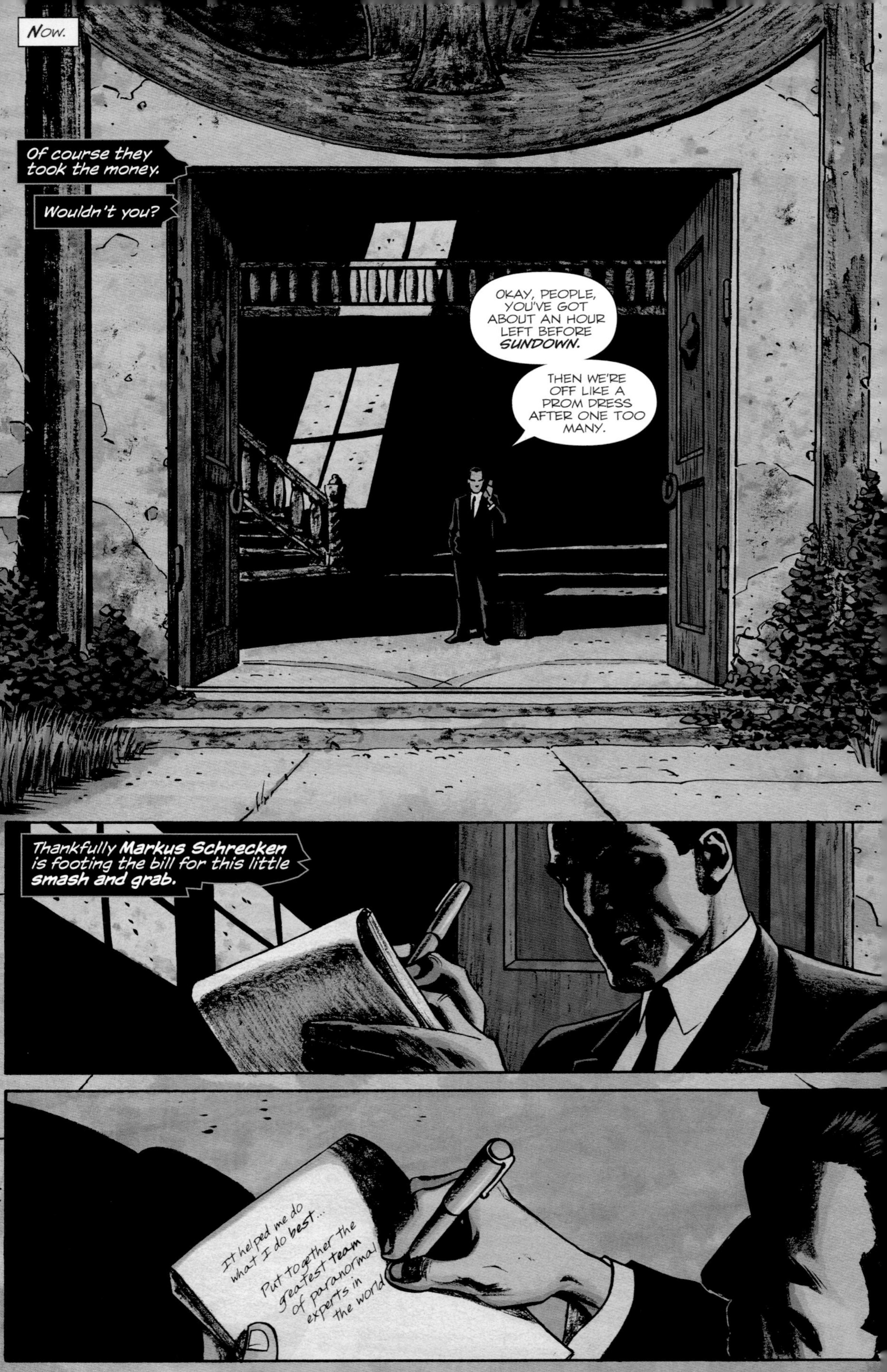
Now.
Of course they took the money.
Wouldn't you?
OKAY, PEOPLE, YOU'VE GOT ABOUT AN HOUR LEFT BEFORE SUNDOWN.
THEN WE'RE OFF LIKE A PROM DRESS AFTER ONE TOO MANY.
Thankfully Markus Schrecken is footing the bill for this little smash and grab.
It helped me do what I do best...
Put together the greatest team of paranormal experts in the world

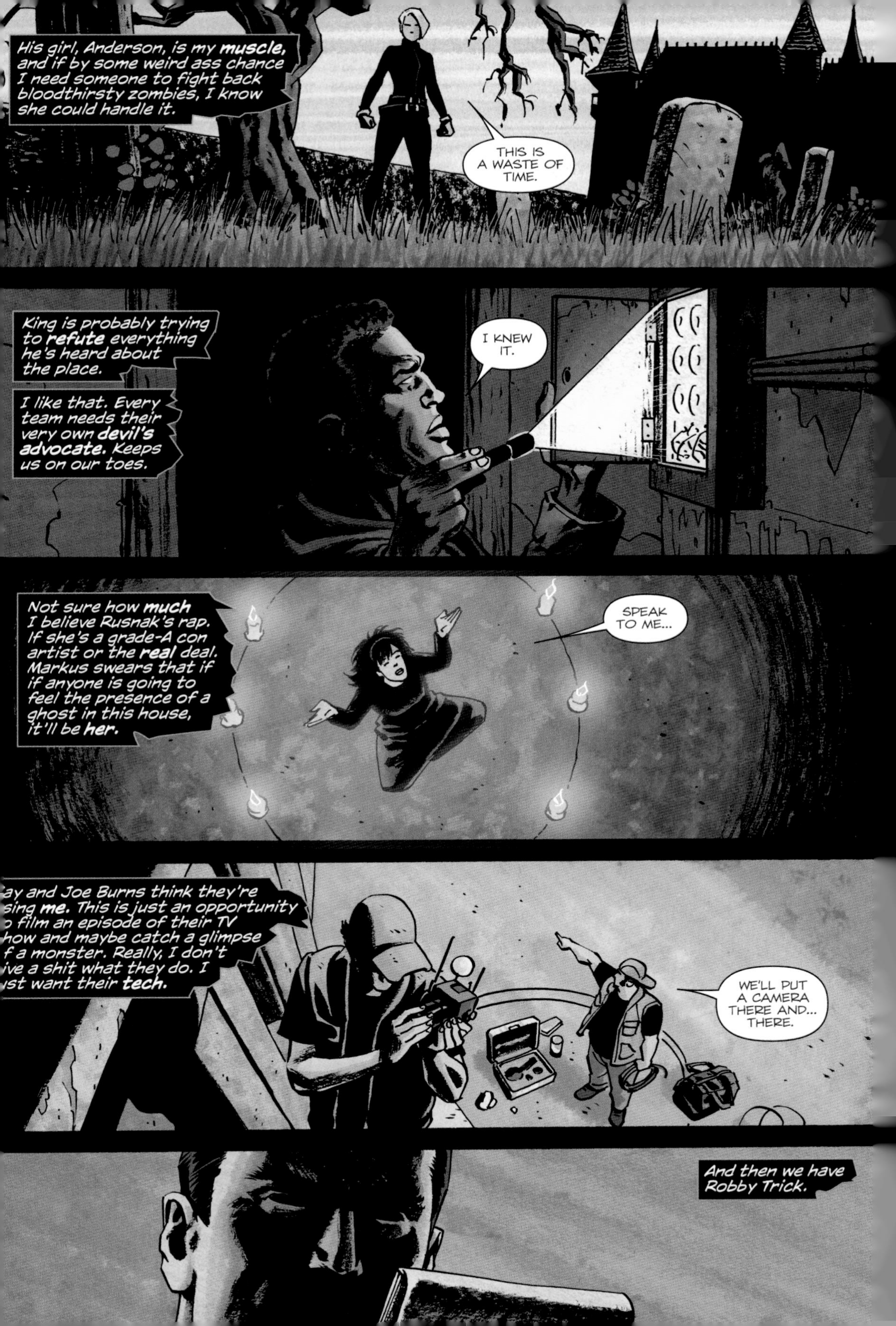
His girl, Anderson, is my muscle, and if by some weird ass chance I need someone to fight back bloodthirsty zombies, I know she could handle it.
THIS IS A WASTE OF TIME.
King is probably trying to refute everything he's heard about the place.
I like that. Every team needs their very own devil's advocate. Keeps us on our toes.
I KNEW IT.
Not sure how much I believe Rusnak's rap. If she's a grade-A con artist or the real deal. Markus swears that if if anyone is going to feel the presence of a ghost in this house, it'll be her.
SPEAK TO ME...
ay and Joe Burns think they're sing me. This is just an opportunity o film an episode of their TV how and maybe catch a glimpse f a monster. Really, I don't ive a shit what they do. I ist want their tech.
WE'LL PUT A CAMERA THERE AND... THERE.
And then we have Robby Trick.

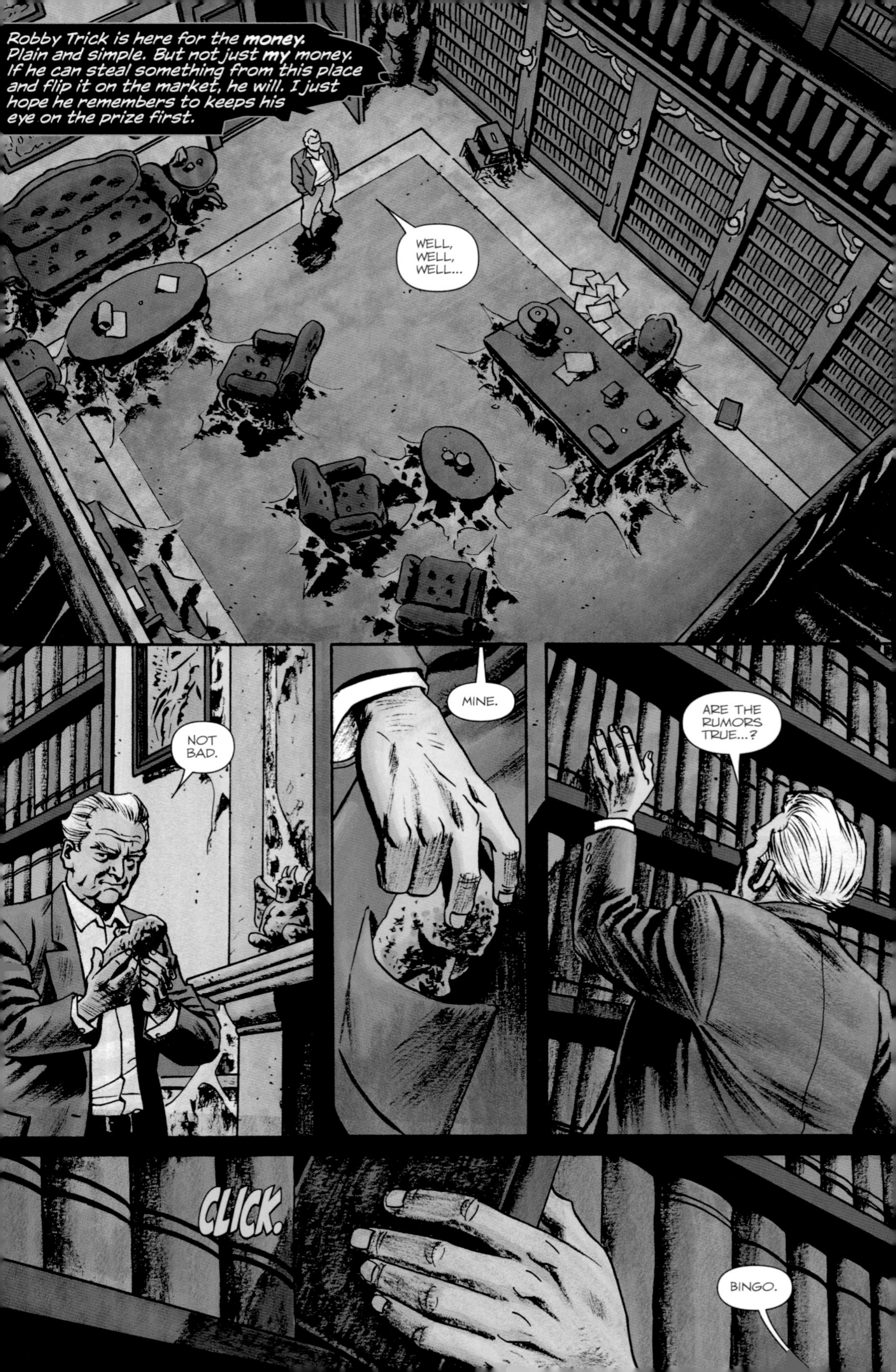
Robby Trick is here for the **money.** Plain and simple. But not just **my** money. If he can steal something from this place and flip it on the market, he will. I just hope he remembers to keeps his eye on the prize first.
WELL, WELL, WELL...
NOT BAD.
MINE.
ARE THE RUMORS TRUE...?
CLICK.
BINGO.

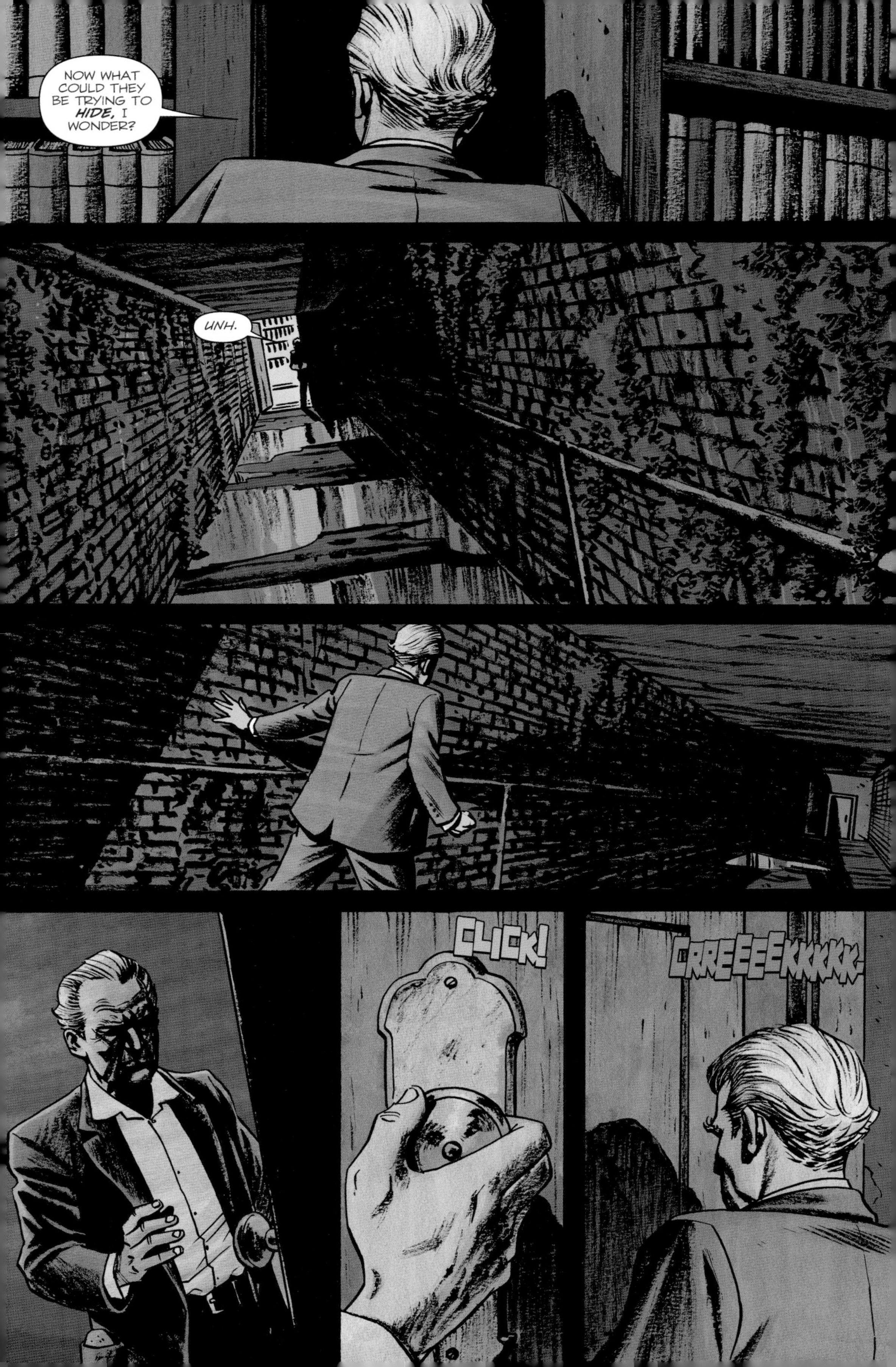
NOW WHAT COULD THEY BE TRYING TO *HIDE,* I WONDER?
UNH.
CLICK!
CRREEEEKKKKK

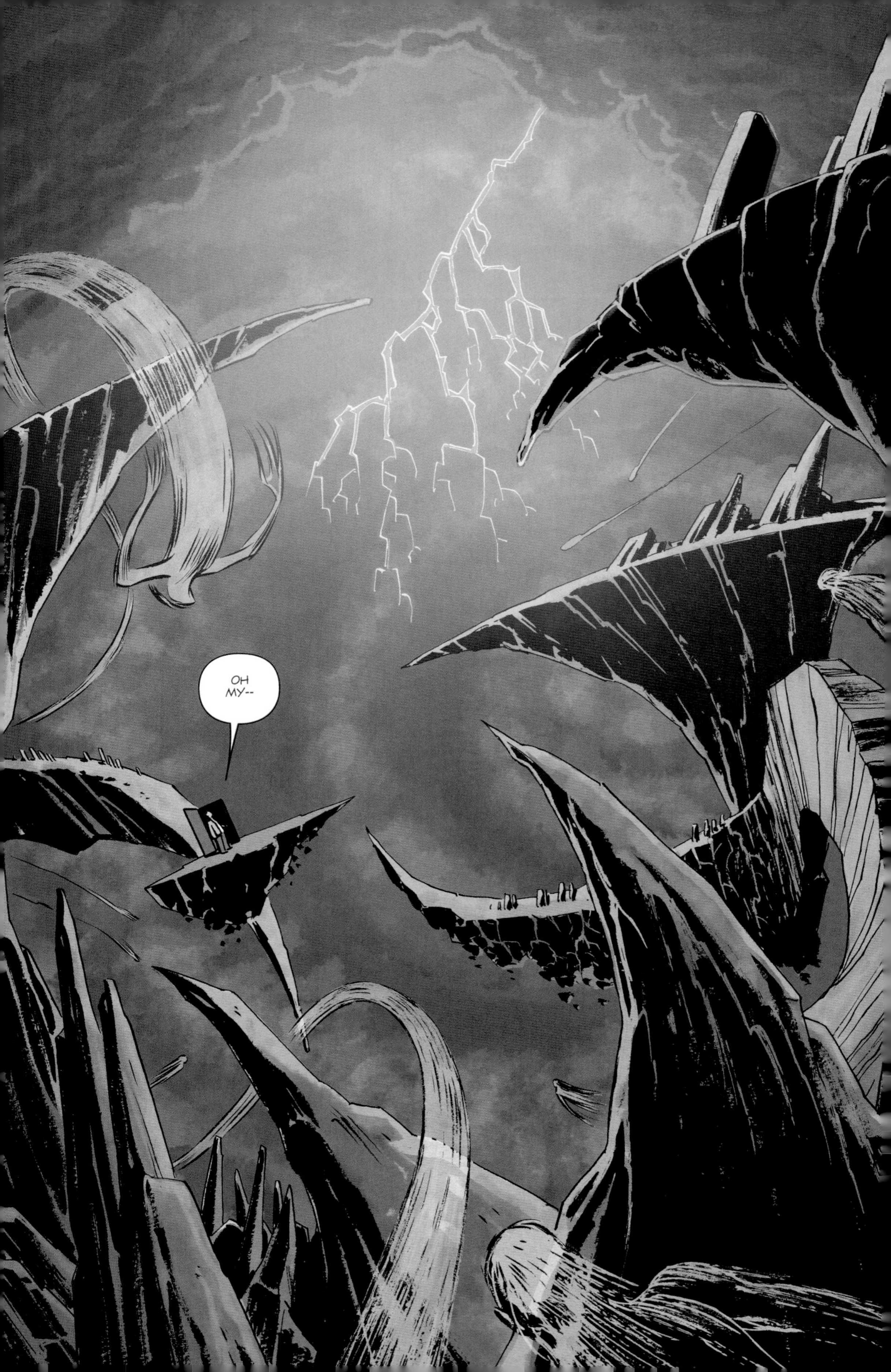
OH MY--

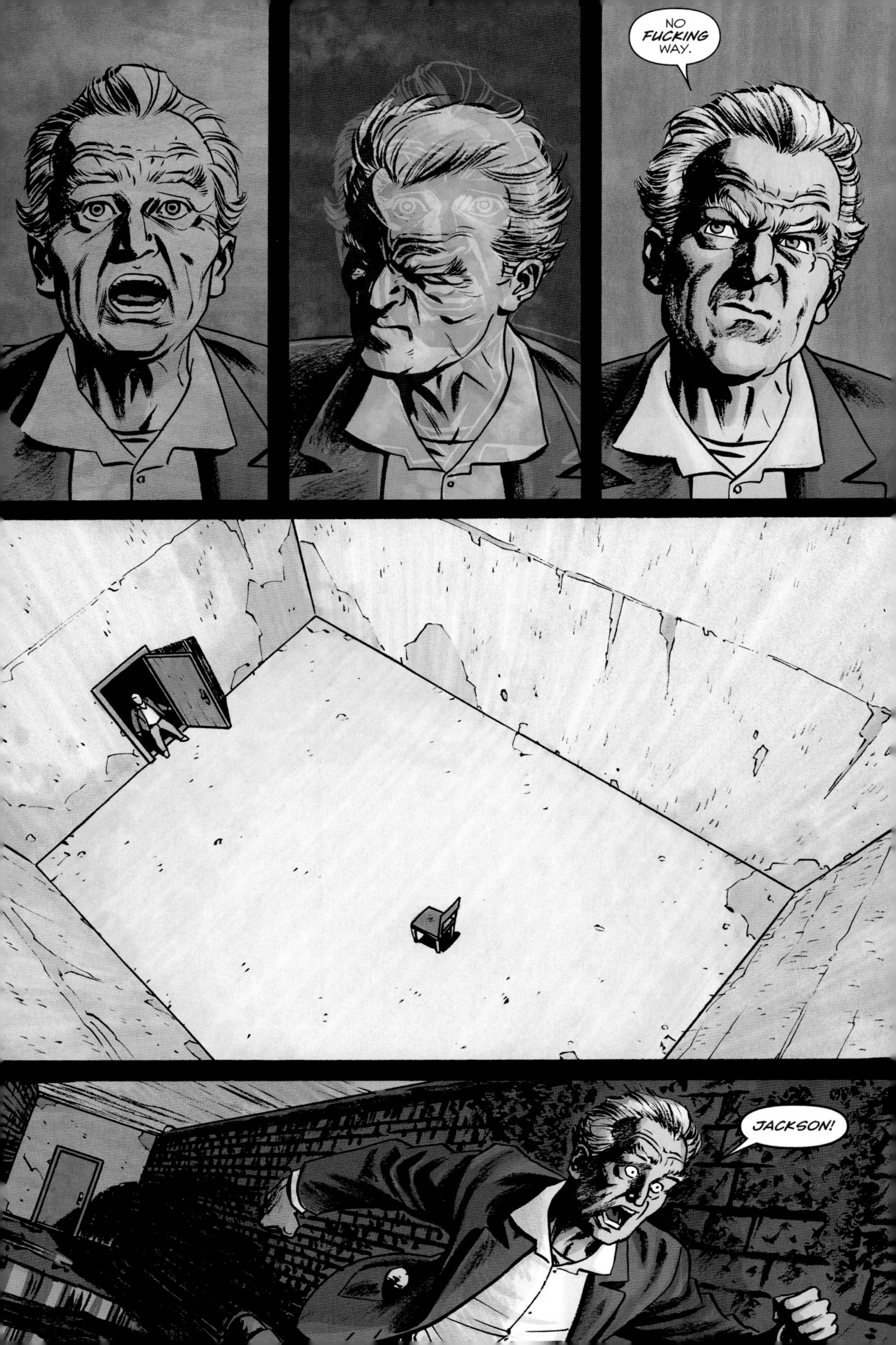
NO FUCKING WAY.
JACKSON!

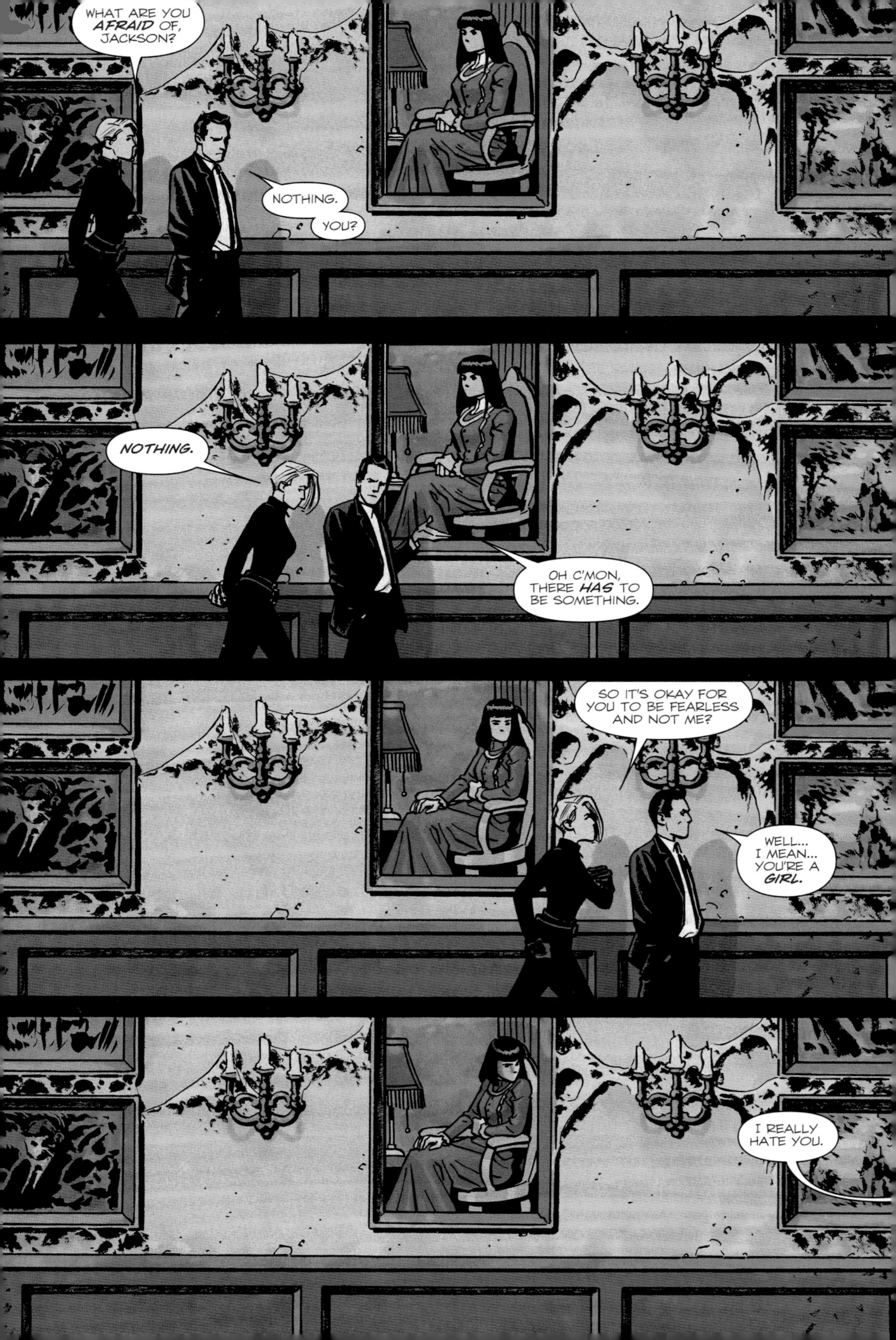
WHAT ARE YOU AFRAID OF, JACKSON?
NOTHING.
YOU?
NOTHING.
OH C'MON, THERE HAS TO BE SOMETHING.
SO IT'S OKAY FOR YOU TO BE FEARLESS AND NOT ME?
WELL... I MEAN... YOU'RE A GIRL.
I REALLY HATE YOU.

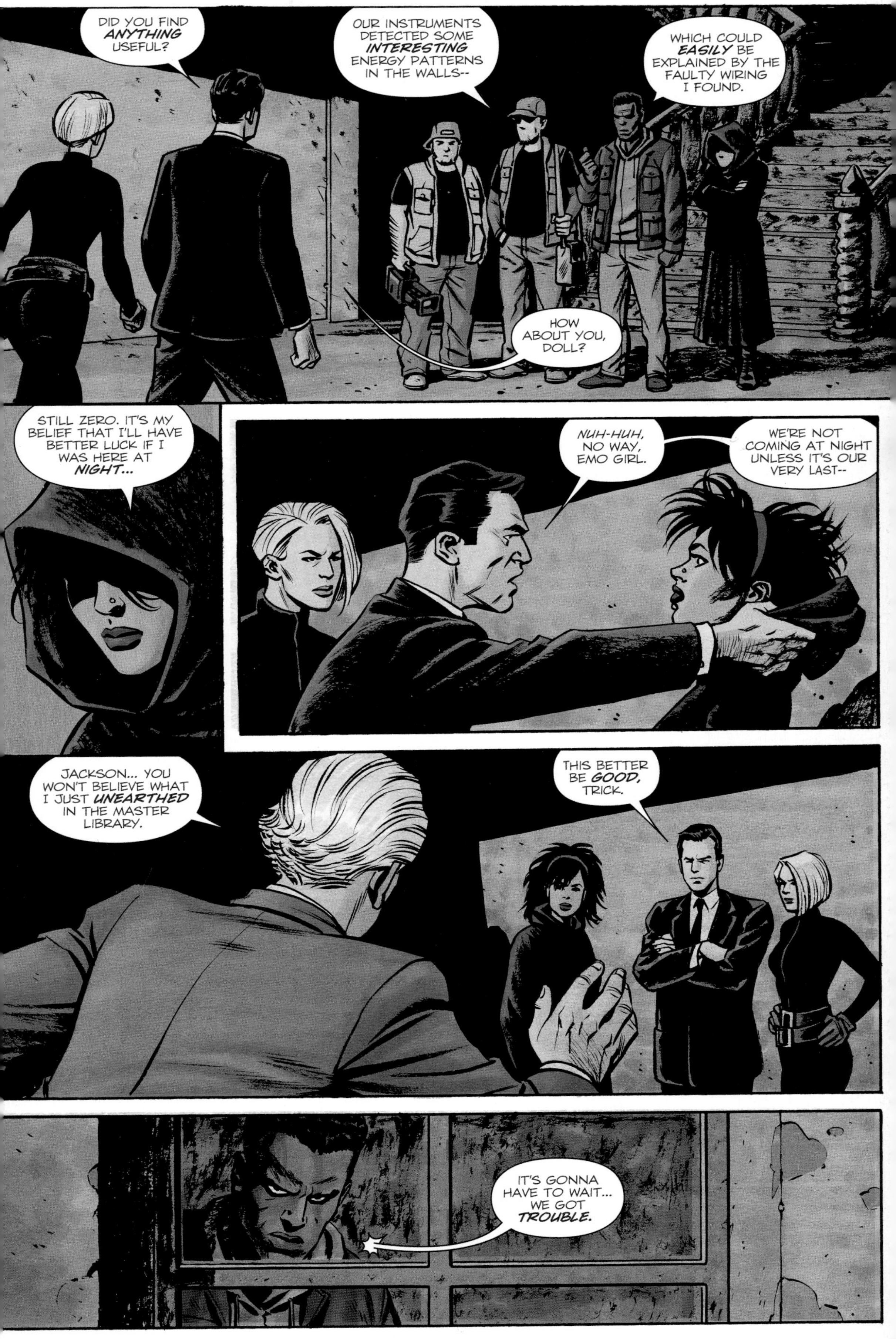
DID YOU FIND ANYTHING USEFUL?
OUR INSTRUMENTS DETECTED SOME INTERESTING ENERGY PATTERNS IN THE WALLS--
WHICH COULD EASILY BE EXPLAINED BY THE FAULTY WIRING I FOUND.
HOW ABOUT YOU, DOLL?
STILL ZERO. IT'S MY BELIEF THAT I'LL HAVE BETTER LUCK IF I WAS HERE AT NIGHT...
NUH-HUH, NO WAY, EMO GIRL.
WE'RE NOT COMING AT NIGHT UNLESS IT'S OUR VERY LAST--
JACKSON... YOU WON'T BELIEVE WHAT I JUST UNEARTHED IN THE MASTER LIBRARY.
THIS BETTER BE GOOD, TRICK.
IT'S GONNA HAVE TO WAIT... WE GOT TROUBLE.

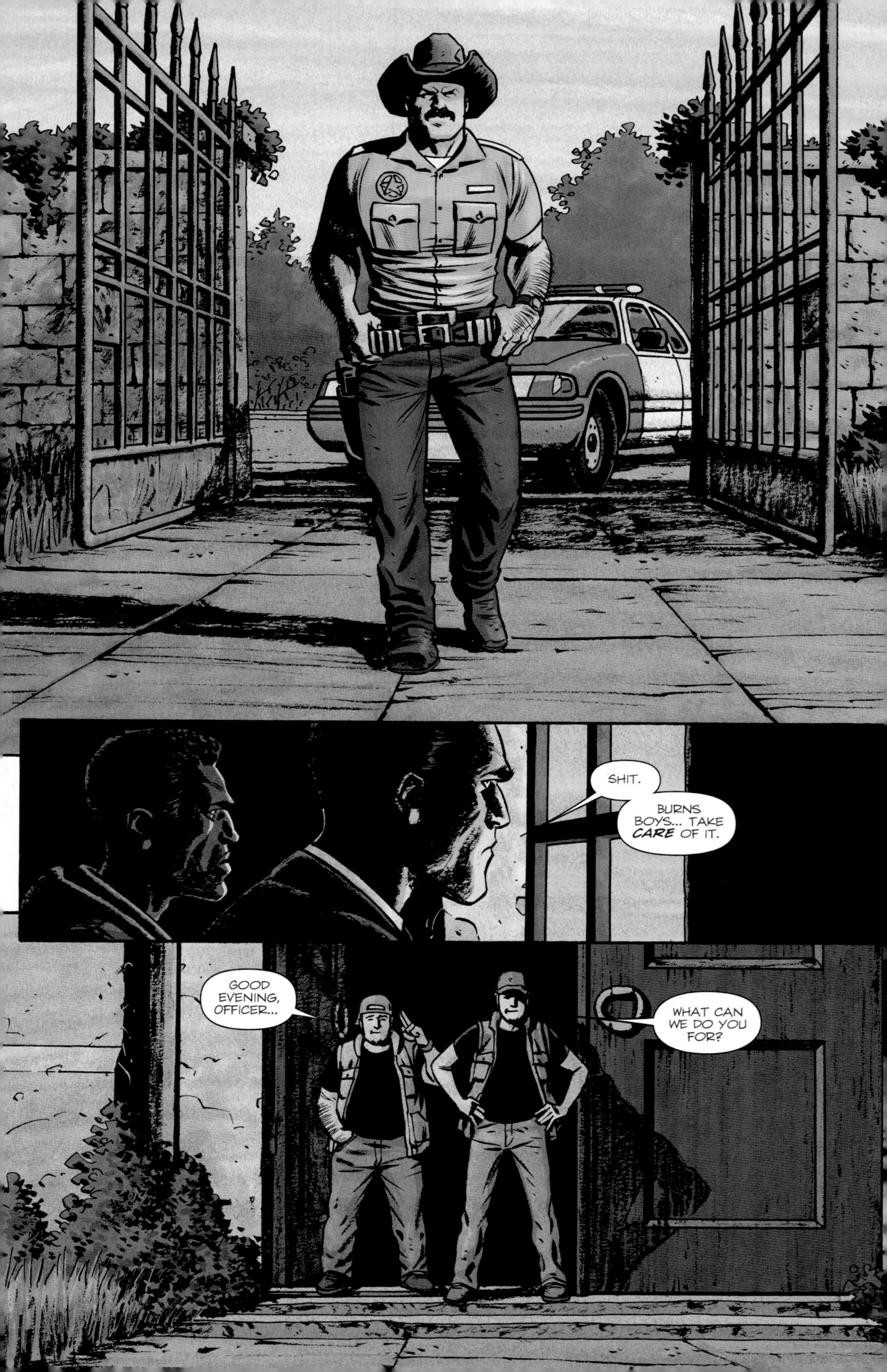
SHIT.
BURNS BOYS... TAKE CARE OF IT.
GOOD EVENING, OFFICER...
WHAT CAN WE DO YOU FOR?

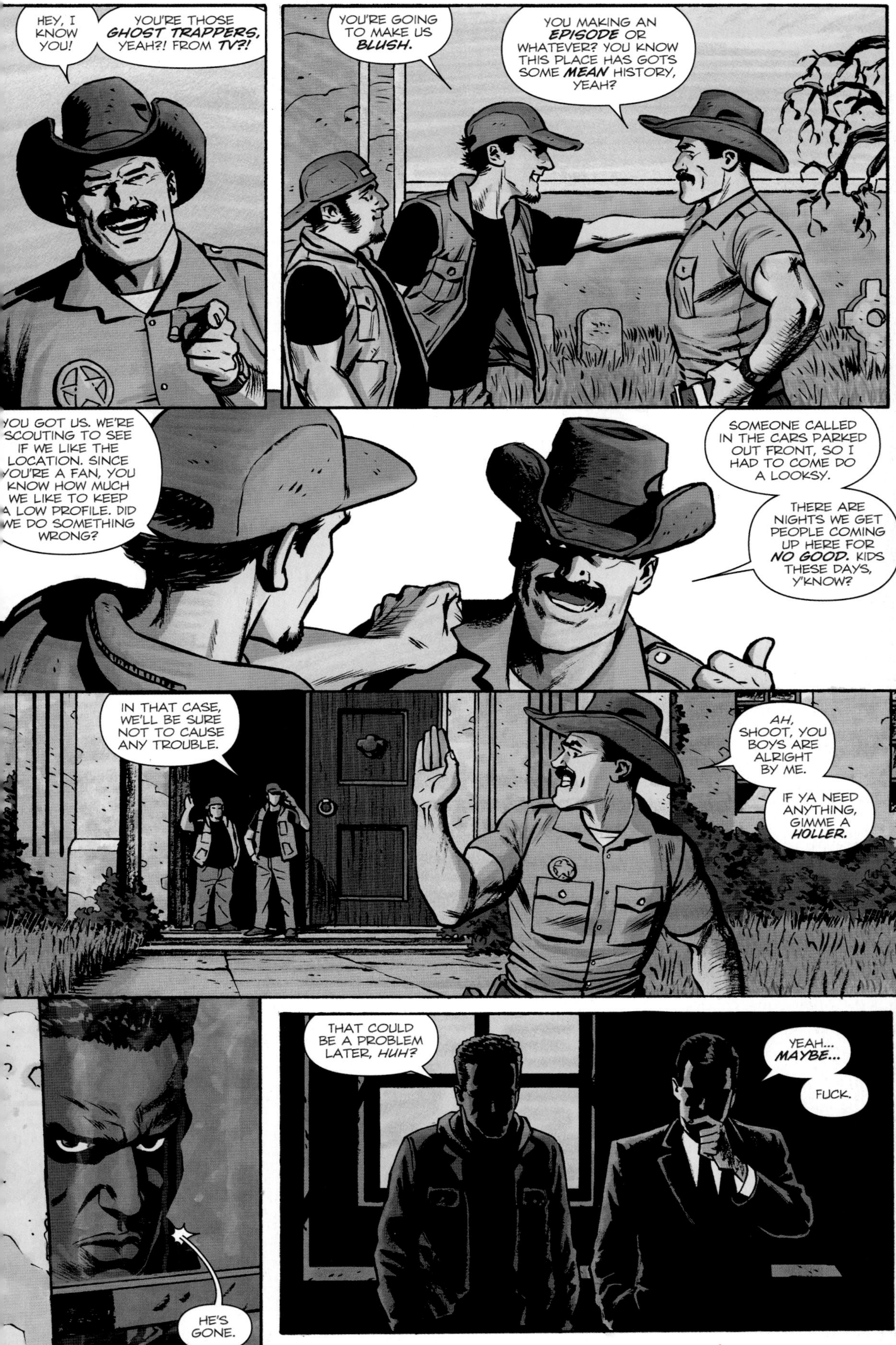
HEY, I KNOW YOU!
YOU'RE THOSE GHOST TRAPPERS, YEAH?! FROM TV?!
YOU'RE GOING TO MAKE US BLUSH.
YOU MAKING AN EPISODE OR WHATEVER? YOU KNOW THIS PLACE HAS GOTS SOME MEAN HISTORY, YEAH?
YOU GOT US. WE'RE SCOUTING TO SEE IF WE LIKE THE LOCATION. SINCE YOU'RE A FAN, YOU KNOW HOW MUCH WE LIKE TO KEEP A LOW PROFILE. DID WE DO SOMETHING WRONG?
SOMEONE CALLED IN THE CARS PARKED OUT FRONT, SO I HAD TO COME DO A LOOKSY.
THERE ARE NIGHTS WE GET PEOPLE COMING UP HERE FOR NO GOOD. KIDS THESE DAYS, Y'KNOW?
IN THAT CASE, WE'LL BE SURE NOT TO CAUSE ANY TROUBLE.
AH, SHOOT, YOU BOYS ARE ALRIGHT BY ME.
IF YA NEED ANYTHING, GIMME A HOLLER.
HE'S GONE.
THAT COULD BE A PROBLEM LATER, HUH?
YEAH... MAYBE...
FUCK.

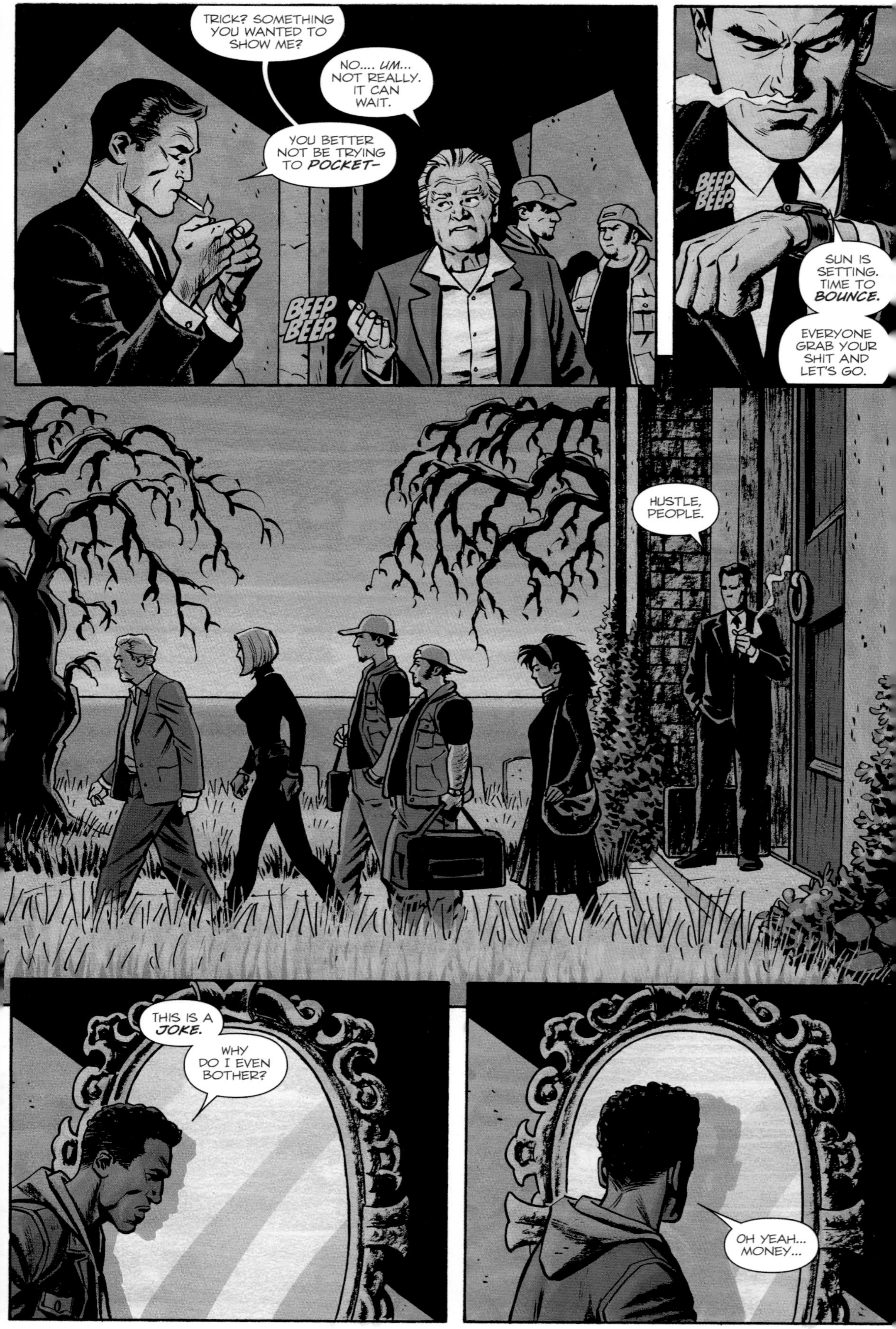
TRICK? SOMETHING YOU WANTED TO SHOW ME?
NO.... UM... NOT REALLY. IT CAN WAIT.
YOU BETTER NOT BE TRYING TO POCKET—
BEEP BEEP.
BEEP BEEP.
SUN IS SETTING. TIME TO BOUNCE.
EVERYONE GRAB YOUR SHIT AND LET'S GO.
HUSTLE, PEOPLE.
THIS IS A JOKE.
WHY DO I EVEN BOTHER?
OH YEAH... MONEY...

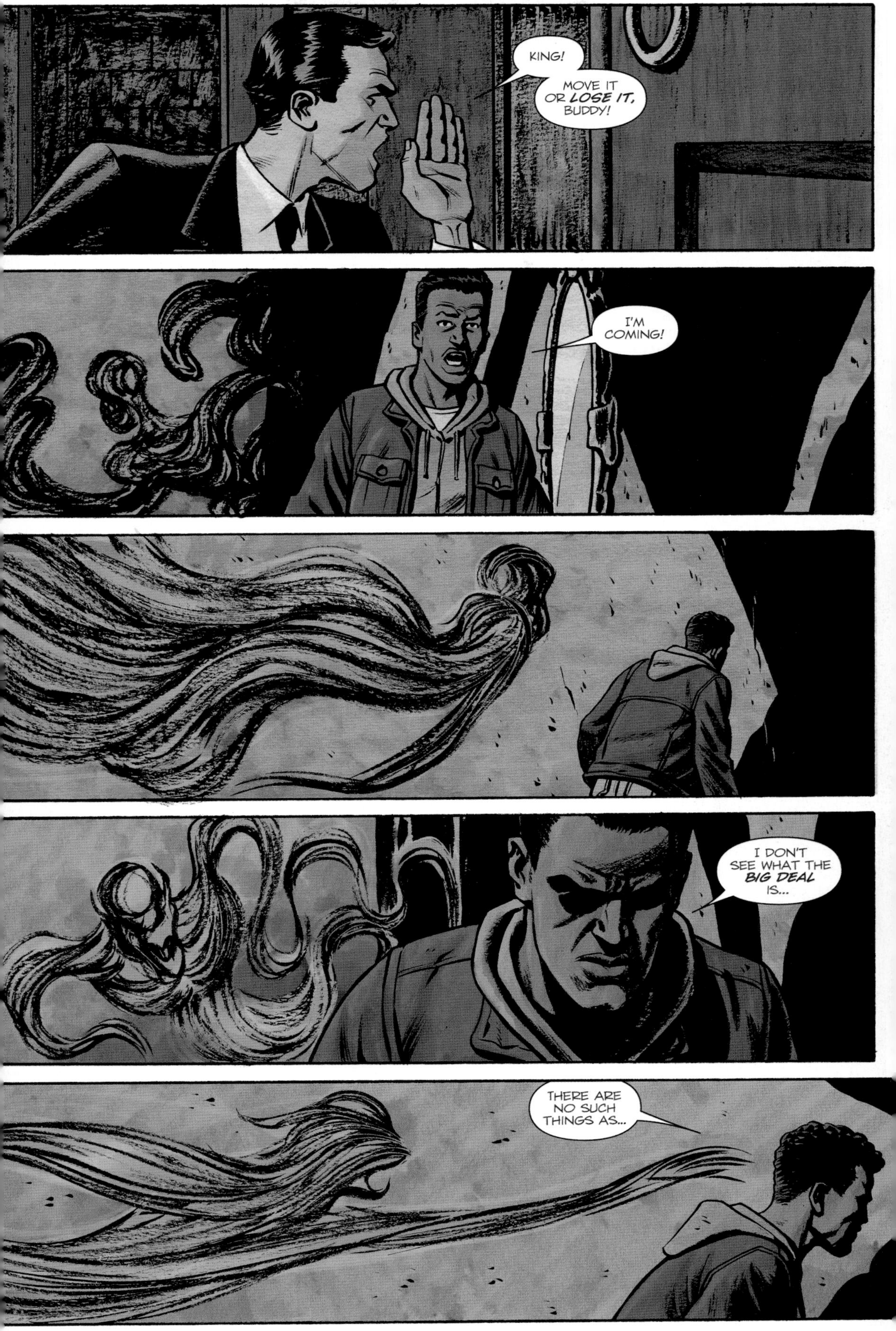
KING!
MOVE IT OR **LOSE IT,** BUDDY!
I'M COMING!
I DON'T SEE WHAT THE **BIG DEAL** IS...
THERE ARE NO SUCH THINGS AS...

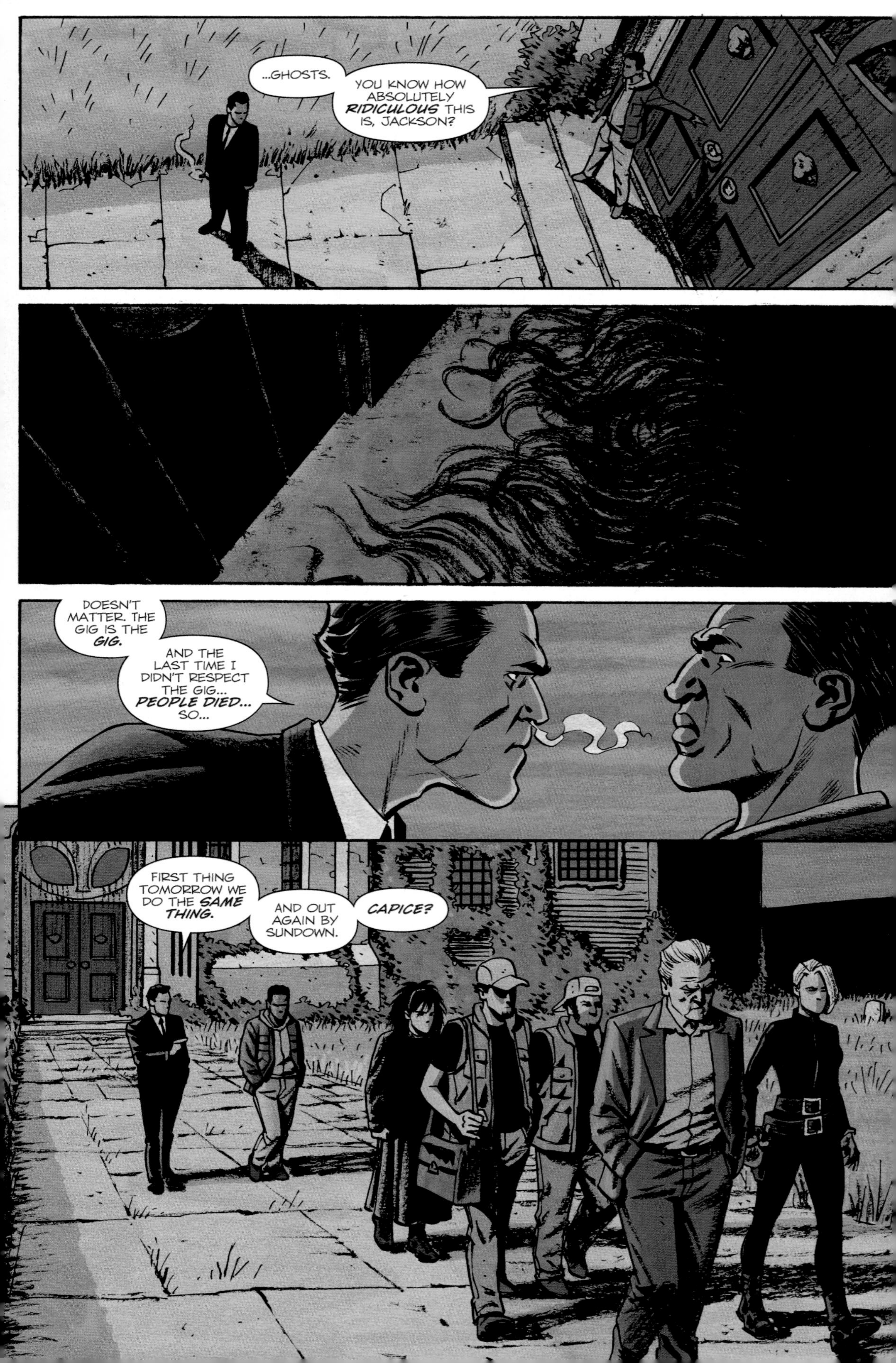
...GHOSTS.
YOU KNOW HOW ABSOLUTELY RIDICULOUS THIS IS, JACKSON?
DOESN'T MATTER. THE GIG IS THE GIG.
AND THE LAST TIME I DIDN'T RESPECT THE GIG... PEOPLE DIED... SO...
FIRST THING TOMORROW WE DO THE SAME THING.
AND OUT AGAIN BY SUNDOWN.
CAPICE?

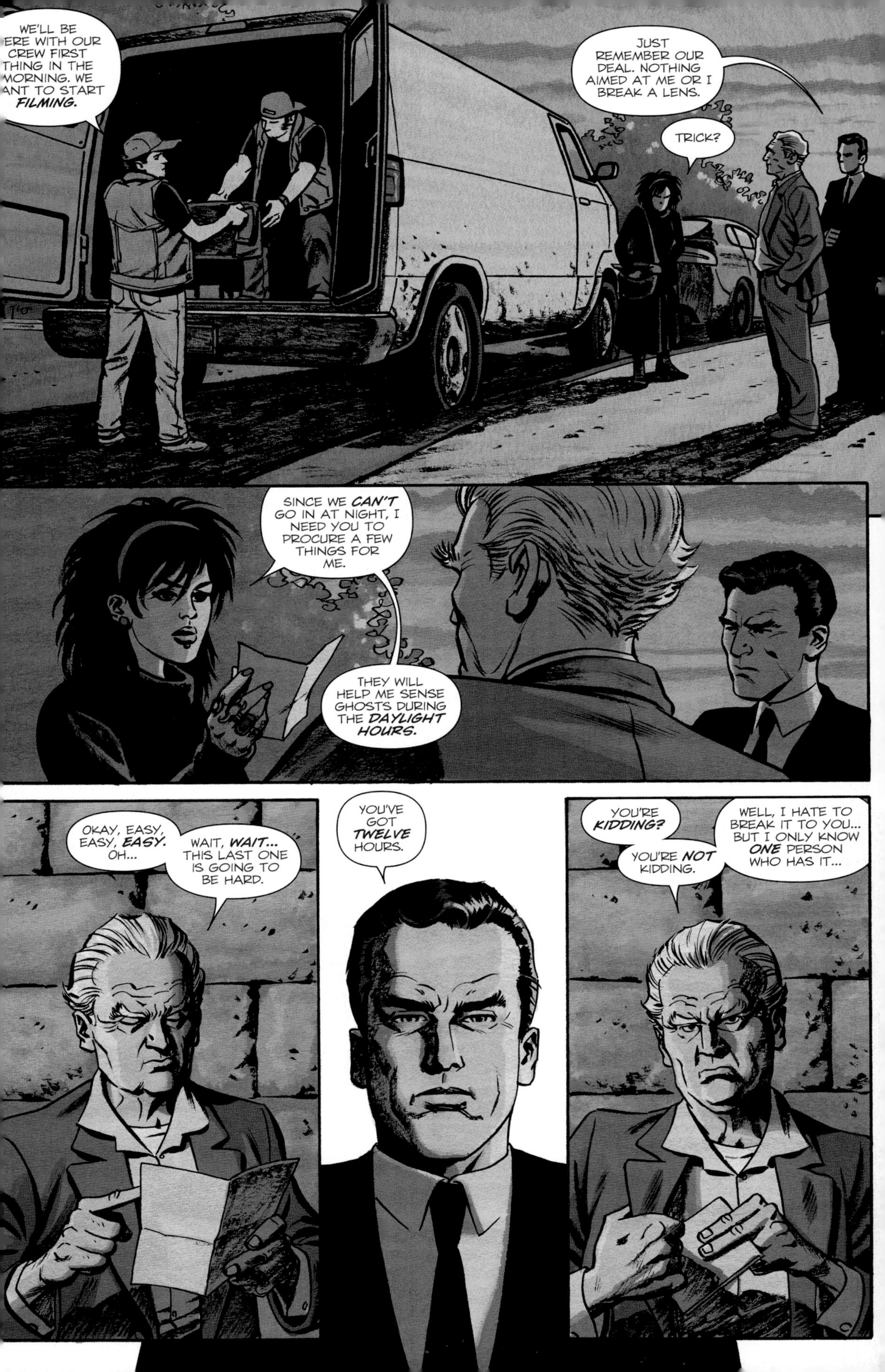
WE'LL BE
ERE WITH OUR CREW FIRST THING IN THE MORNING. WE ANT TO START *FILMING.*
JUST REMEMBER OUR DEAL. NOTHING AIMED AT ME OR I BREAK A LENS.
TRICK?
SINCE WE *CAN'T* GO IN AT NIGHT, I NEED YOU TO PROCURE A FEW THINGS FOR ME.
THEY WILL HELP ME SENSE GHOSTS DURING THE *DAYLIGHT HOURS.*
OKAY, EASY, EASY, *EASY.* OH...
WAIT, *WAIT...* THIS LAST ONE IS GOING TO BE HARD.
YOU'VE GOT *TWELVE* HOURS.
YOU'RE *KIDDING?*
YOU'RE *NOT* KIDDING.
WELL, I HATE TO BREAK IT TO YOU... BUT I ONLY KNOW *ONE* PERSON WHO HAS IT...

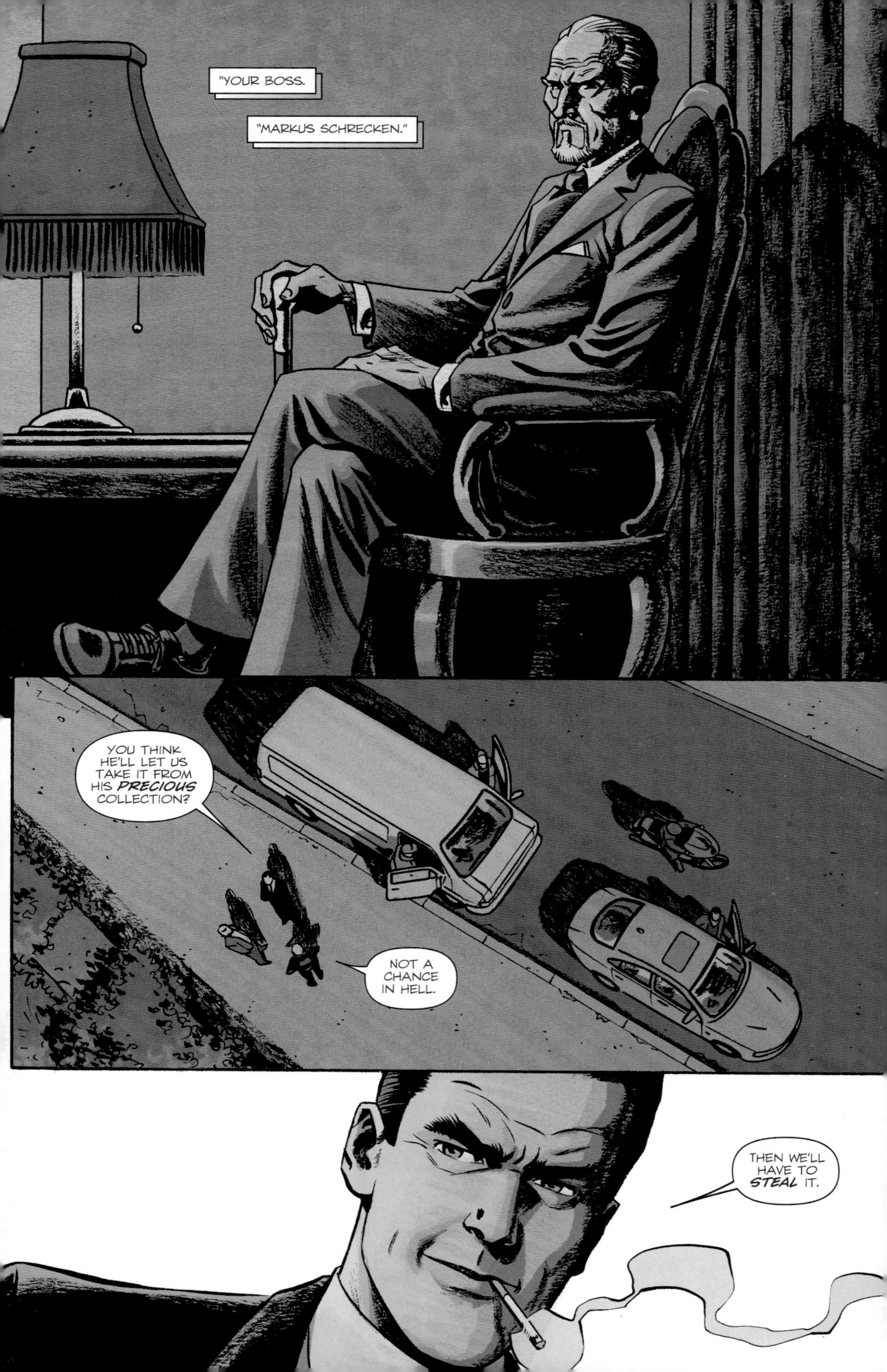
"YOUR BOSS.
"MARKUS SCHRECKEN."
YOU THINK HE'LL LET US TAKE IT FROM HIS *PRECIOUS* COLLECTION?
NOT A CHANCE IN HELL.
THEN WE'LL HAVE TO *STEAL* IT.

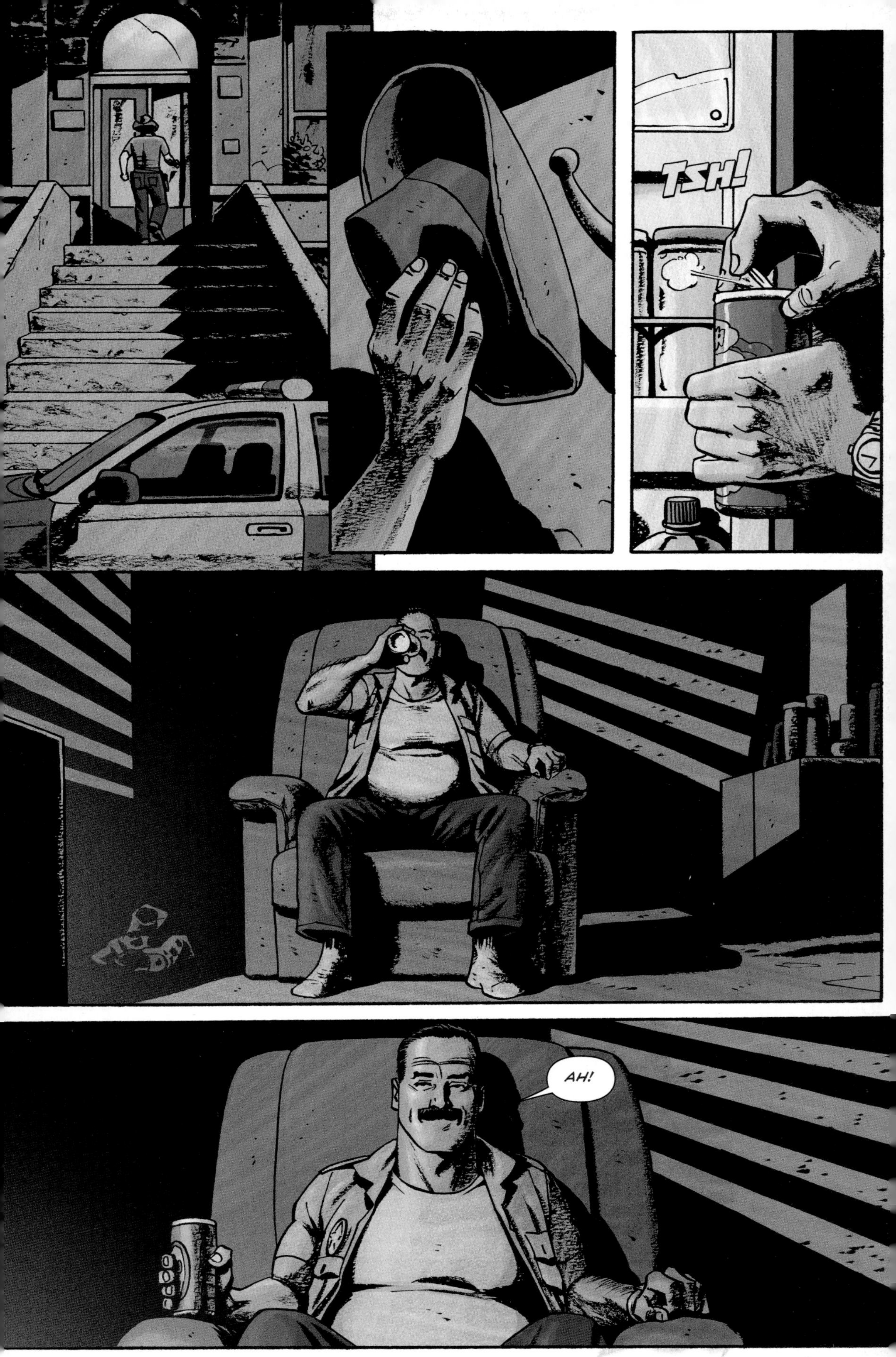
TSH!
AH!

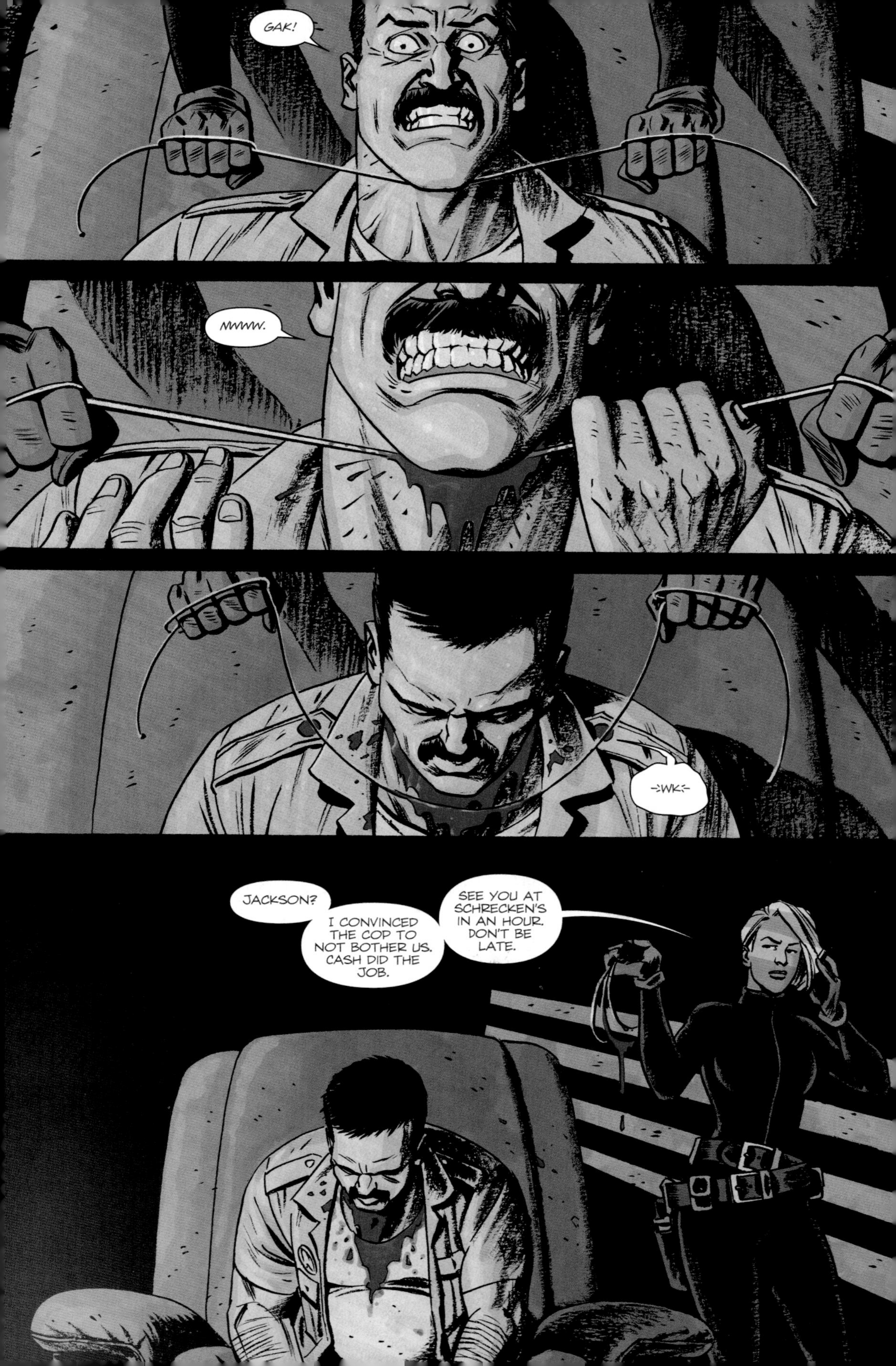
GAK!
NWWW.
-:WK:-
JACKSON?
I CONVINCED THE COP TO NOT BOTHER US. CASH DID THE JOB.
SEE YOU AT SCHRECKEN'S IN AN HOUR. DON'T BE LATE.

CHAPTER THREE

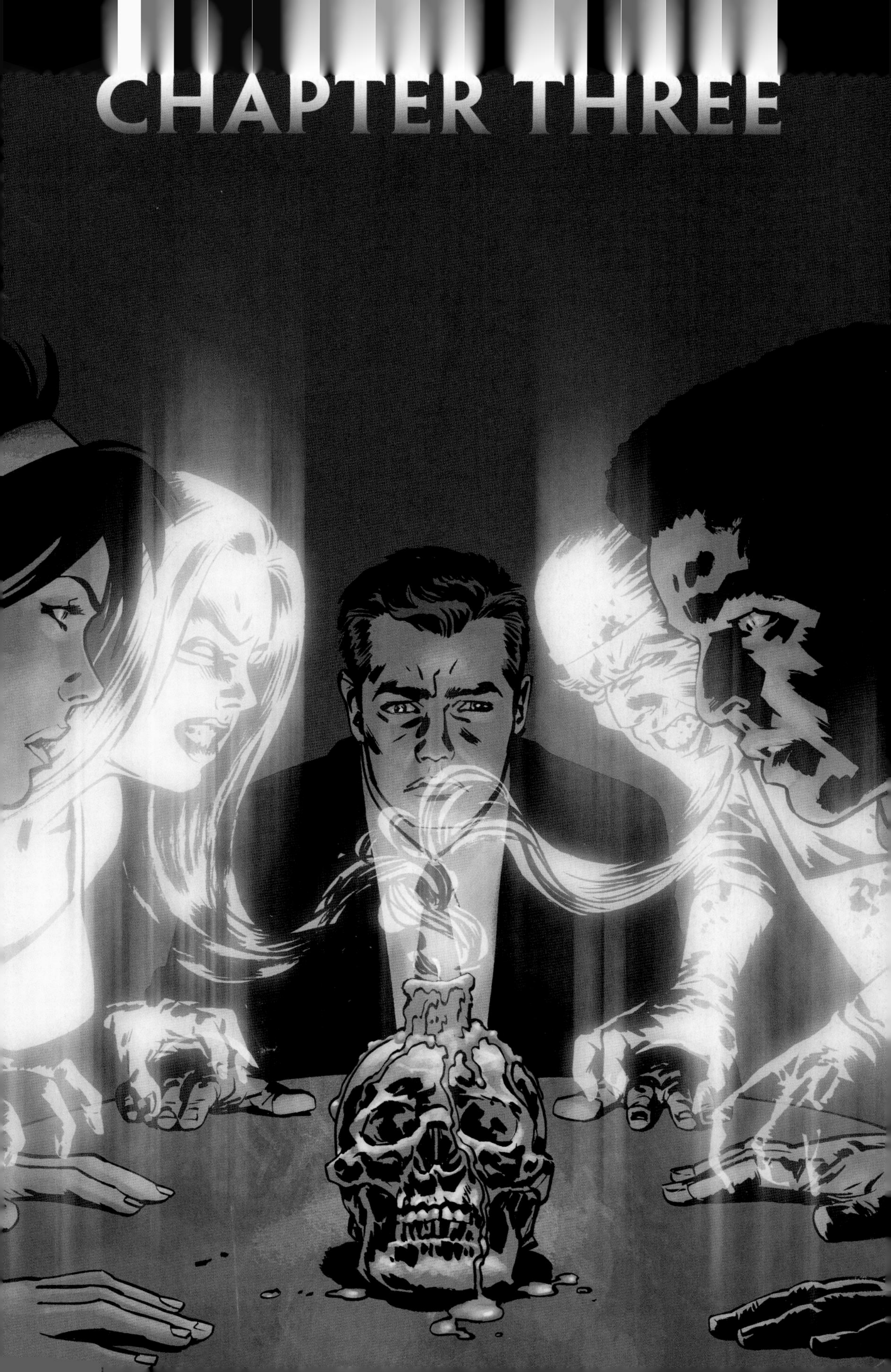

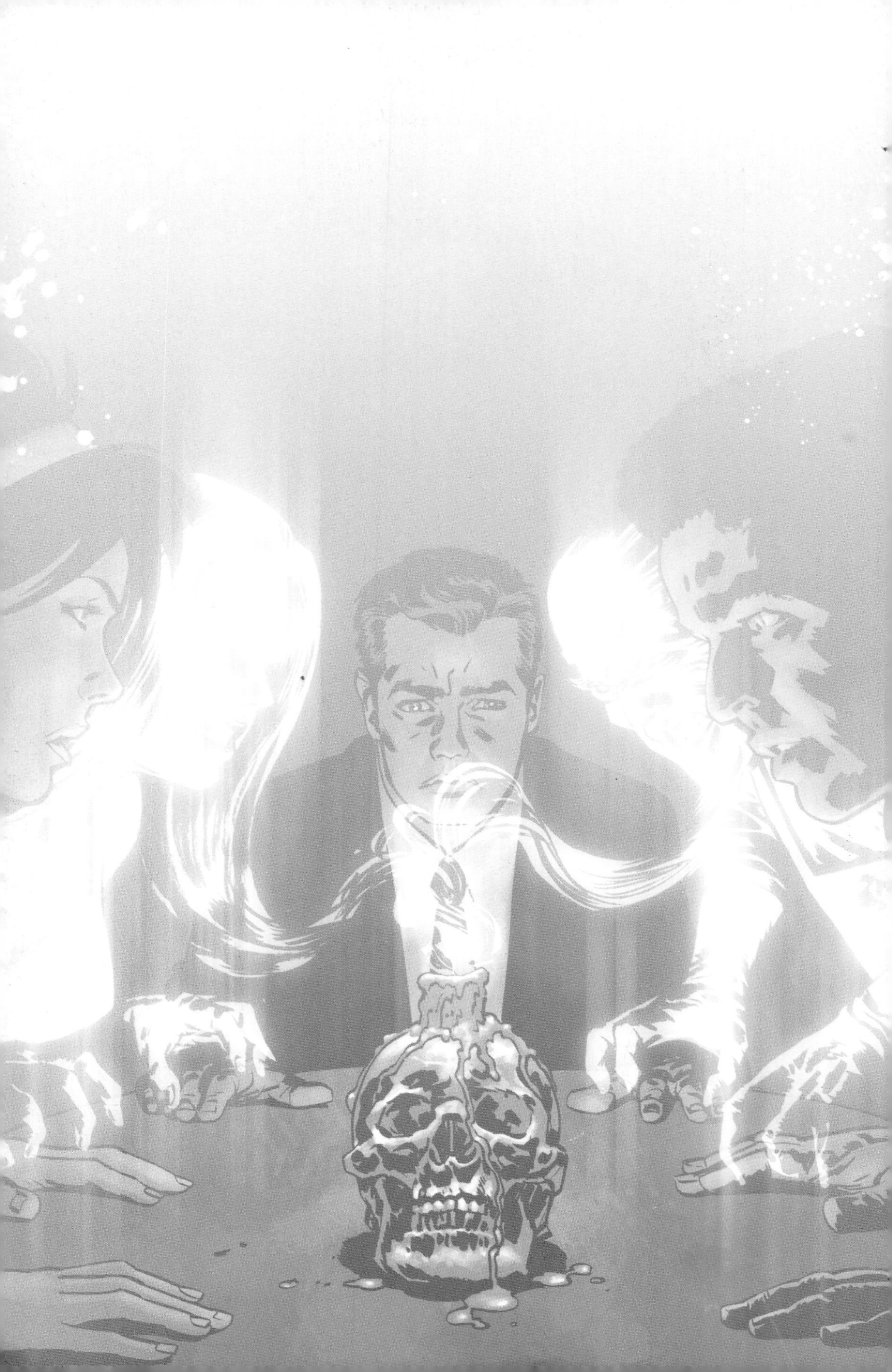

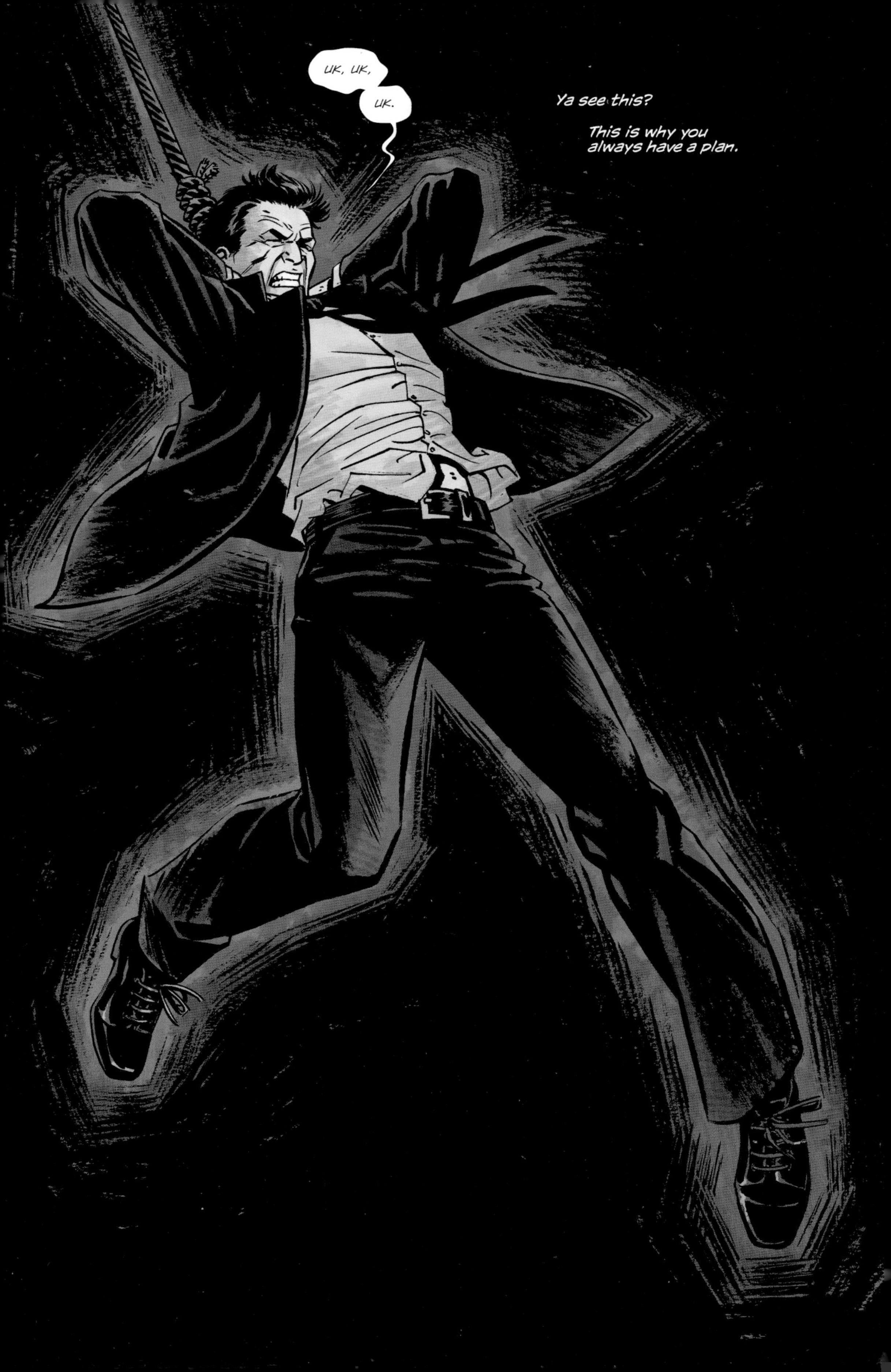
UK, UK,
UK.
Ya see this?
This is why you always have a plan.

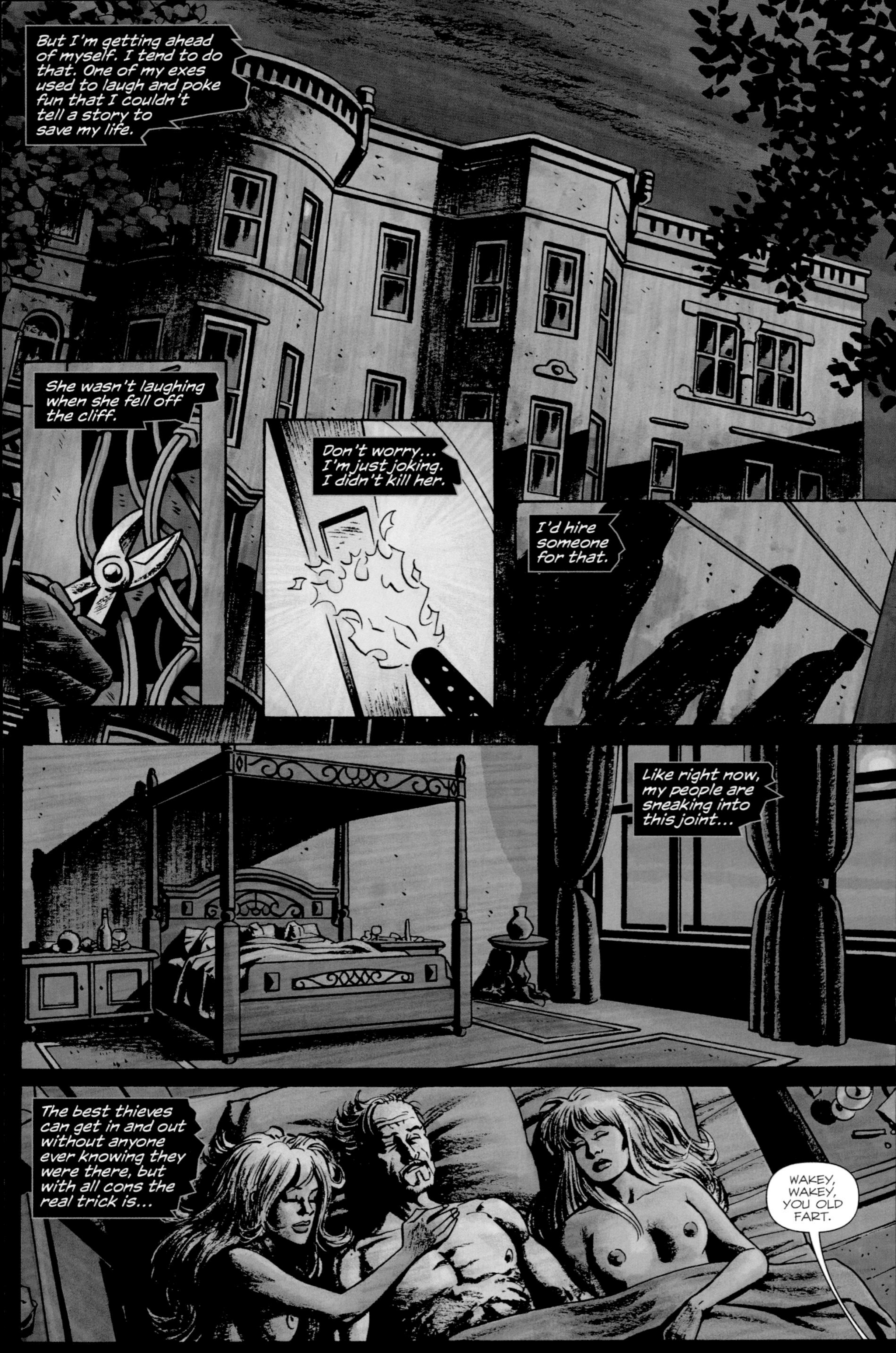
But I'm getting ahead of myself. I tend to do that. One of my exes used to laugh and poke fun that I couldn't tell a story to save my life.
She wasn't laughing when she fell off the cliff.
Don't worry... I'm just joking. I didn't kill her.
I'd hire someone for that.
Like right now, my people are sneaking into this joint...
The best thieves can get in and out without anyone ever knowing they were there, but with all cons the real trick is...
WAKEY, WAKEY, YOU OLD FART.

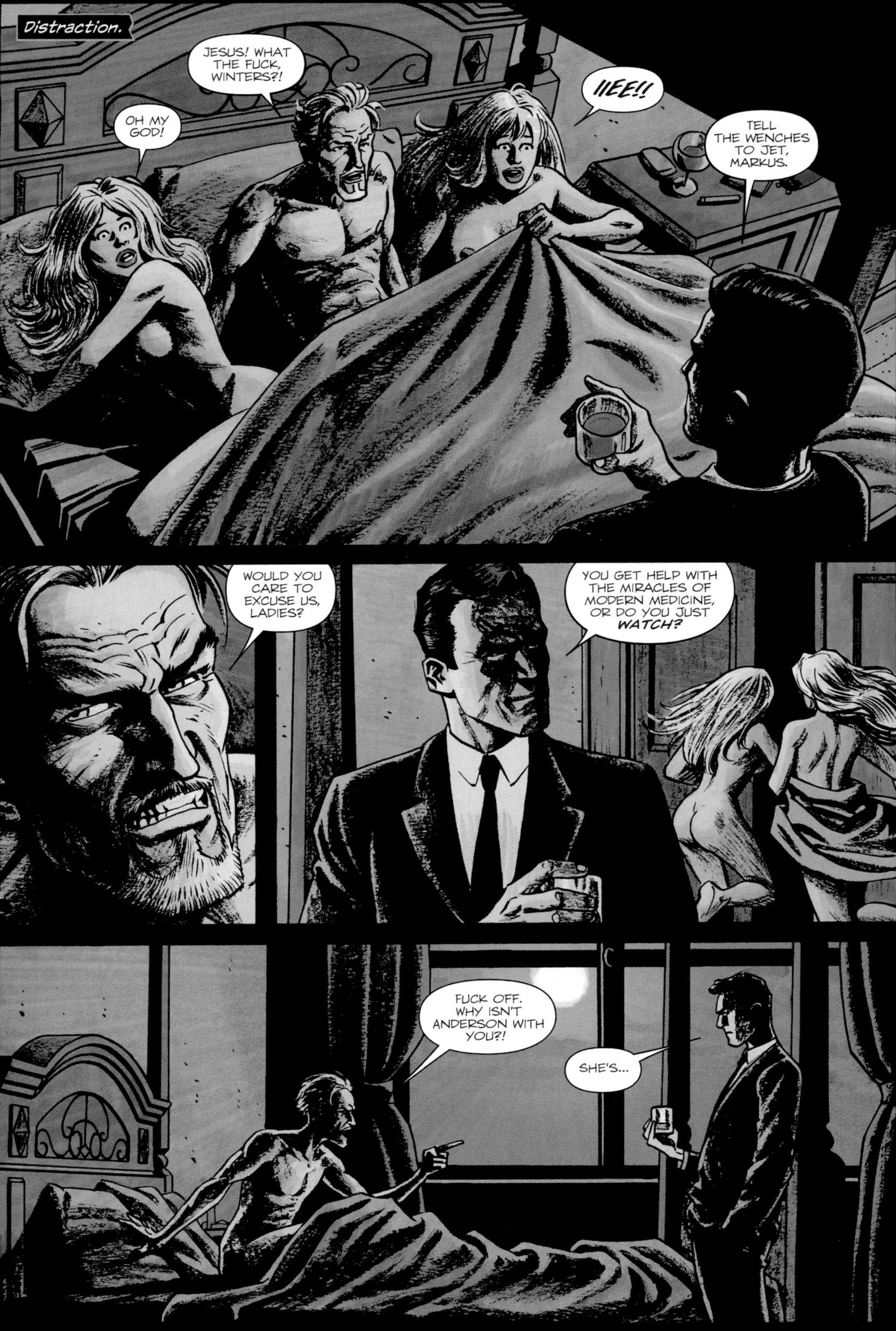

Distraction.
JESUS! WHAT THE FUCK, WINTERS?!
OH MY GOD!
IIEE!!
TELL THE WENCHES TO JET, MARKUS.
WOULD YOU CARE TO EXCUSE US, LADIES?
YOU GET HELP WITH THE MIRACLES OF MODERN MEDICINE, OR DO YOU JUST *WATCH?*
FUCK OFF. WHY ISN'T ANDERSON WITH YOU?!
SHE'S...

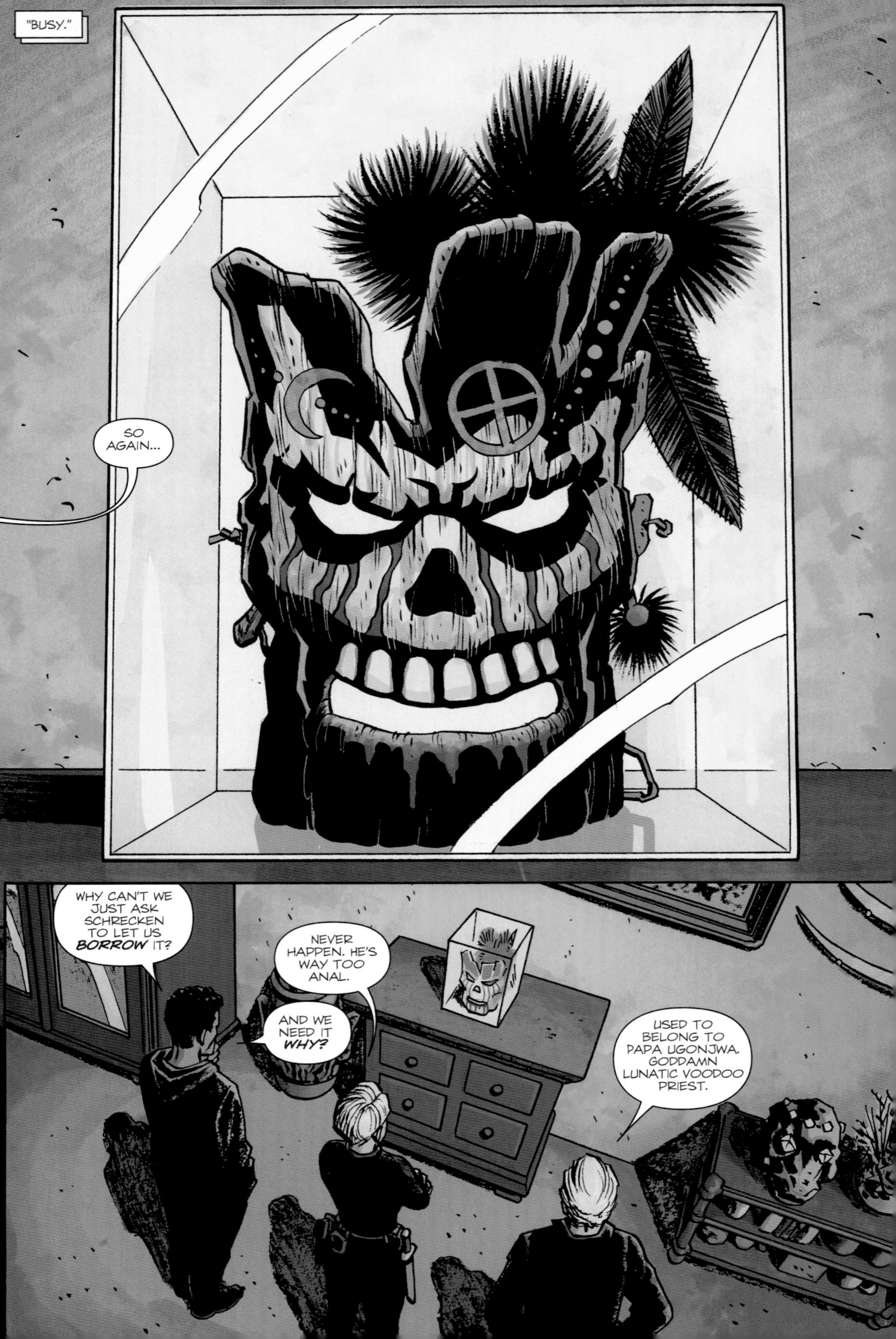
"BUSY."
SO AGAIN...
WHY CAN'T WE JUST ASK SCHRECKEN TO LET US BORROW IT?
NEVER HAPPEN. HE'S WAY TOO ANAL.
AND WE NEED IT WHY?
USED TO BELONG TO PAPA UGONJWA. GODDAMN LUNATIC VOODOO PRIEST.

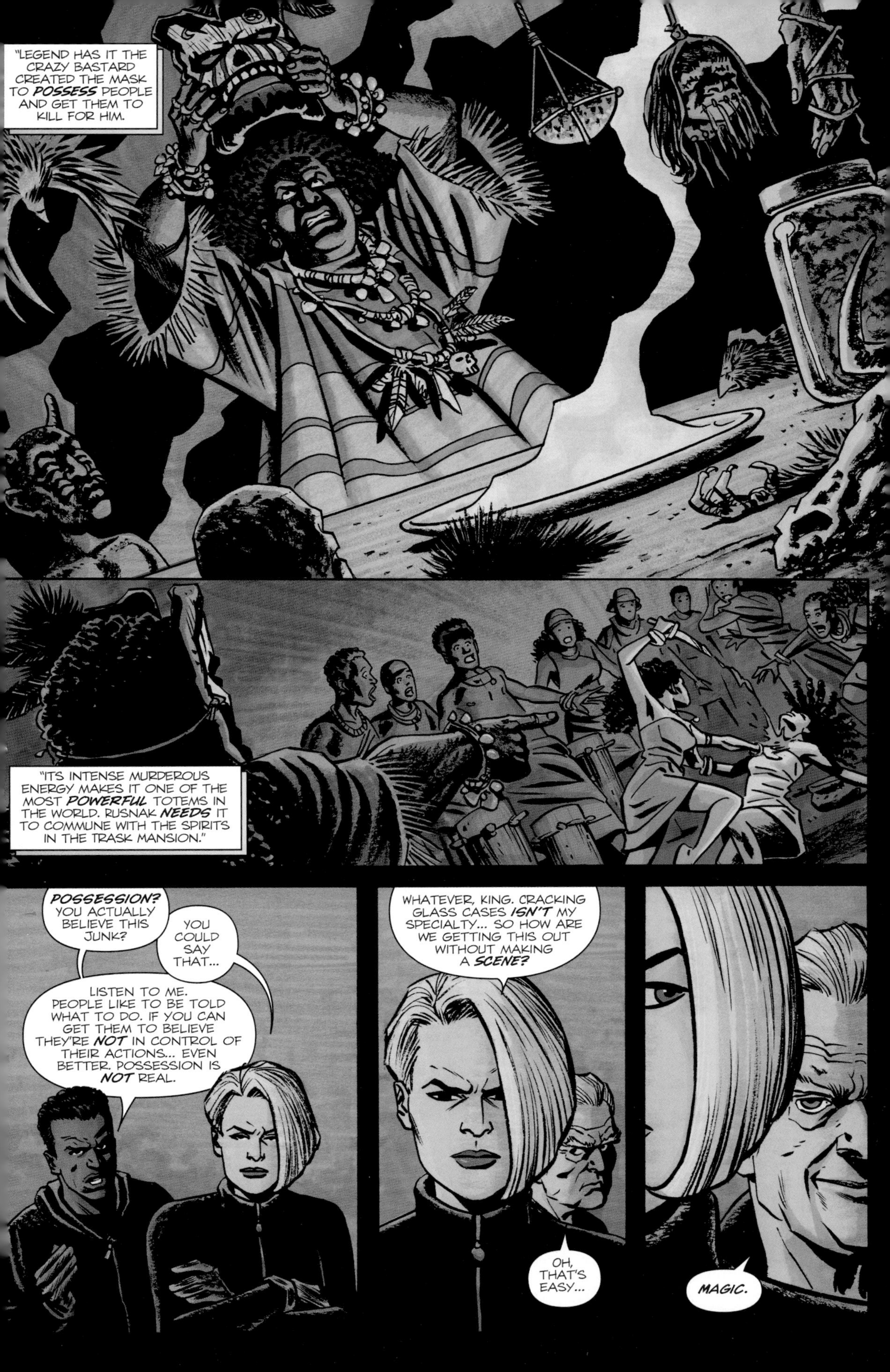
"LEGEND HAS IT THE CRAZY BASTARD CREATED THE MASK TO POSSESS PEOPLE AND GET THEM TO KILL FOR HIM.
"ITS INTENSE MURDEROUS ENERGY MAKES IT ONE OF THE MOST POWERFUL TOTEMS IN THE WORLD. RUSNAK NEEDS IT TO COMMUNE WITH THE SPIRITS IN THE TRASK MANSION."
POSSESSION? YOU ACTUALLY BELIEVE THIS JUNK?
YOU COULD SAY THAT...
LISTEN TO ME. PEOPLE LIKE TO BE TOLD WHAT TO DO. IF YOU CAN GET THEM TO BELIEVE THEY'RE NOT IN CONTROL OF THEIR ACTIONS... EVEN BETTER. POSSESSION IS NOT REAL.
WHATEVER, KING. CRACKING GLASS CASES ISN'T MY SPECIALTY... SO HOW ARE WE GETTING THIS OUT WITHOUT MAKING A SCENE?
OH, THAT'S EASY...
MAGIC.

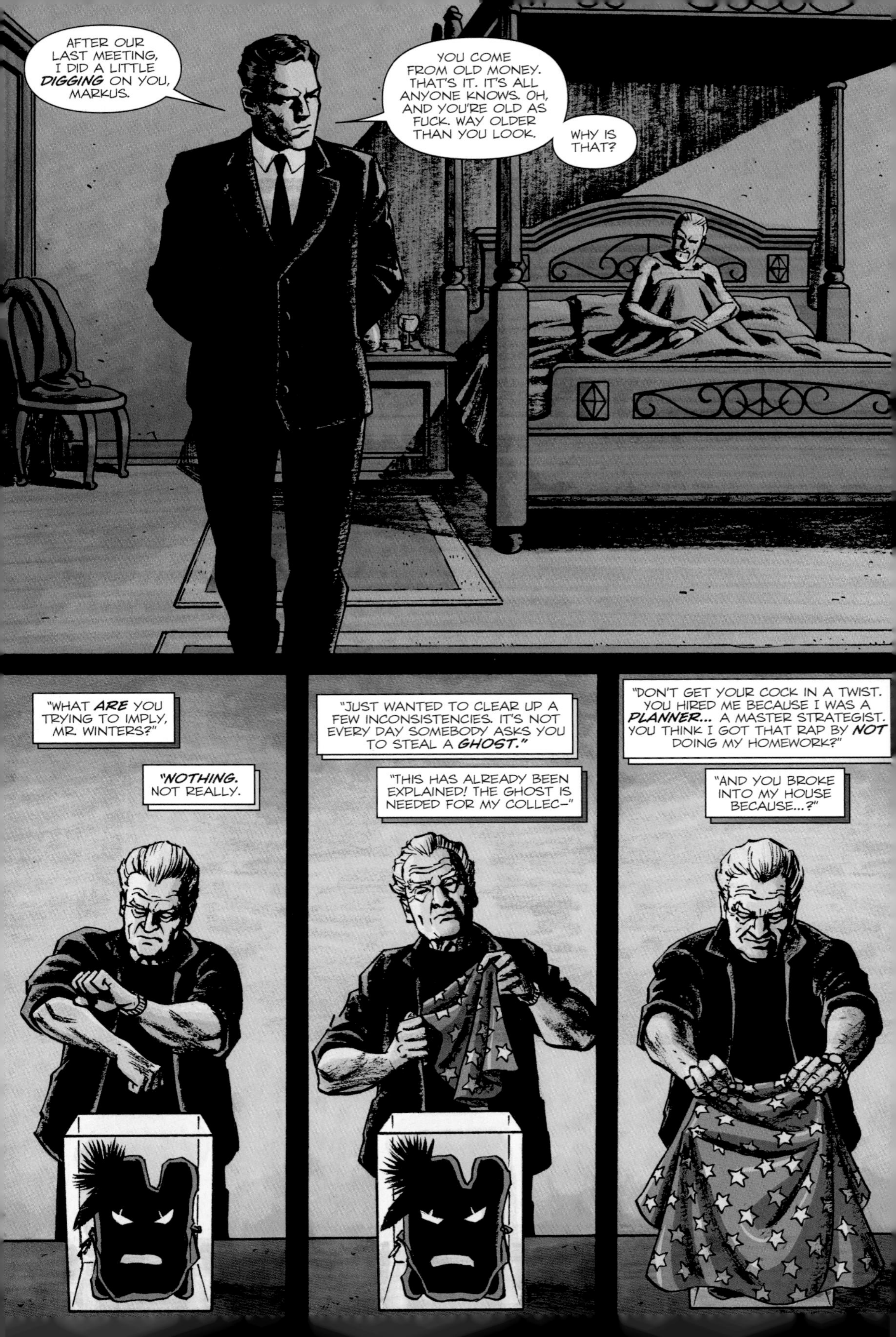

AFTER OUR LAST MEETING, I DID A LITTLE DIGGING ON YOU, MARKUS.
YOU COME FROM OLD MONEY. THAT'S IT. IT'S ALL ANYONE KNOWS. OH, AND YOU'RE OLD AS FUCK. WAY OLDER THAN YOU LOOK.
WHY IS THAT?
"WHAT ARE YOU TRYING TO IMPLY, MR. WINTERS?"
"NOTHING. NOT REALLY.
"JUST WANTED TO CLEAR UP A FEW INCONSISTENCIES. IT'S NOT EVERY DAY SOMEBODY ASKS YOU TO STEAL A GHOST."
"THIS HAS ALREADY BEEN EXPLAINED! THE GHOST IS NEEDED FOR MY COLLEC–"
"DON'T GET YOUR COCK IN A TWIST. YOU HIRED ME BECAUSE I WAS A PLANNER... A MASTER STRATEGIST. YOU THINK I GOT THAT RAP BY NOT DOING MY HOMEWORK?"
"AND YOU BROKE INTO MY HOUSE BECAUSE...?"

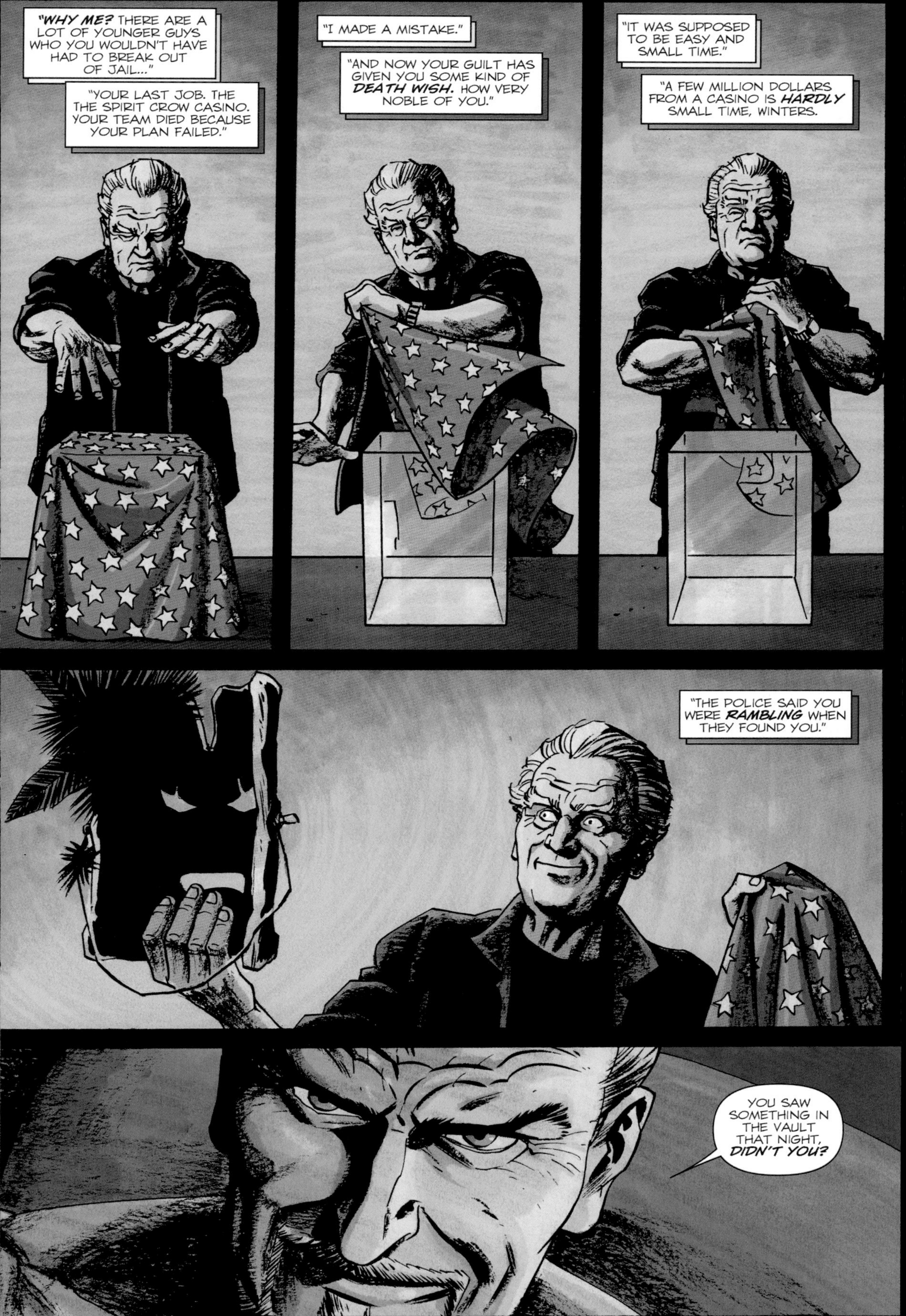
"WHY ME? THERE ARE A LOT OF YOUNGER GUYS WHO YOU WOULDN'T HAVE HAD TO BREAK OUT OF JAIL..."
"YOUR LAST JOB. THE THE SPIRIT CROW CASINO. YOUR TEAM DIED BECAUSE YOUR PLAN FAILED."
"I MADE A MISTAKE."
"AND NOW YOUR GUILT HAS GIVEN YOU SOME KIND OF DEATH WISH. HOW VERY NOBLE OF YOU."
"IT WAS SUPPOSED TO BE EASY AND SMALL TIME."
"A FEW MILLION DOLLARS FROM A CASINO IS HARDLY SMALL TIME, WINTERS.
"THE POLICE SAID YOU WERE RAMBLING WHEN THEY FOUND YOU."
YOU SAW SOMETHING IN THE VAULT THAT NIGHT, DIDN'T YOU?

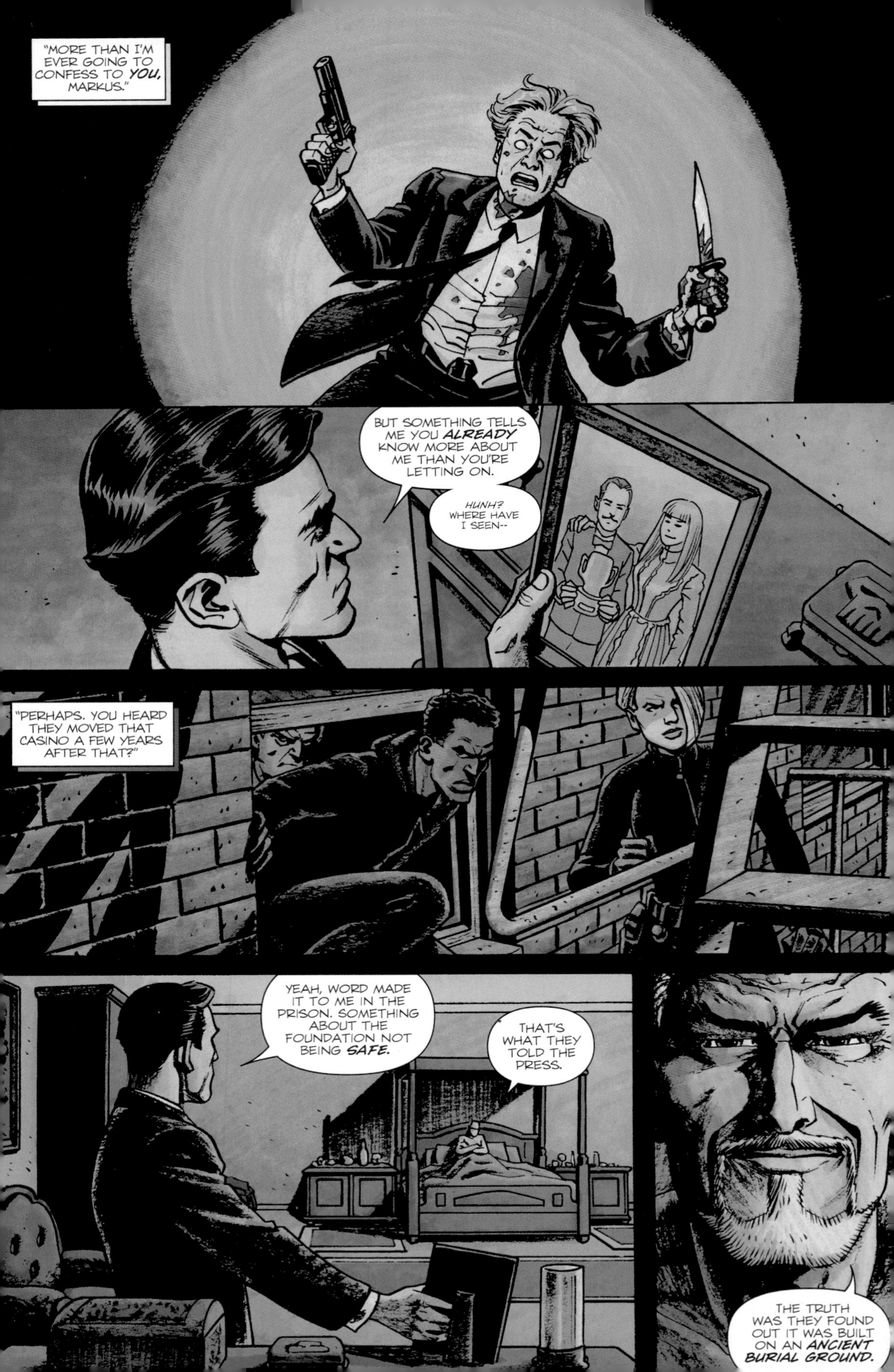
"MORE THAN I'M EVER GOING TO CONFESS TO ***YOU,*** MARKUS."
BUT SOMETHING TELLS ME YOU ***ALREADY*** KNOW MORE ABOUT ME THAN YOU'RE LETTING ON.
HUNH? WHERE HAVE I SEEN--
"PERHAPS. YOU HEARD THEY MOVED THAT CASINO A FEW YEARS AFTER THAT?"
YEAH, WORD MADE IT TO ME IN THE PRISON. SOMETHING ABOUT THE FOUNDATION NOT BEING ***SAFE.***
THAT'S WHAT THEY TOLD THE PRESS.
THE TRUTH WAS THEY FOUND OUT IT WAS BUILT ON AN ***ANCIENT BURIAL GROUND.***

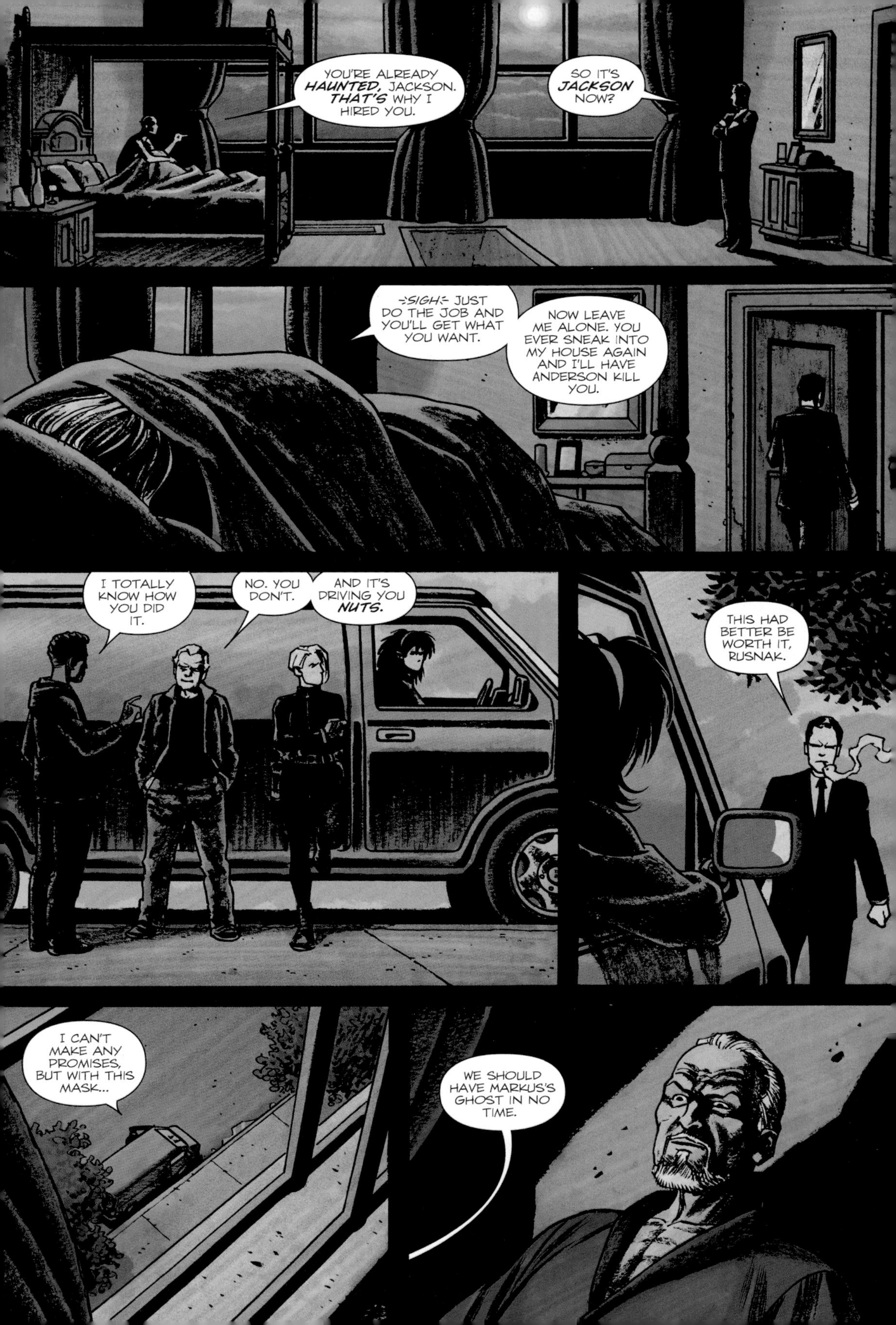
YOU'RE ALREADY **HAUNTED,** JACKSON. **THAT'S** WHY I HIRED YOU.
SO IT'S **JACKSON** NOW?
-SIGH- JUST DO THE JOB AND YOU'LL GET WHAT YOU WANT.
NOW LEAVE ME ALONE. YOU EVER SNEAK INTO MY HOUSE AGAIN AND I'LL HAVE ANDERSON KILL YOU.
I TOTALLY KNOW HOW YOU DID IT.
NO. YOU DON'T.
AND IT'S DRIVING YOU **NUTS.**
THIS HAD BETTER BE WORTH IT, RUSNAK.
I CAN'T MAKE ANY PROMISES, BUT WITH THIS MASK...
WE SHOULD HAVE MARKUS'S GHOST IN NO TIME.

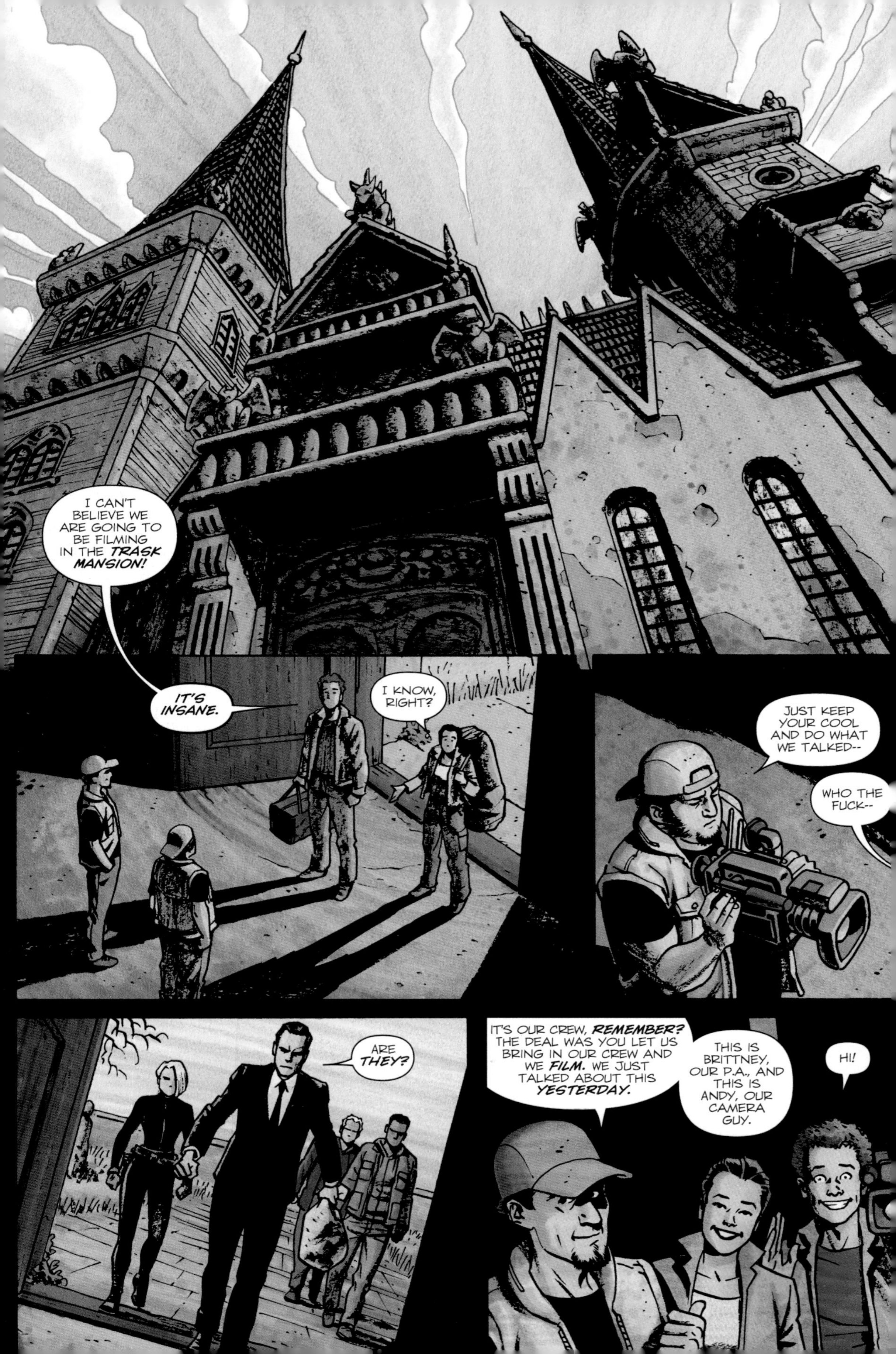
I CAN'T BELIEVE WE ARE GOING TO BE FILMING IN THE *TRASK MANSION!*
IT'S INSANE.
I KNOW, RIGHT?
JUST KEEP YOUR COOL AND DO WHAT WE TALKED--
WHO THE FUCK--
ARE *THEY?*
IT'S OUR CREW, *REMEMBER?* THE DEAL WAS YOU LET US BRING IN OUR CREW AND WE *FILM.* WE JUST TALKED ABOUT THIS *YESTERDAY.*
THIS IS BRITTNEY, OUR P.A., AND THIS IS ANDY, OUR CAMERA GUY.
HI!

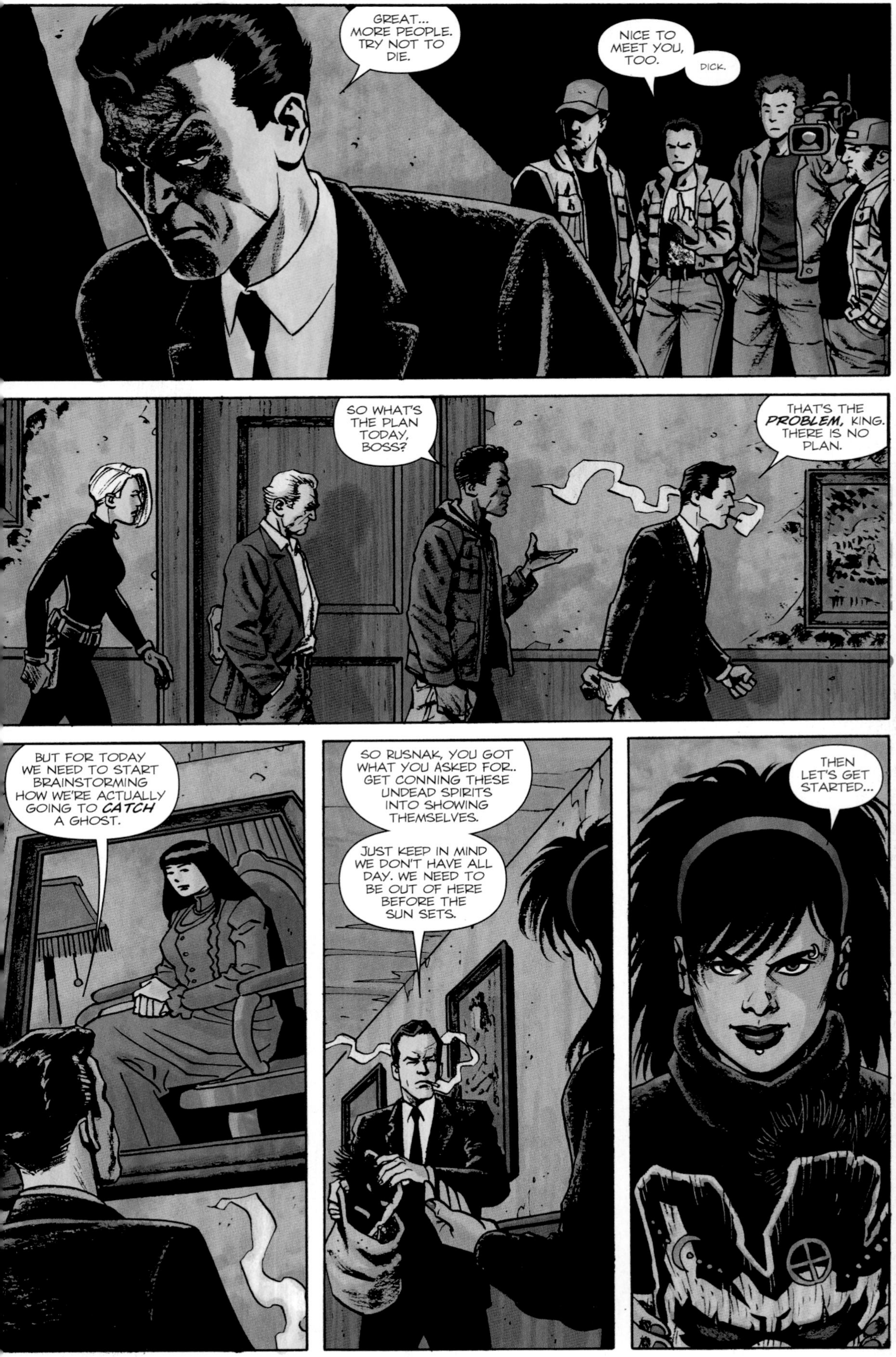
GREAT... MORE PEOPLE. TRY NOT TO DIE.
NICE TO MEET YOU, TOO.
DICK.
SO WHAT'S THE PLAN TODAY, BOSS?
THAT'S THE PROBLEM, KING. THERE IS NO PLAN.
BUT FOR TODAY WE NEED TO START BRAINSTORMING HOW WE'RE ACTUALLY GOING TO CATCH A GHOST.
SO RUSNAK, YOU GOT WHAT YOU ASKED FOR.. GET CONNING THESE UNDEAD SPIRITS INTO SHOWING THEMSELVES.
JUST KEEP IN MIND WE DON'T HAVE ALL DAY. WE NEED TO BE OUT OF HERE BEFORE THE SUN SETS.
THEN LET'S GET STARTED...

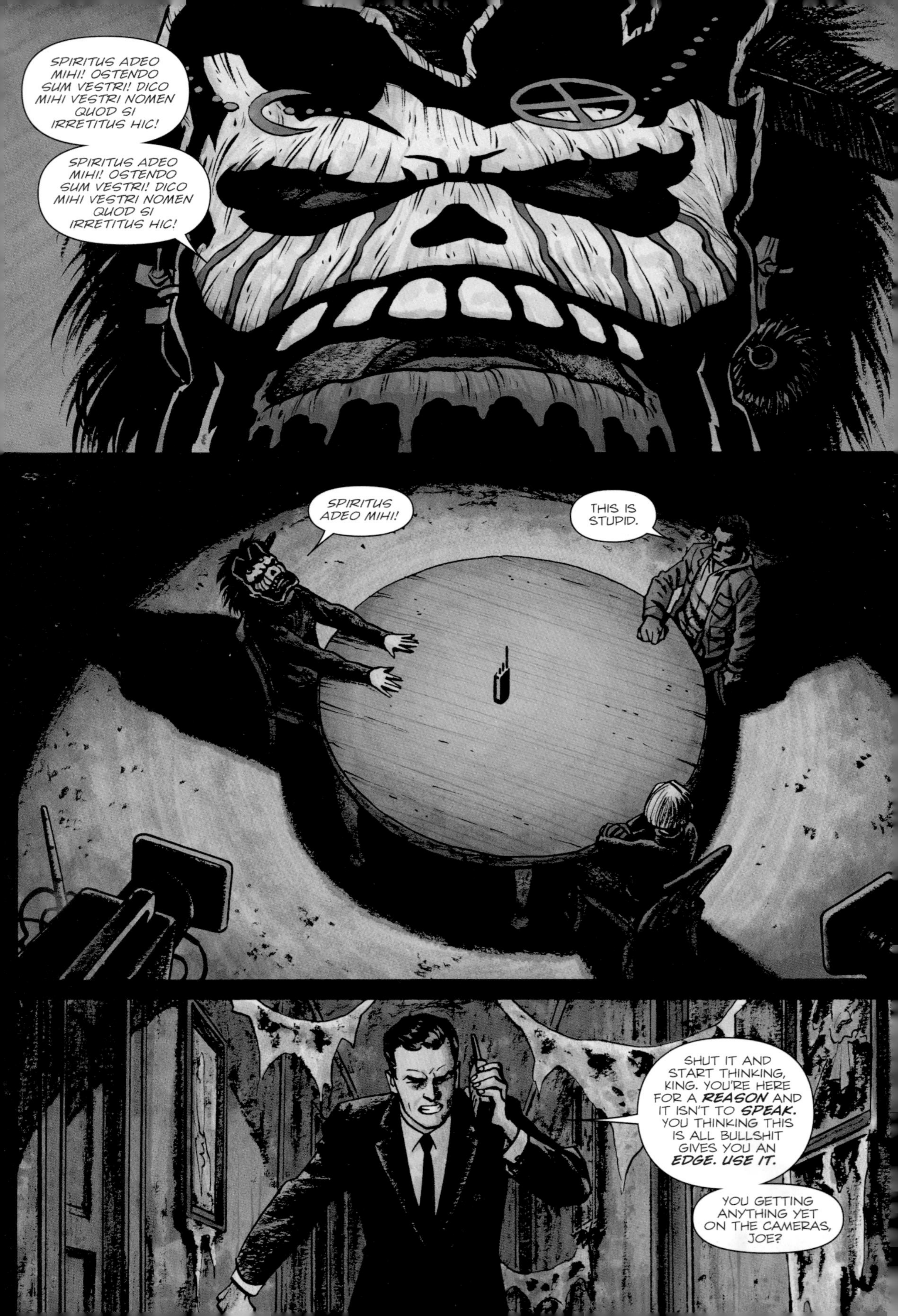
SPIRITUS ADEO MIHI! OSTENDO SUM VESTRI! DICO MIHI VESTRI NOMEN QUOD SI IRRETITUS HIC!
SPIRITUS ADEO MIHI! OSTENDO SUM VESTRI! DICO MIHI VESTRI NOMEN QUOD SI IRRETITUS HIC!
SPIRITUS ADEO MIHI!
THIS IS STUPID.
SHUT IT AND START THINKING, KING. YOU'RE HERE FOR A **REASON** AND IT ISN'T TO **SPEAK.** YOU THINKING THIS IS ALL BULLSHIT GIVES YOU AN **EDGE. USE IT.**
YOU GETTING ANYTHING YET ON THE CAMERAS, JOE?

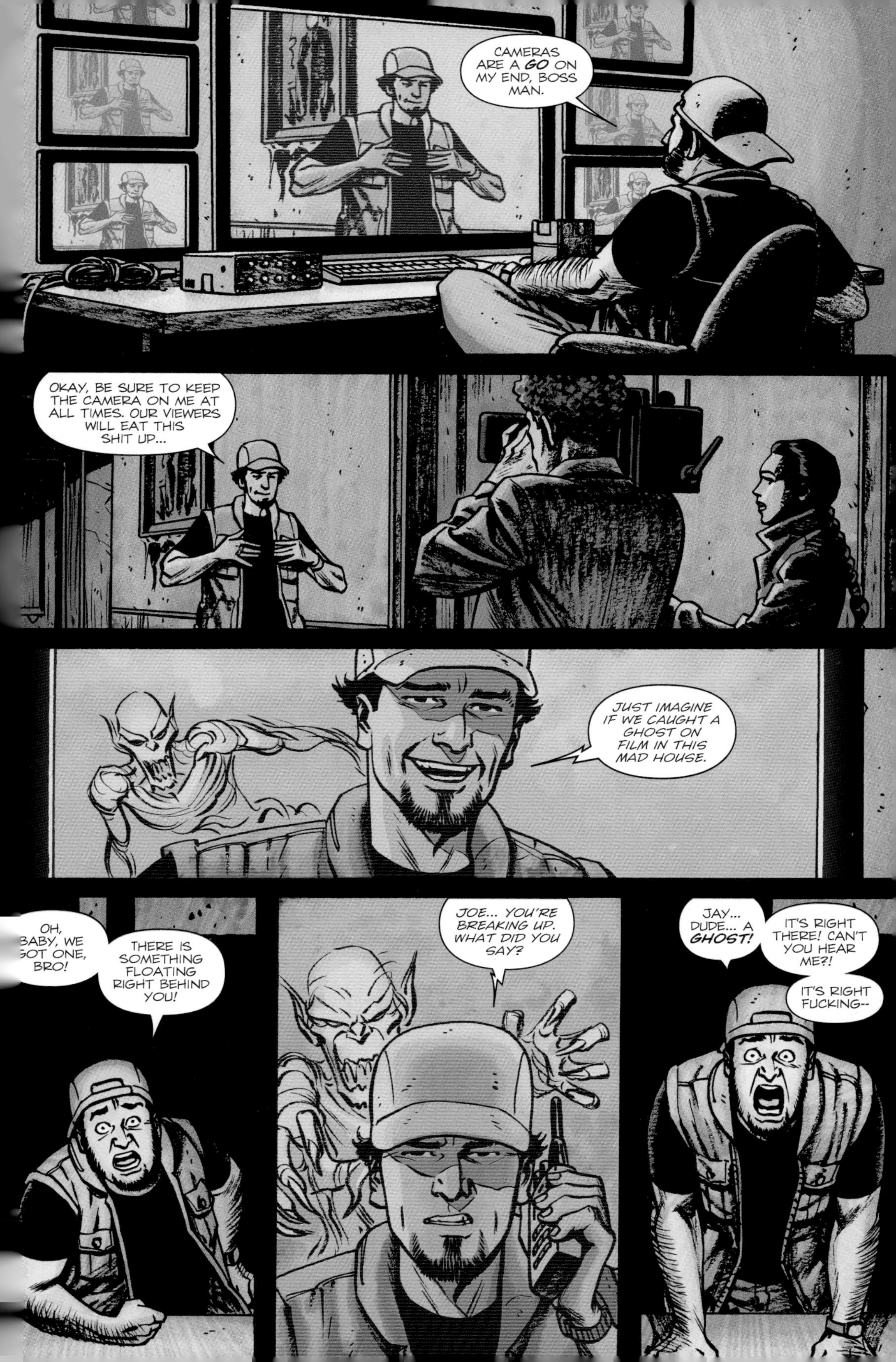
CAMERAS ARE A GO ON MY END, BOSS MAN.
OKAY, BE SURE TO KEEP THE CAMERA ON ME AT ALL TIMES. OUR VIEWERS WILL EAT THIS SHIT UP...
JUST IMAGINE IF WE CAUGHT A GHOST ON FILM IN THIS MAD HOUSE.
OH, BABY, WE GOT ONE, BRO!
THERE IS SOMETHING FLOATING RIGHT BEHIND YOU!
JOE... YOU'RE BREAKING UP. WHAT DID YOU SAY?
JAY... DUDE... A GHOST!
IT'S RIGHT THERE! CAN'T YOU HEAR ME?!
IT'S RIGHT FUCKING--

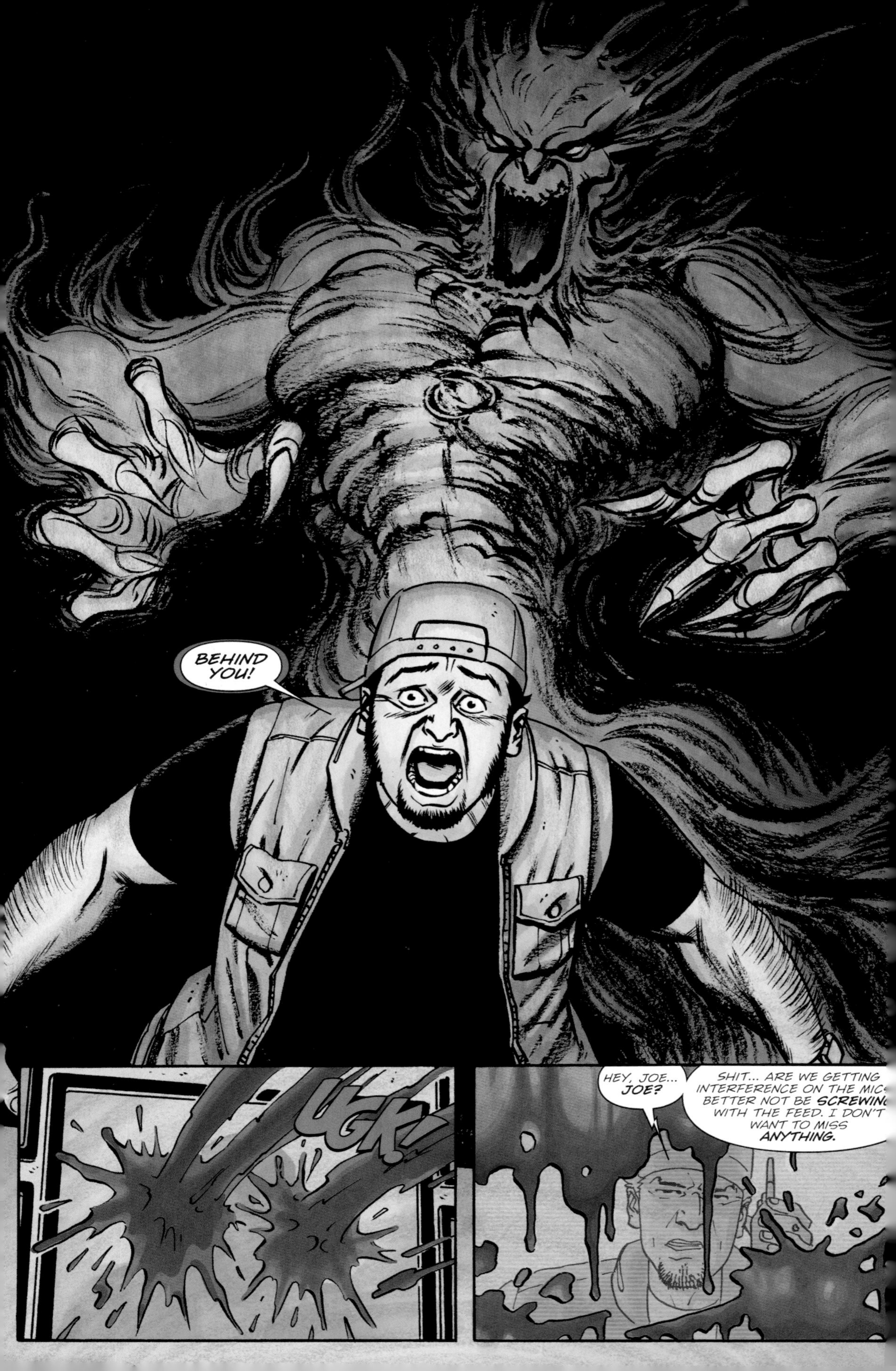
BEHIND YOU!
UGK!
HEY, JOE... JOE?
SHIT... ARE WE GETTING INTERFERENCE ON THE MICS BETTER NOT BE SCREWING WITH THE FEED. I DON'T WANT TO MISS ANYTHING.

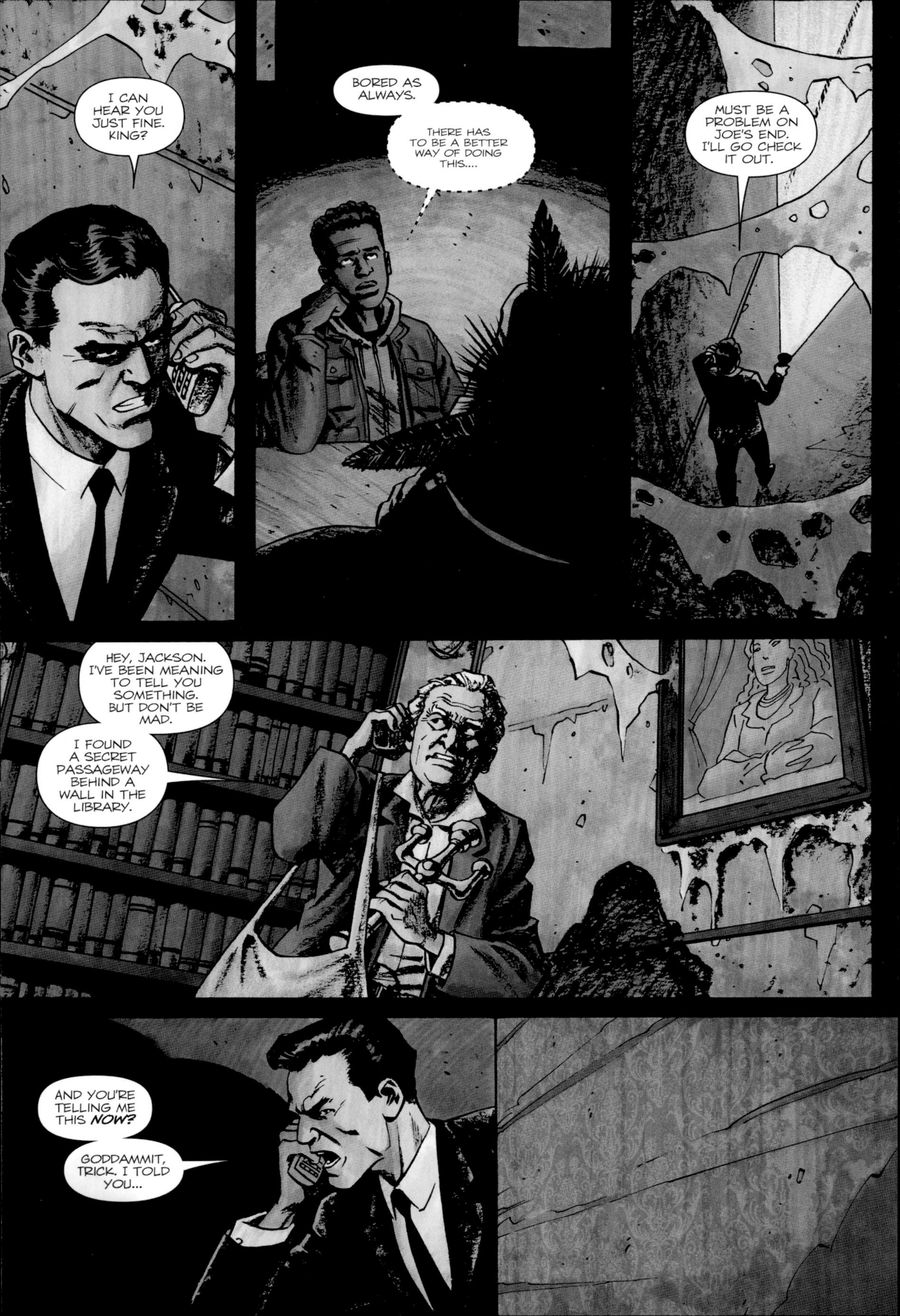

I CAN HEAR YOU JUST FINE. KING?
BORED AS ALWAYS.
THERE HAS TO BE A BETTER WAY OF DOING THIS....
MUST BE A PROBLEM ON JOE'S END. I'LL GO CHECK IT OUT.
HEY, JACKSON. I'VE BEEN MEANING TO TELL YOU SOMETHING. BUT DON'T BE MAD.
I FOUND A SECRET PASSAGEWAY BEHIND A WALL IN THE LIBRARY.
AND YOU'RE TELLING ME THIS NOW?
GODDAMMIT, TRICK. I TOLD YOU...

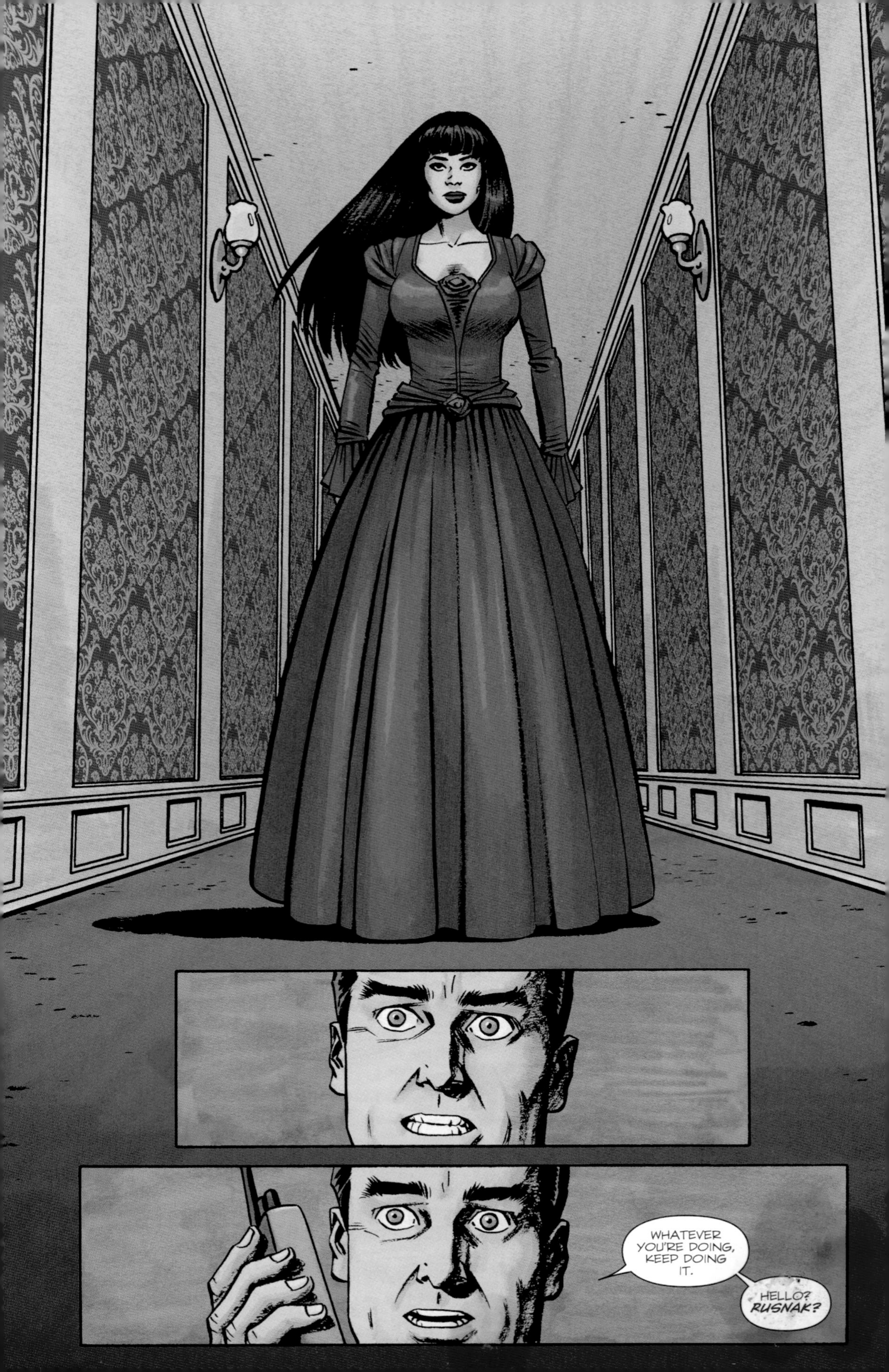
WHATEVER YOU'RE DOING, KEEP DOING IT.
HELLO? RUSNAK?

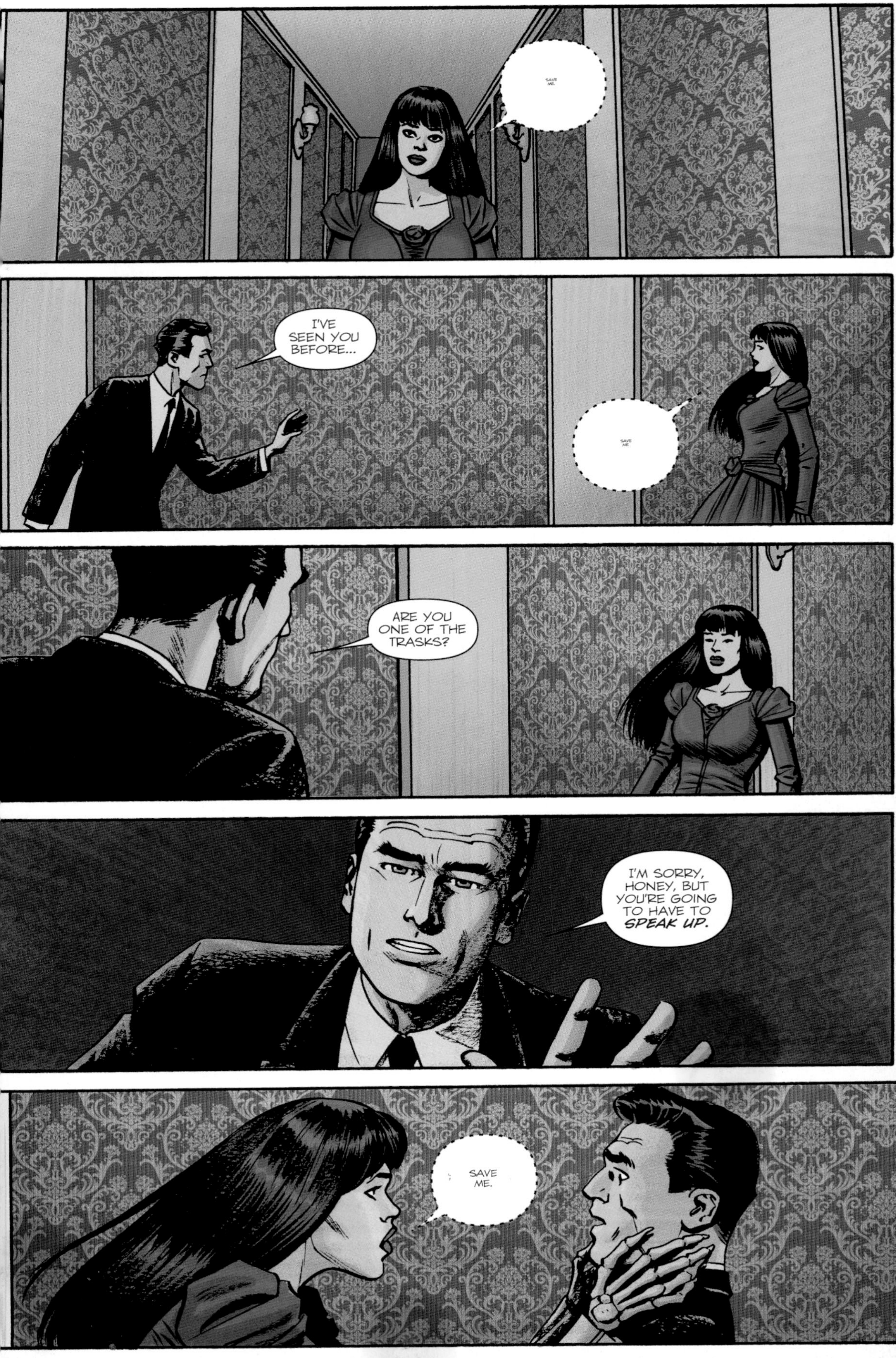
SAVE ME.
I'VE SEEN YOU BEFORE...
SAVE ME.
ARE YOU ONE OF THE TRASKS?
I'M SORRY, HONEY, BUT YOU'RE GOING TO HAVE TO *SPEAK UP.*
SAVE ME.

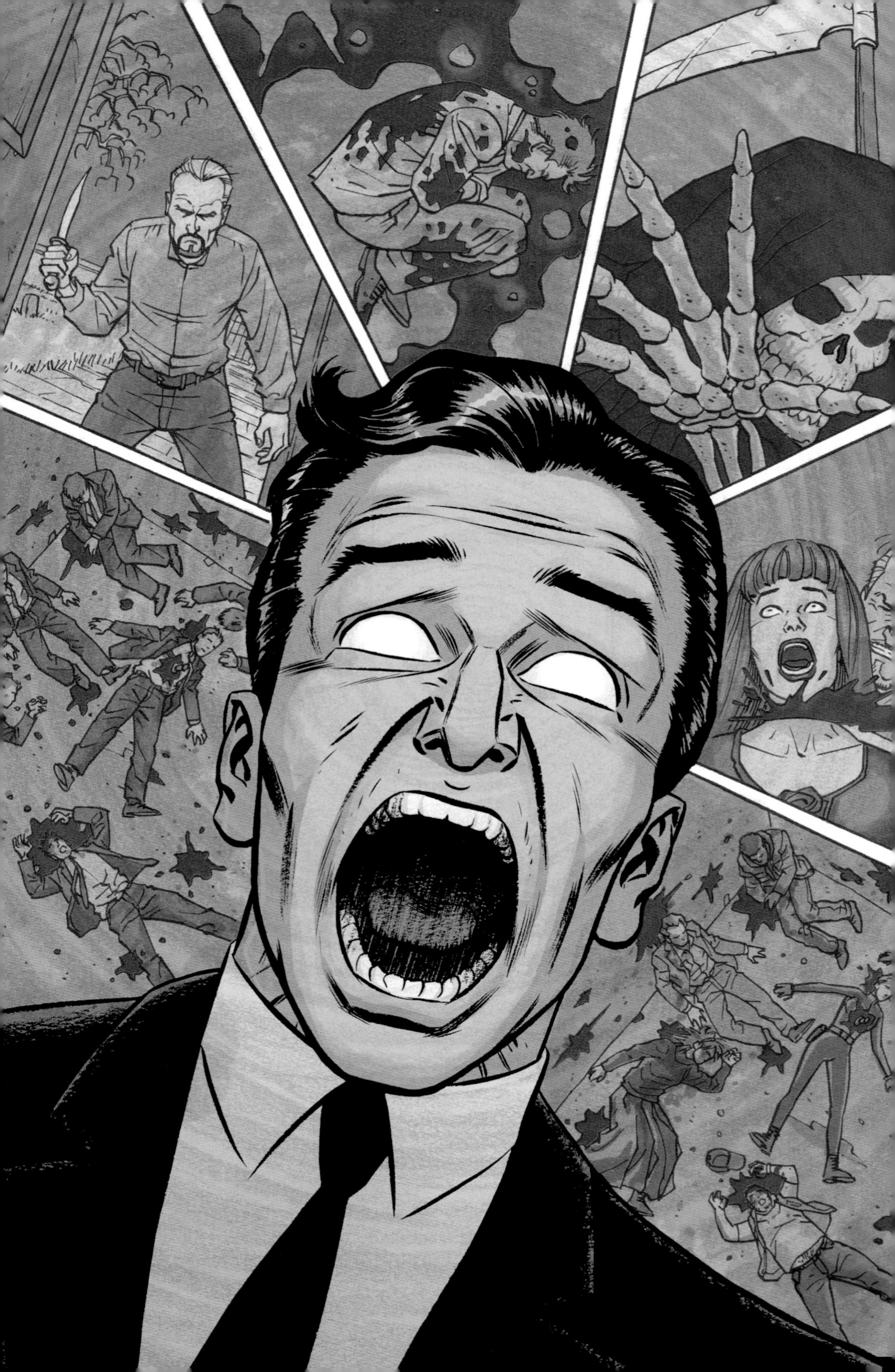

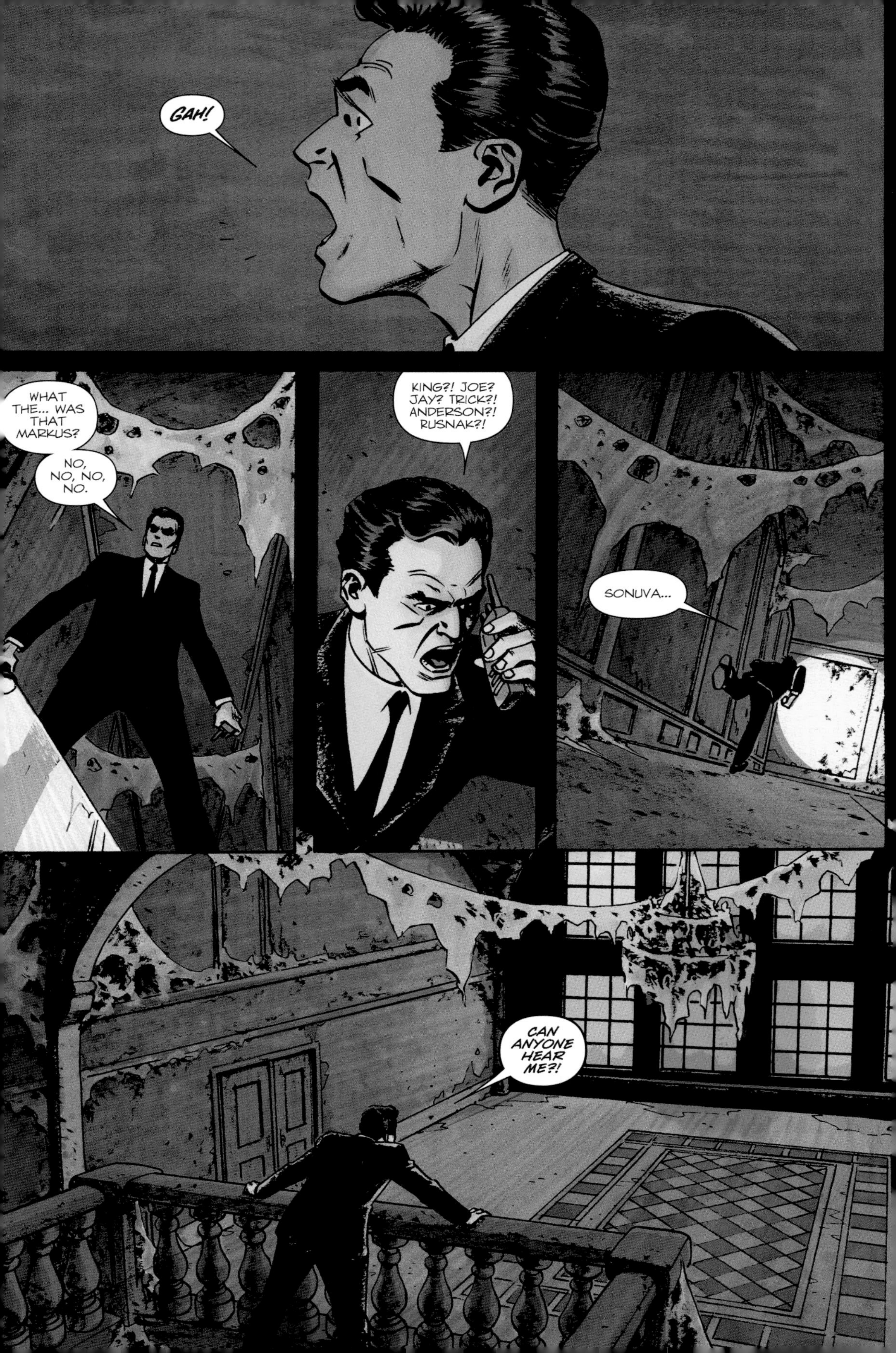
GAH!
WHAT THE... WAS THAT MARKUS?
NO, NO, NO, NO.
KING?! JOE? JAY? TRICK?! ANDERSON?! RUSNAK?!
SONUVA...
CAN ANYONE HEAR ME?!

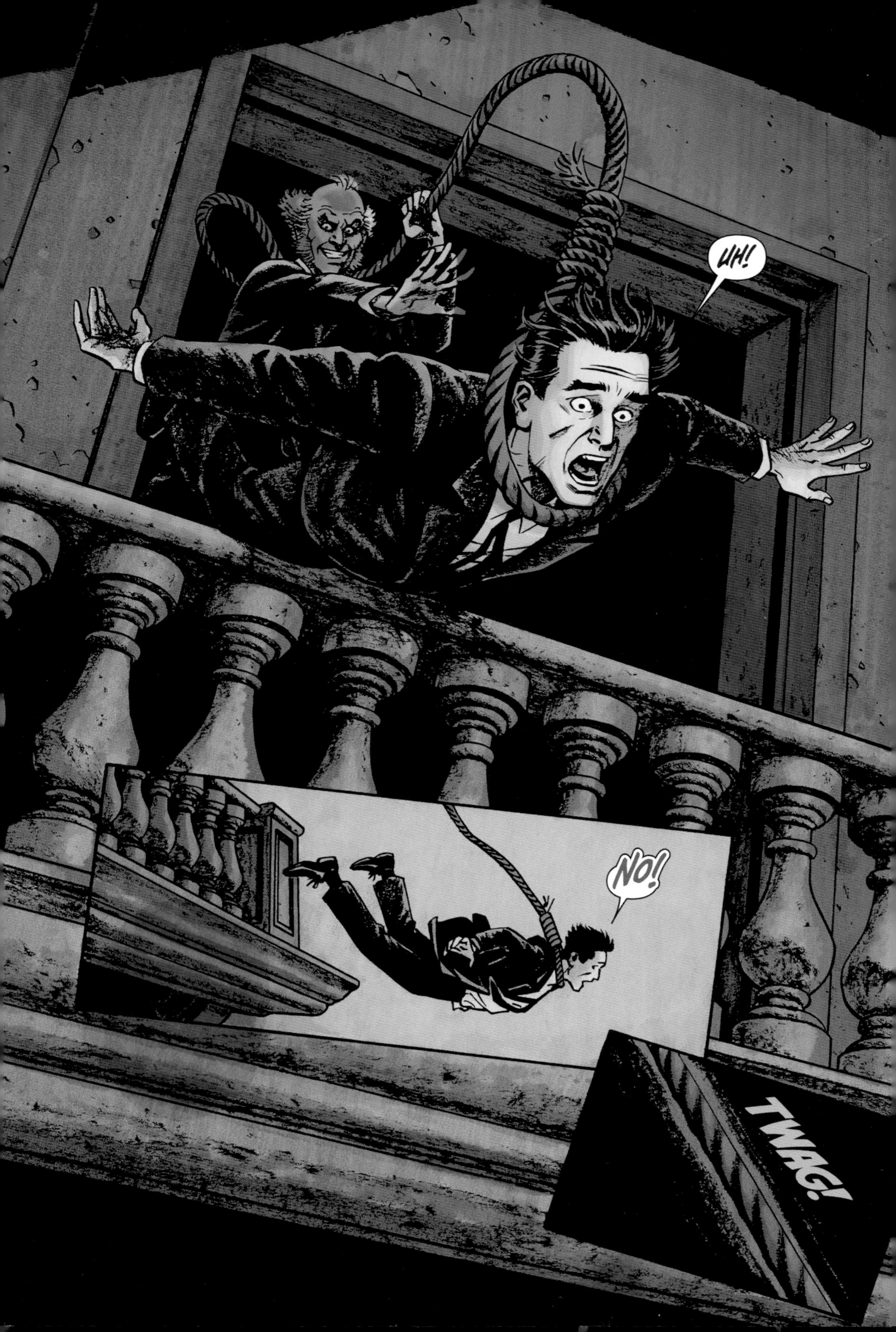
UH!
NO!
TWAG!

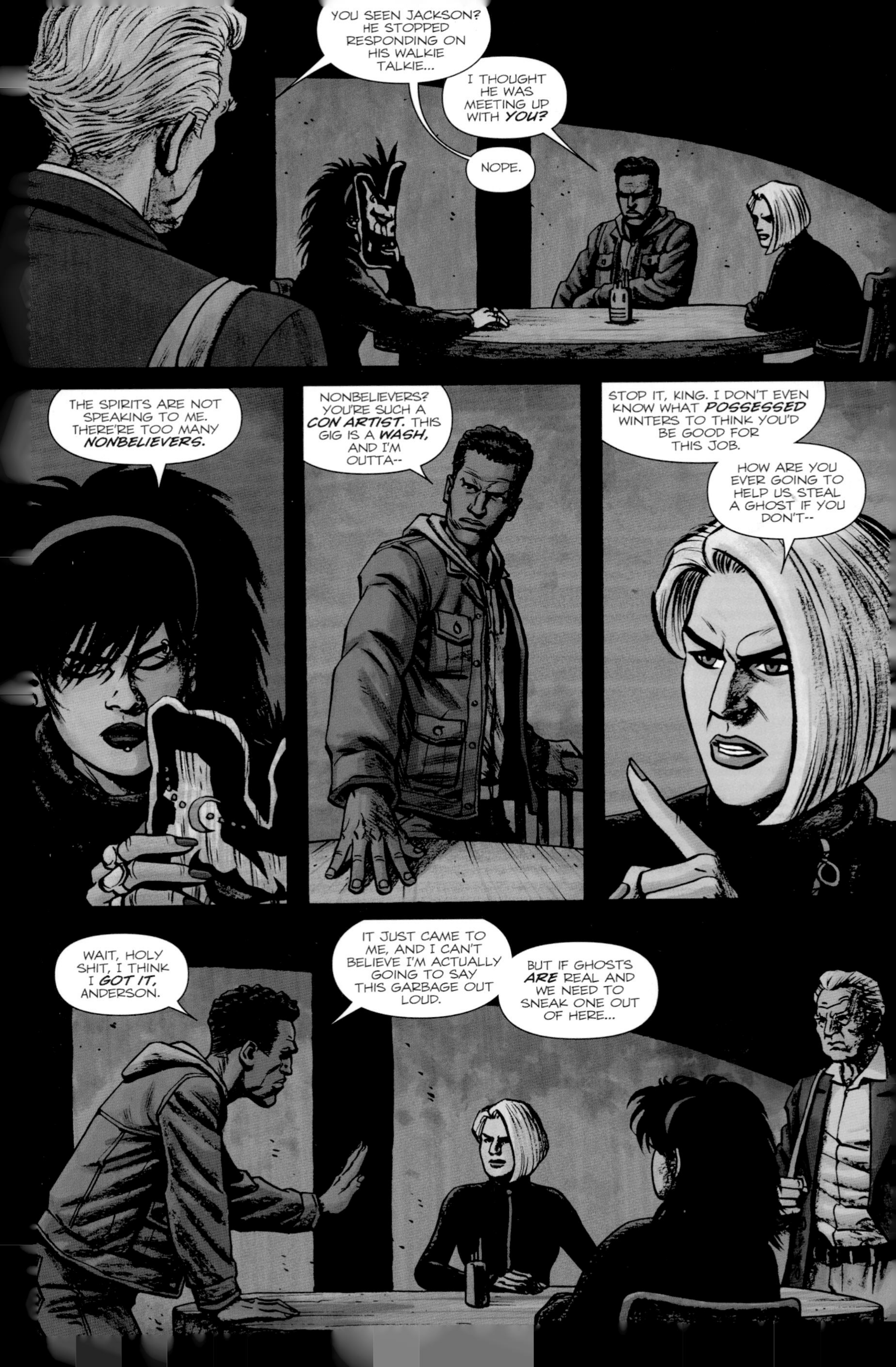
YOU SEEN JACKSON? HE STOPPED RESPONDING ON HIS WALKIE TALKIE...
I THOUGHT HE WAS MEETING UP WITH YOU?
NOPE.
THE SPIRITS ARE NOT SPEAKING TO ME. THERE'RE TOO MANY NONBELIEVERS.
NONBELIEVERS? YOU'RE SUCH A CON ARTIST. THIS GIG IS A WASH, AND I'M OUTTA--
STOP IT, KING. I DON'T EVEN KNOW WHAT POSSESSED WINTERS TO THINK YOU'D BE GOOD FOR THIS JOB.
HOW ARE YOU EVER GOING TO HELP US STEAL A GHOST IF YOU DON'T--
WAIT, HOLY SHIT, I THINK I GOT IT, ANDERSON.
IT JUST CAME TO ME, AND I CAN'T BELIEVE I'M ACTUALLY GOING TO SAY THIS GARBAGE OUT LOUD.
BUT IF GHOSTS ARE REAL AND WE NEED TO SNEAK ONE OUT OF HERE...

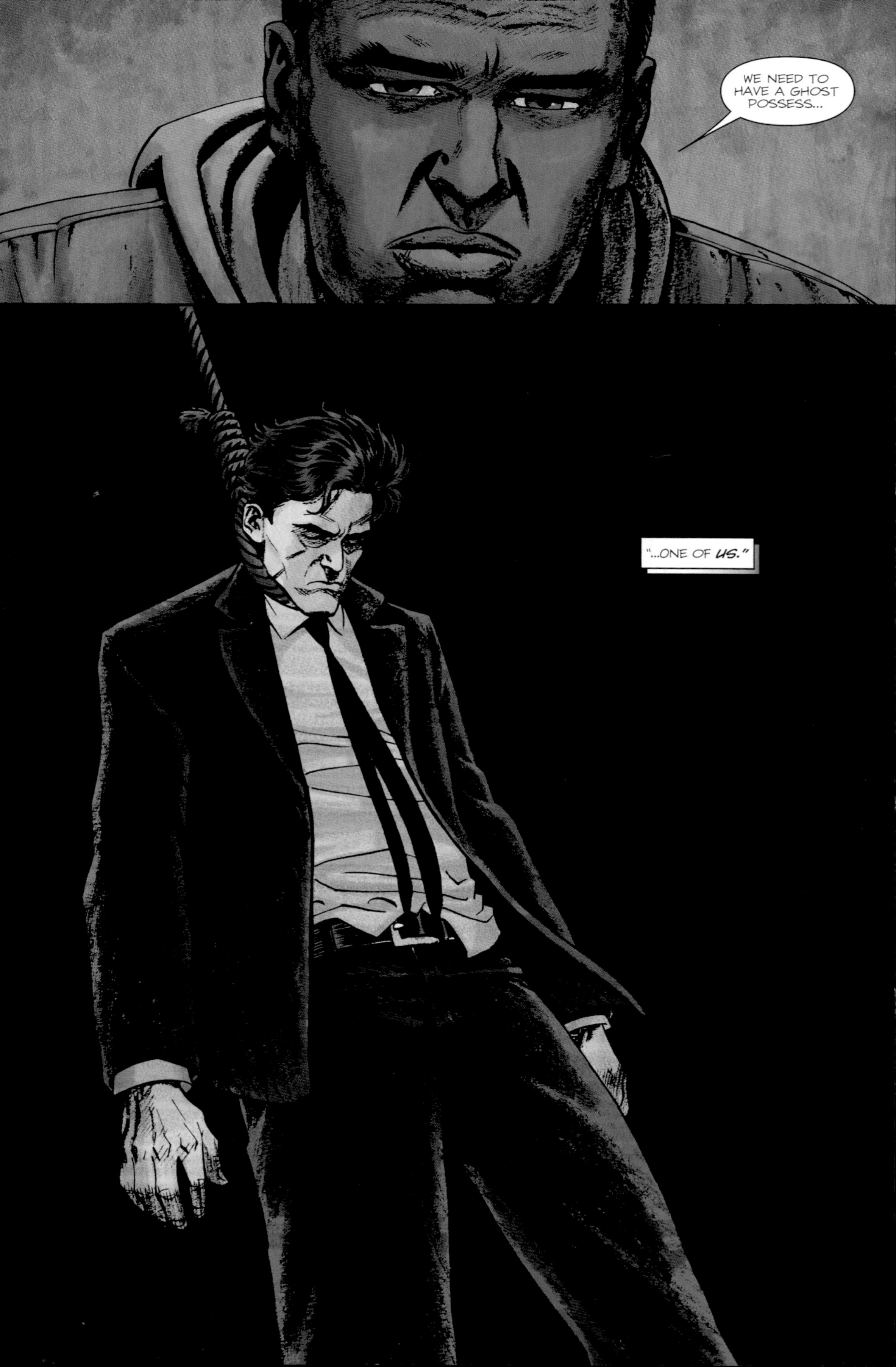
WE NEED TO HAVE A GHOST POSSESS...
"...ONE OF *US.*"

CHAPTER FOUR

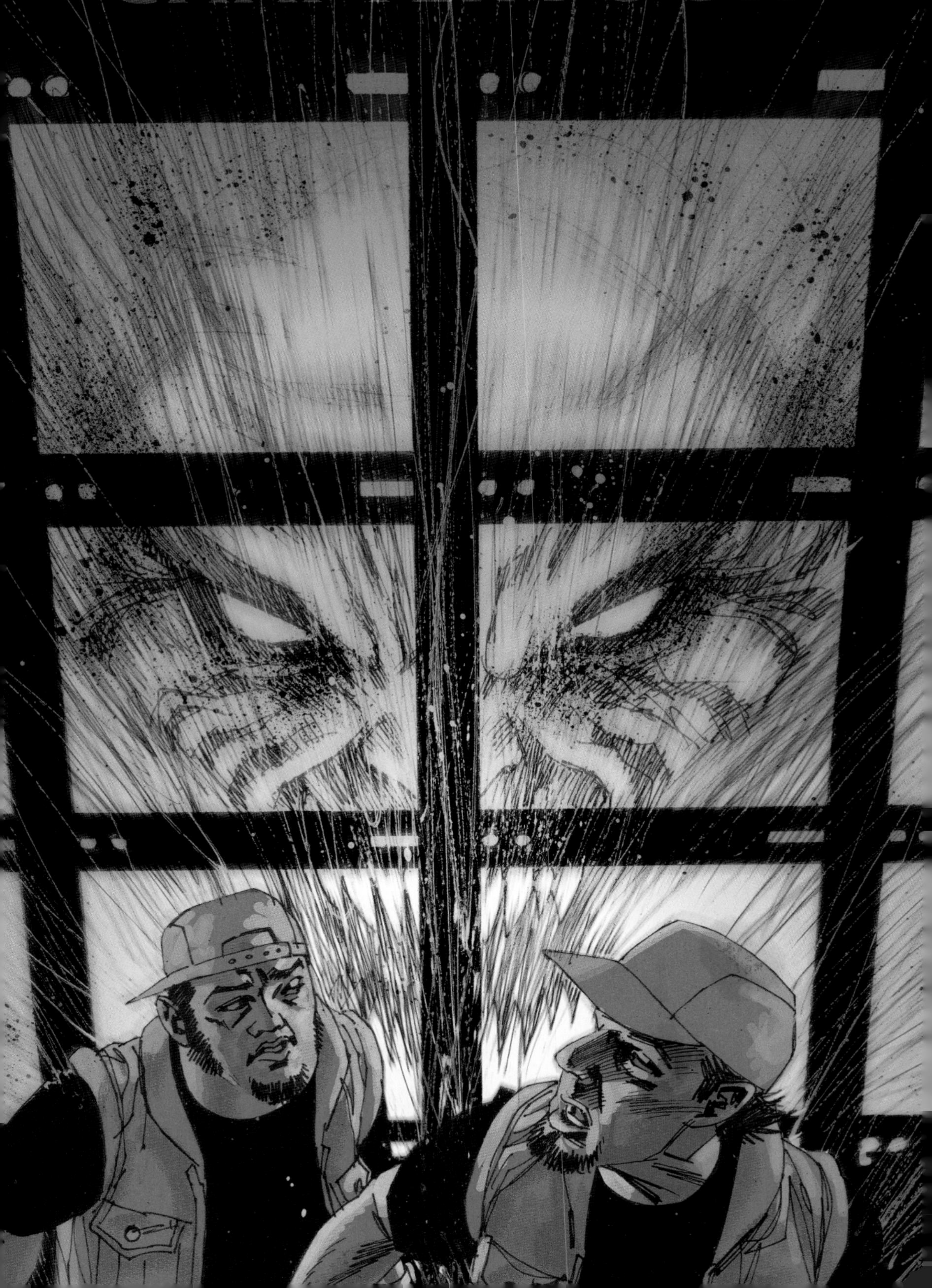

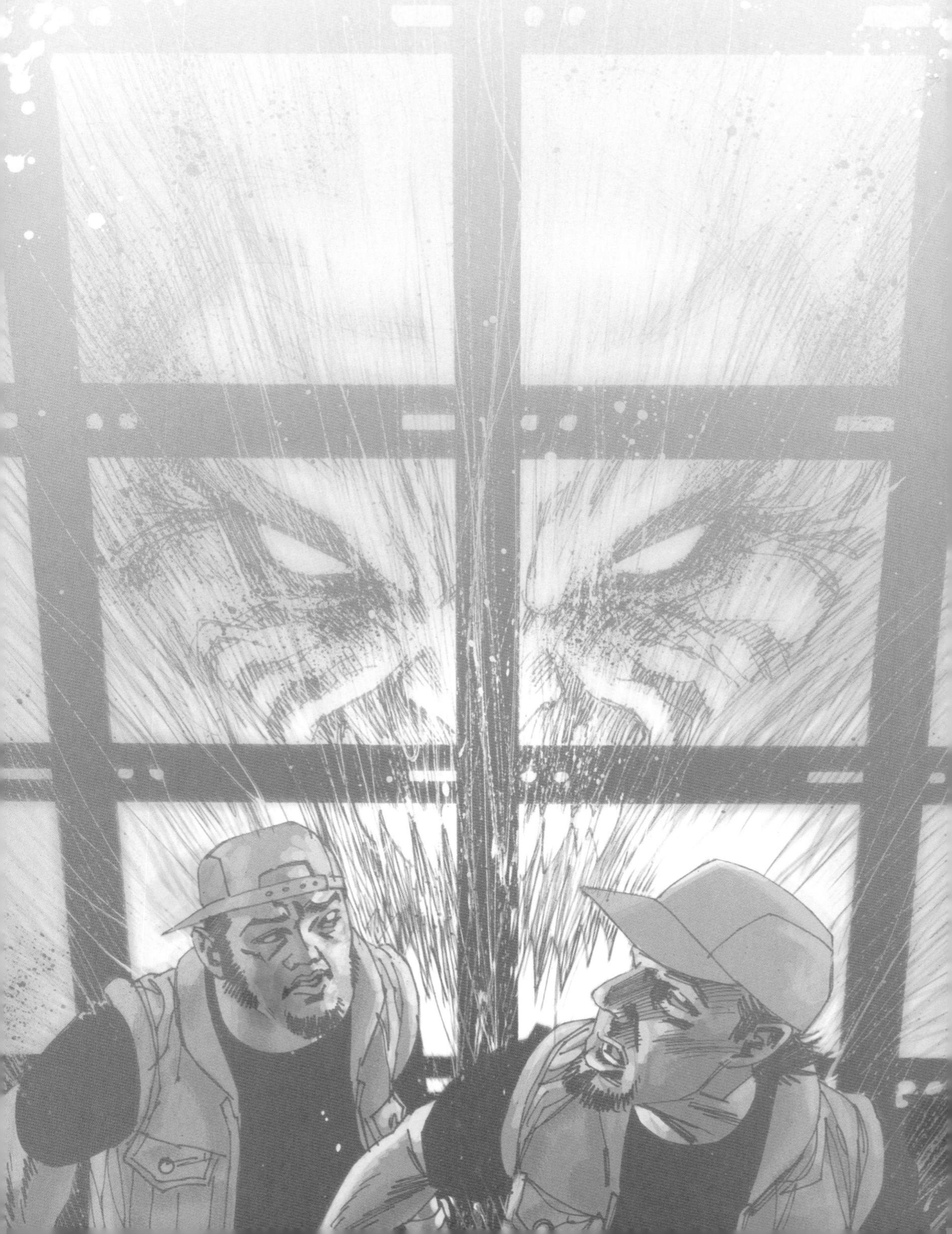

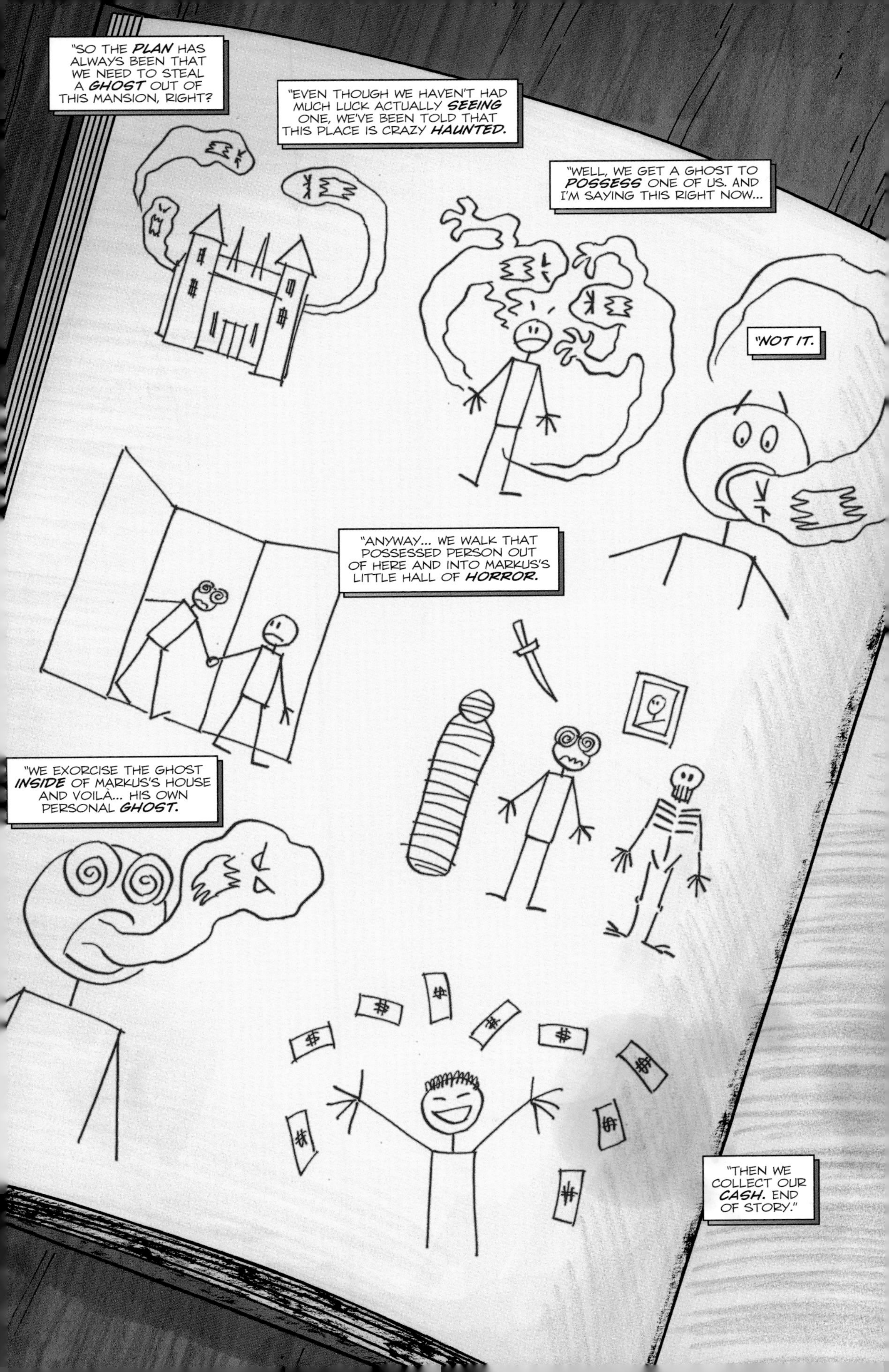
"SO THE PLAN HAS ALWAYS BEEN THAT WE NEED TO STEAL A GHOST OUT OF THIS MANSION, RIGHT?
"EVEN THOUGH WE HAVEN'T HAD MUCH LUCK ACTUALLY SEEING ONE, WE'VE BEEN TOLD THAT THIS PLACE IS CRAZY HAUNTED.
"WELL, WE GET A GHOST TO POSSESS ONE OF US. AND I'M SAYING THIS RIGHT NOW...
"NOT IT.
"ANYWAY... WE WALK THAT POSSESSED PERSON OUT OF HERE AND INTO MARKUS'S LITTLE HALL OF HORROR.
"WE EXORCISE THE GHOST INSIDE OF MARKUS'S HOUSE AND VOILÀ... HIS OWN PERSONAL GHOST.
"THEN WE COLLECT OUR CASH. END OF STORY."

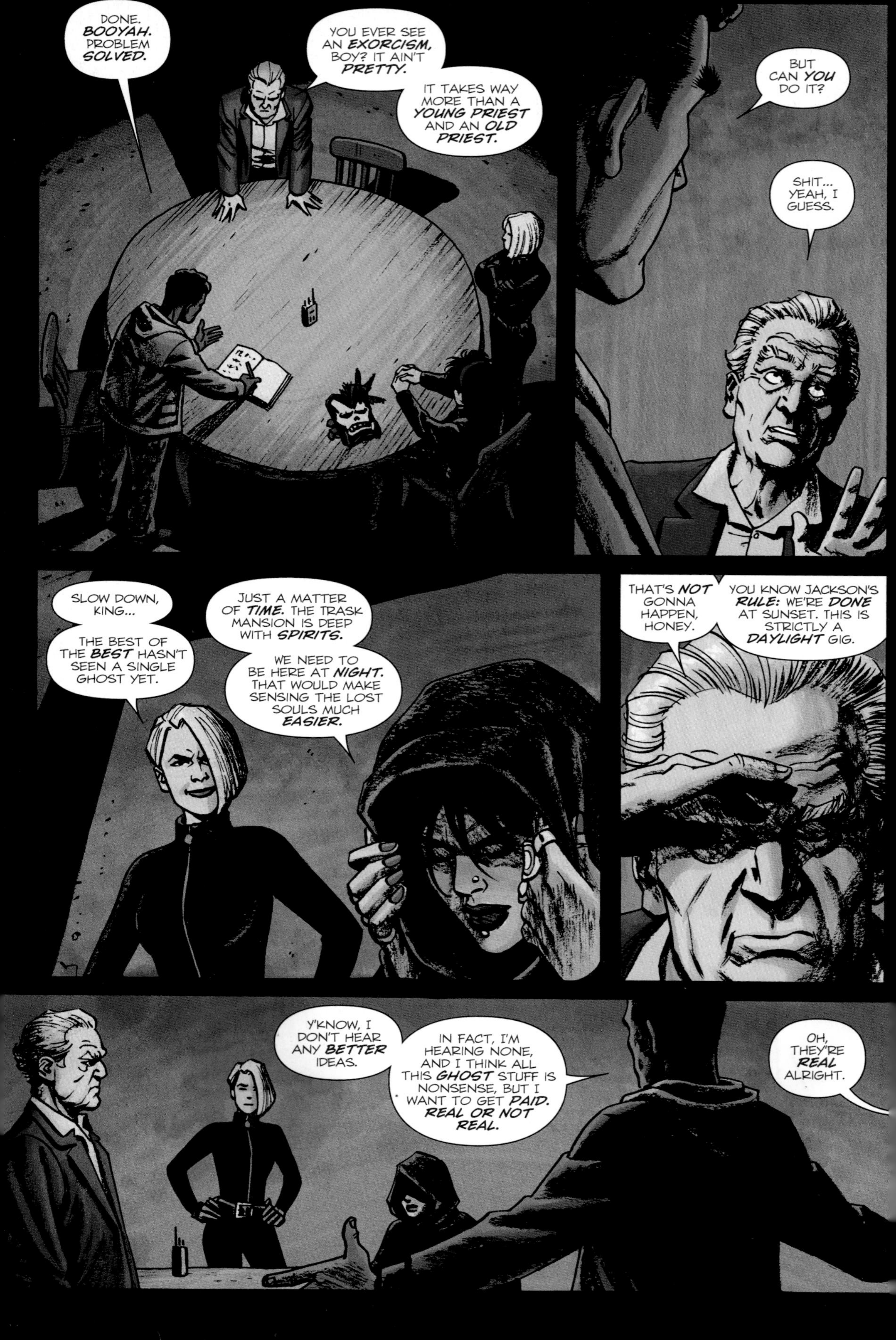
DONE. BOOYAH. PROBLEM SOLVED.
YOU EVER SEE AN EXORCISM, BOY? IT AIN'T PRETTY.
IT TAKES WAY MORE THAN A YOUNG PRIEST AND AN OLD PRIEST.
BUT CAN YOU DO IT?
SHIT... YEAH, I GUESS.
SLOW DOWN, KING...
THE BEST OF THE BEST HASN'T SEEN A SINGLE GHOST YET.
JUST A MATTER OF TIME. THE TRASK MANSION IS DEEP WITH SPIRITS.
WE NEED TO BE HERE AT NIGHT. THAT WOULD MAKE SENSING THE LOST SOULS MUCH EASIER.
THAT'S NOT GONNA HAPPEN, HONEY.
YOU KNOW JACKSON'S RULE: WE'RE DONE AT SUNSET. THIS IS STRICTLY A DAYLIGHT GIG.
Y'KNOW, I DON'T HEAR ANY BETTER IDEAS.
IN FACT, I'M HEARING NONE, AND I THINK ALL THIS GHOST STUFF IS NONSENSE, BUT I WANT TO GET PAID. REAL OR NOT REAL.
OH, THEY'RE REAL ALRIGHT.

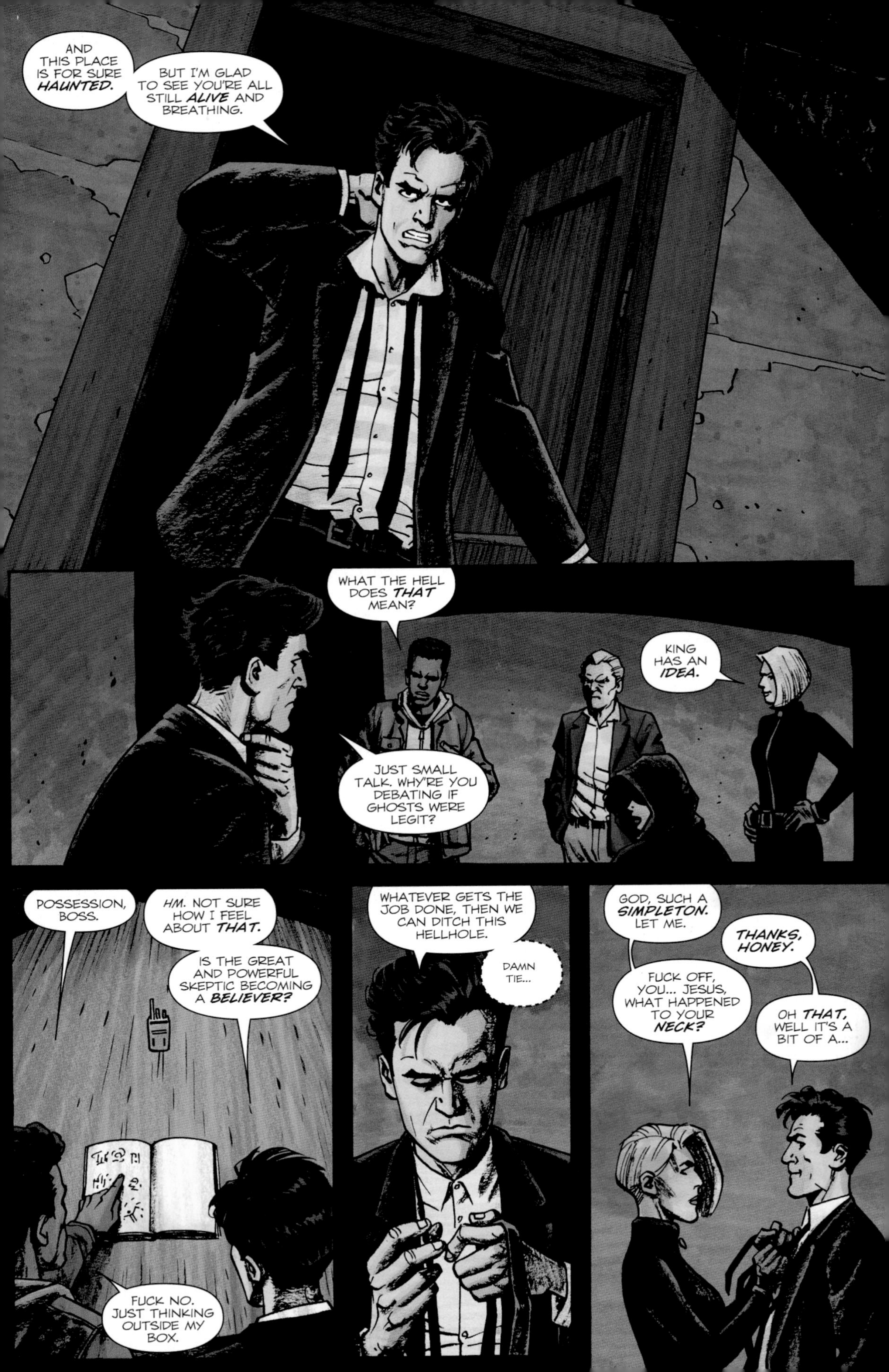
AND THIS PLACE IS FOR SURE *HAUNTED.*
BUT I'M GLAD TO SEE YOU'RE ALL STILL *ALIVE* AND BREATHING.
WHAT THE HELL DOES *THAT* MEAN?
KING HAS AN *IDEA.*
JUST SMALL TALK. WHY'RE YOU DEBATING IF GHOSTS WERE LEGIT?
POSSESSION, BOSS.
HM. NOT SURE HOW I FEEL ABOUT *THAT.*
IS THE GREAT AND POWERFUL SKEPTIC BECOMING A *BELIEVER?*
FUCK NO. JUST THINKING OUTSIDE MY BOX.
WHATEVER GETS THE JOB DONE, THEN WE CAN DITCH THIS HELLHOLE.
DAMN TIE...
GOD, SUCH A *SIMPLETON.* LET ME.
THANKS, HONEY.
FUCK OFF, YOU... JESUS, WHAT HAPPENED TO YOUR *NECK?*
OH *THAT,* WELL IT'S A BIT OF A...

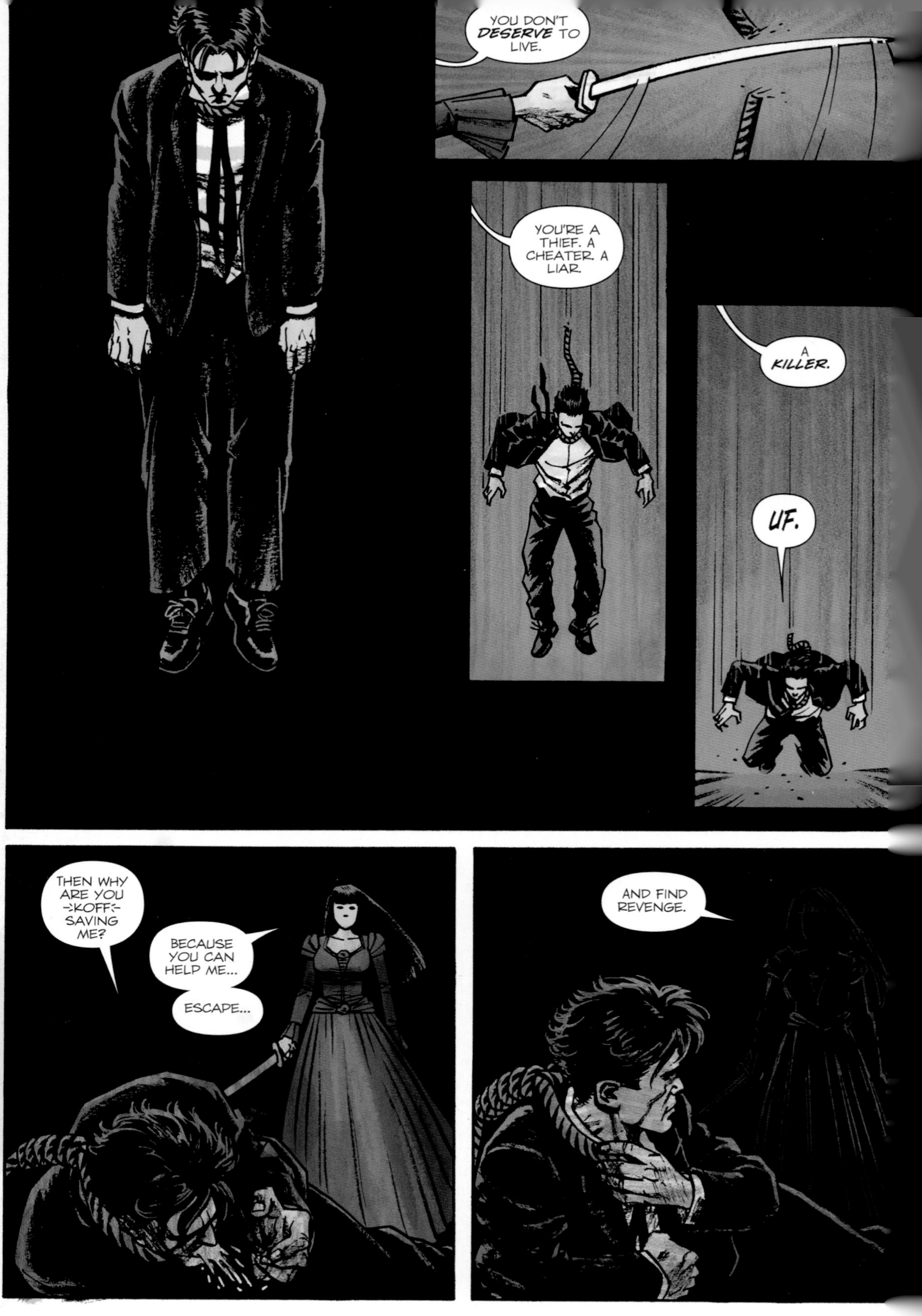
YOU DON'T DESERVE TO LIVE.
YOU'RE A THIEF. A CHEATER. A LIAR.
A KILLER.
UF.
THEN WHY ARE YOU -KOFF- SAVING ME?
BECAUSE YOU CAN HELP ME...
ESCAPE...
AND FIND REVENGE.

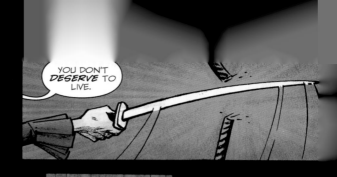

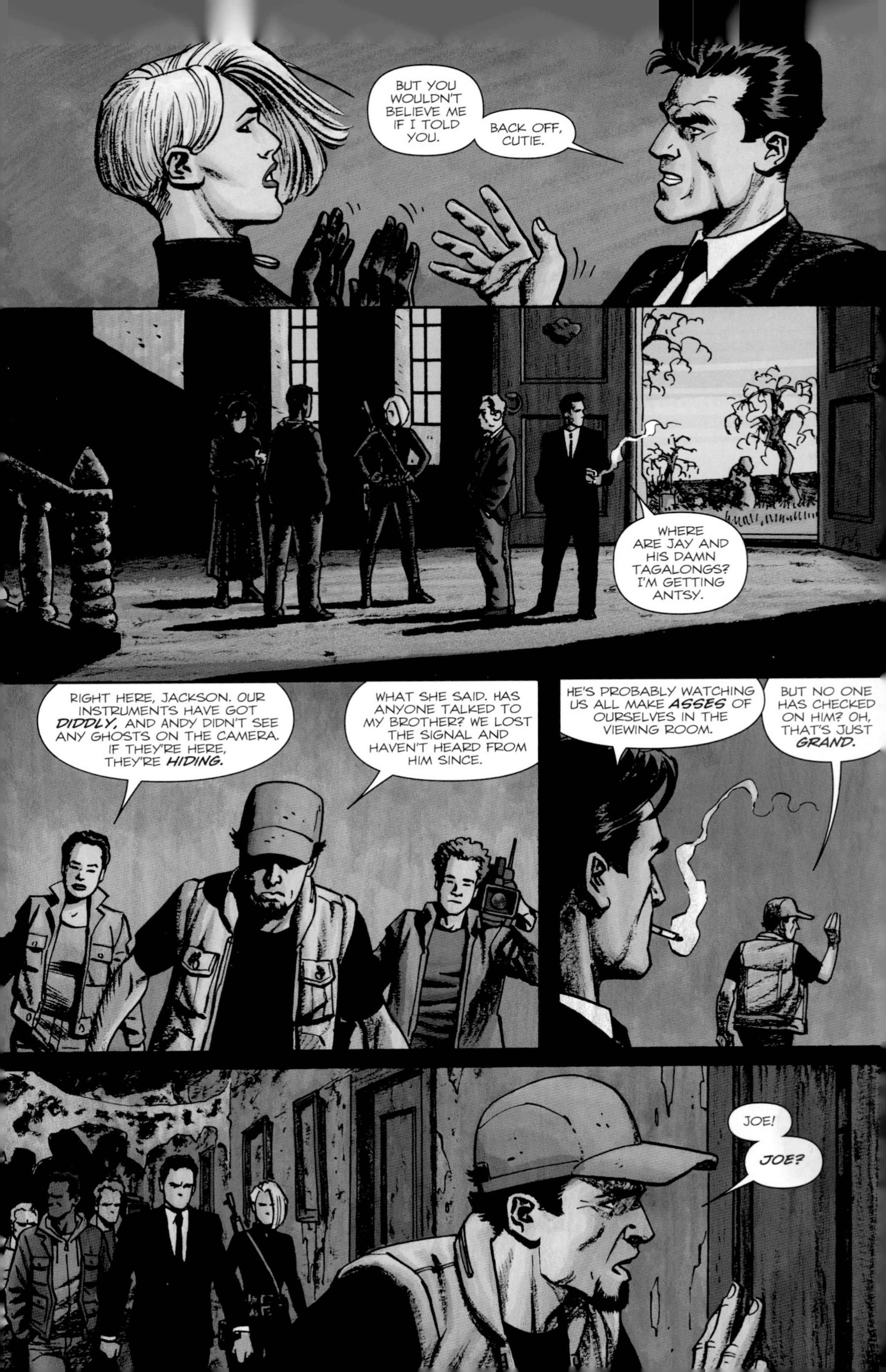
BUT YOU WOULDN'T BELIEVE ME IF I TOLD YOU.
BACK OFF, CUTIE.
WHERE ARE JAY AND HIS DAMN TAGALONGS? I'M GETTING ANTSY.
RIGHT HERE, JACKSON. OUR INSTRUMENTS HAVE GOT DIDDLY, AND ANDY DIDN'T SEE ANY GHOSTS ON THE CAMERA. IF THEY'RE HERE, THEY'RE HIDING.
WHAT SHE SAID. HAS ANYONE TALKED TO MY BROTHER? WE LOST THE SIGNAL AND HAVEN'T HEARD FROM HIM SINCE.
HE'S PROBABLY WATCHING US ALL MAKE ASSES OF OURSELVES IN THE VIEWING ROOM.
BUT NO ONE HAS CHECKED ON HIM? OH, THAT'S JUST GRAND.
JOE!
JOE?

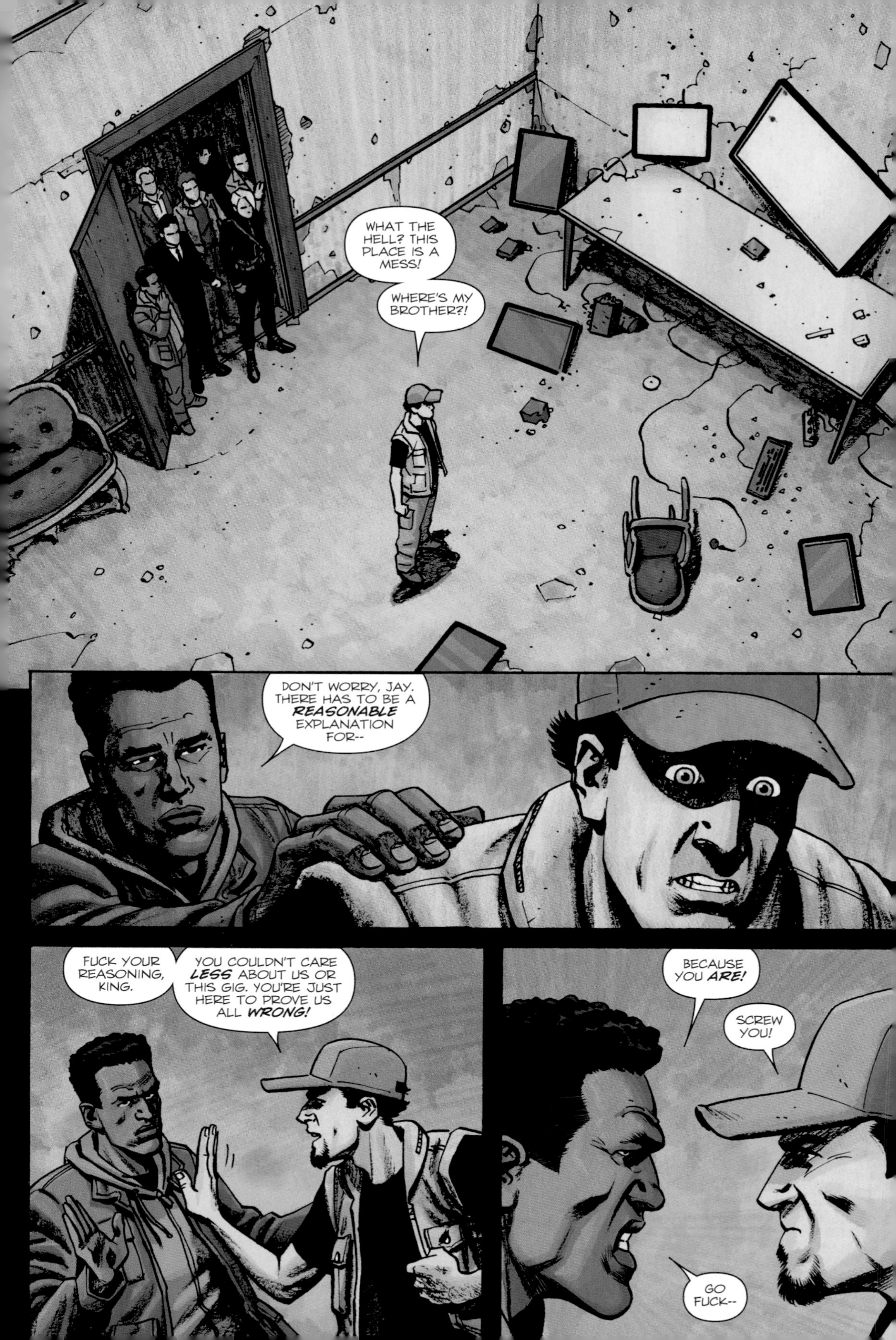
WHAT THE HELL? THIS PLACE IS A MESS!
WHERE'S MY BROTHER?!
DON'T WORRY, JAY. THERE HAS TO BE A *REASONABLE* EXPLANATION FOR--
FUCK YOUR REASONING, KING.
YOU COULDN'T CARE *LESS* ABOUT US OR THIS GIG. YOU'RE JUST HERE TO PROVE US ALL *WRONG!*
BECAUSE YOU *ARE!*
SCREW YOU!
GO FUCK--

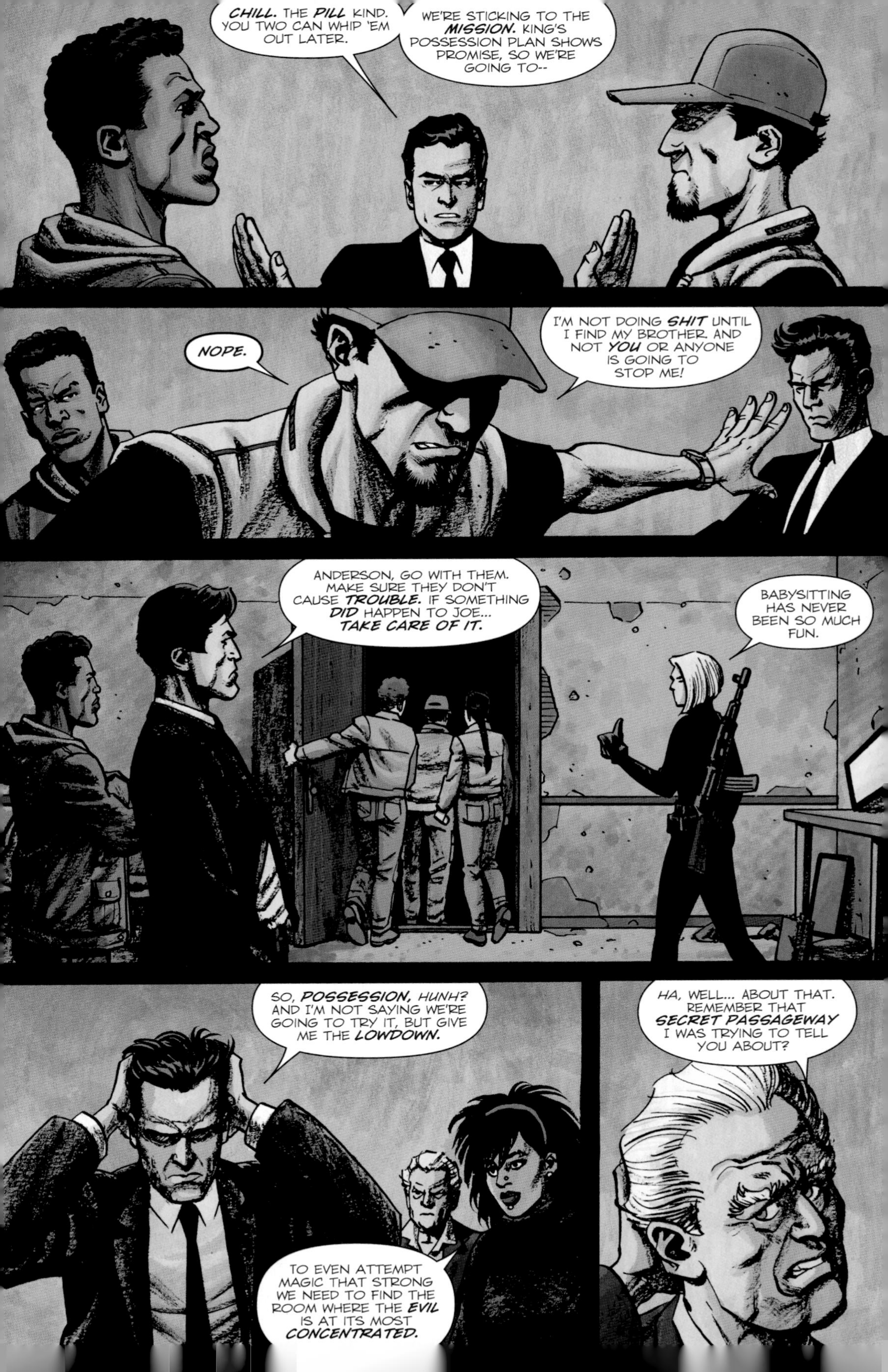
CHILL. THE PILL KIND. YOU TWO CAN WHIP 'EM OUT LATER.
WE'RE STICKING TO THE MISSION. KING'S POSSESSION PLAN SHOWS PROMISE, SO WE'RE GOING TO--
NOPE.
I'M NOT DOING SHIT UNTIL I FIND MY BROTHER. AND NOT YOU OR ANYONE IS GOING TO STOP ME!
ANDERSON, GO WITH THEM. MAKE SURE THEY DON'T CAUSE TROUBLE. IF SOMETHING DID HAPPEN TO JOE... TAKE CARE OF IT.
BABYSITTING HAS NEVER BEEN SO MUCH FUN.
SO, POSSESSION, HUNH? AND I'M NOT SAYING WE'RE GOING TO TRY IT, BUT GIVE ME THE LOWDOWN.
TO EVEN ATTEMPT MAGIC THAT STRONG WE NEED TO FIND THE ROOM WHERE THE EVIL IS AT ITS MOST CONCENTRATED.
HA, WELL... ABOUT THAT. REMEMBER THAT SECRET PASSAGEWAY I WAS TRYING TO TELL YOU ABOUT?

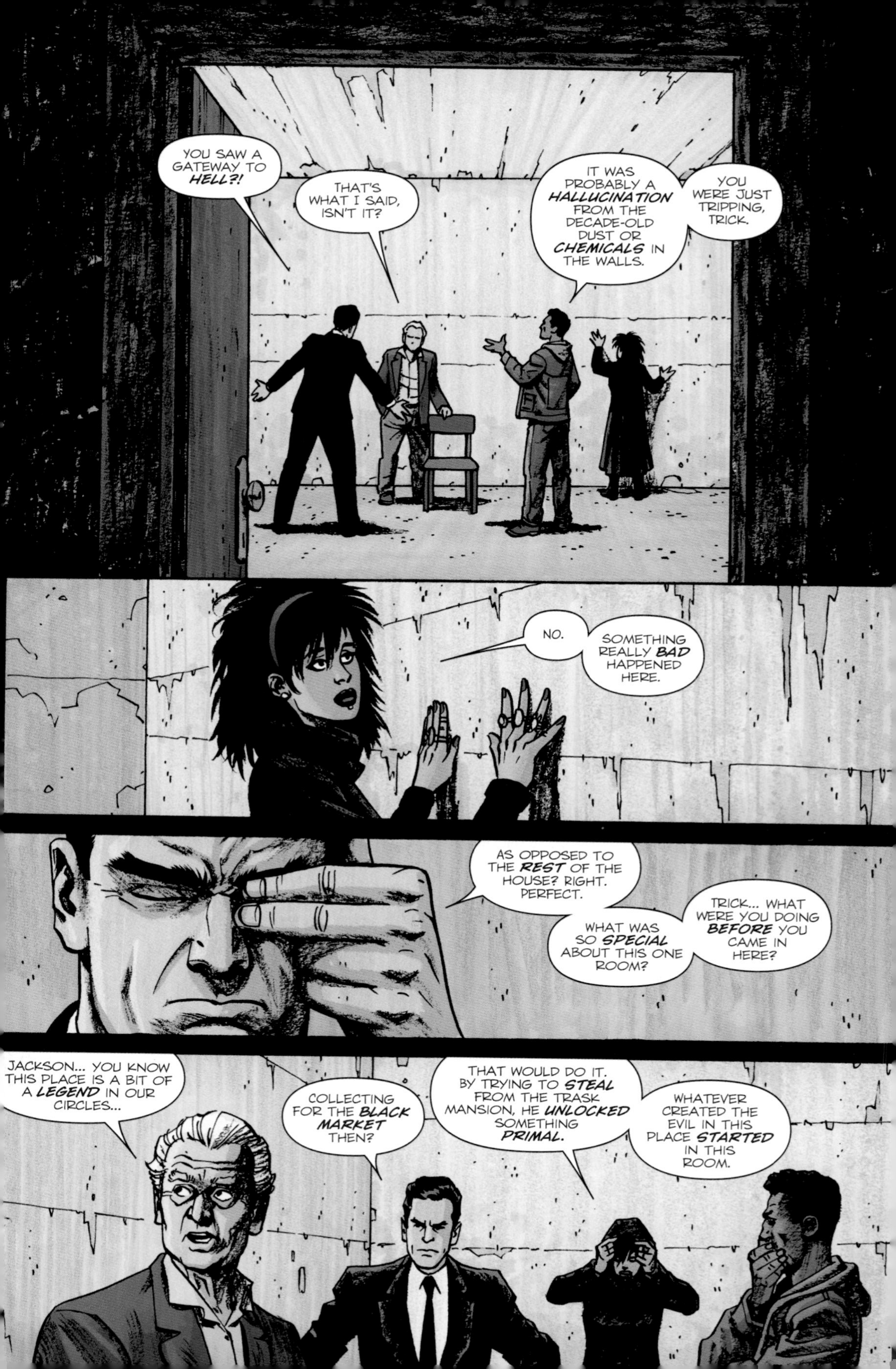
YOU SAW A GATEWAY TO HELL?!
THAT'S WHAT I SAID, ISN'T IT?
IT WAS PROBABLY A HALLUCINATION FROM THE DECADE-OLD DUST OR CHEMICALS IN THE WALLS.
YOU WERE JUST TRIPPING, TRICK.
NO.
SOMETHING REALLY BAD HAPPENED HERE.
AS OPPOSED TO THE REST OF THE HOUSE? RIGHT. PERFECT.
WHAT WAS SO SPECIAL ABOUT THIS ONE ROOM?
TRICK... WHAT WERE YOU DOING BEFORE YOU CAME IN HERE?
JACKSON... YOU KNOW THIS PLACE IS A BIT OF A LEGEND IN OUR CIRCLES...
COLLECTING FOR THE BLACK MARKET THEN?
THAT WOULD DO IT. BY TRYING TO STEAL FROM THE TRASK MANSION, HE UNLOCKED SOMETHING PRIMAL.
WHATEVER CREATED THE EVIL IN THIS PLACE STARTED IN THIS ROOM.

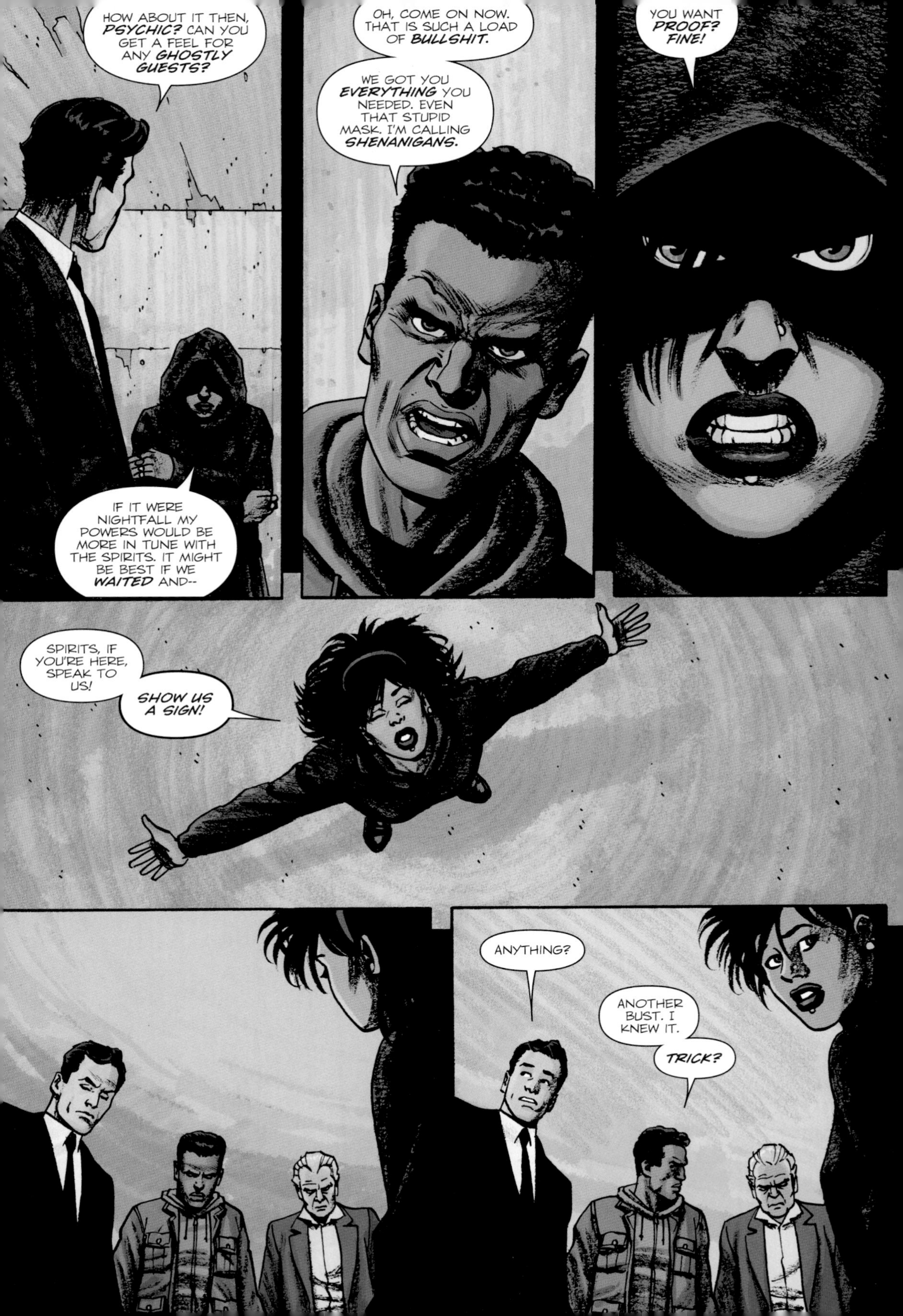
HOW ABOUT IT THEN, PSYCHIC? CAN YOU GET A FEEL FOR ANY GHOSTLY GUESTS?
IF IT WERE NIGHTFALL MY POWERS WOULD BE MORE IN TUNE WITH THE SPIRITS. IT MIGHT BE BEST IF WE WAITED AND--
OH, COME ON NOW. THAT IS SUCH A LOAD OF BULLSHIT.
WE GOT YOU EVERYTHING YOU NEEDED. EVEN THAT STUPID MASK. I'M CALLING SHENANIGANS.
YOU WANT PROOF? FINE!
SPIRITS, IF YOU'RE HERE, SPEAK TO US!
SHOW US A SIGN!
ANYTHING?
ANOTHER BUST. I KNEW IT.
TRICK?

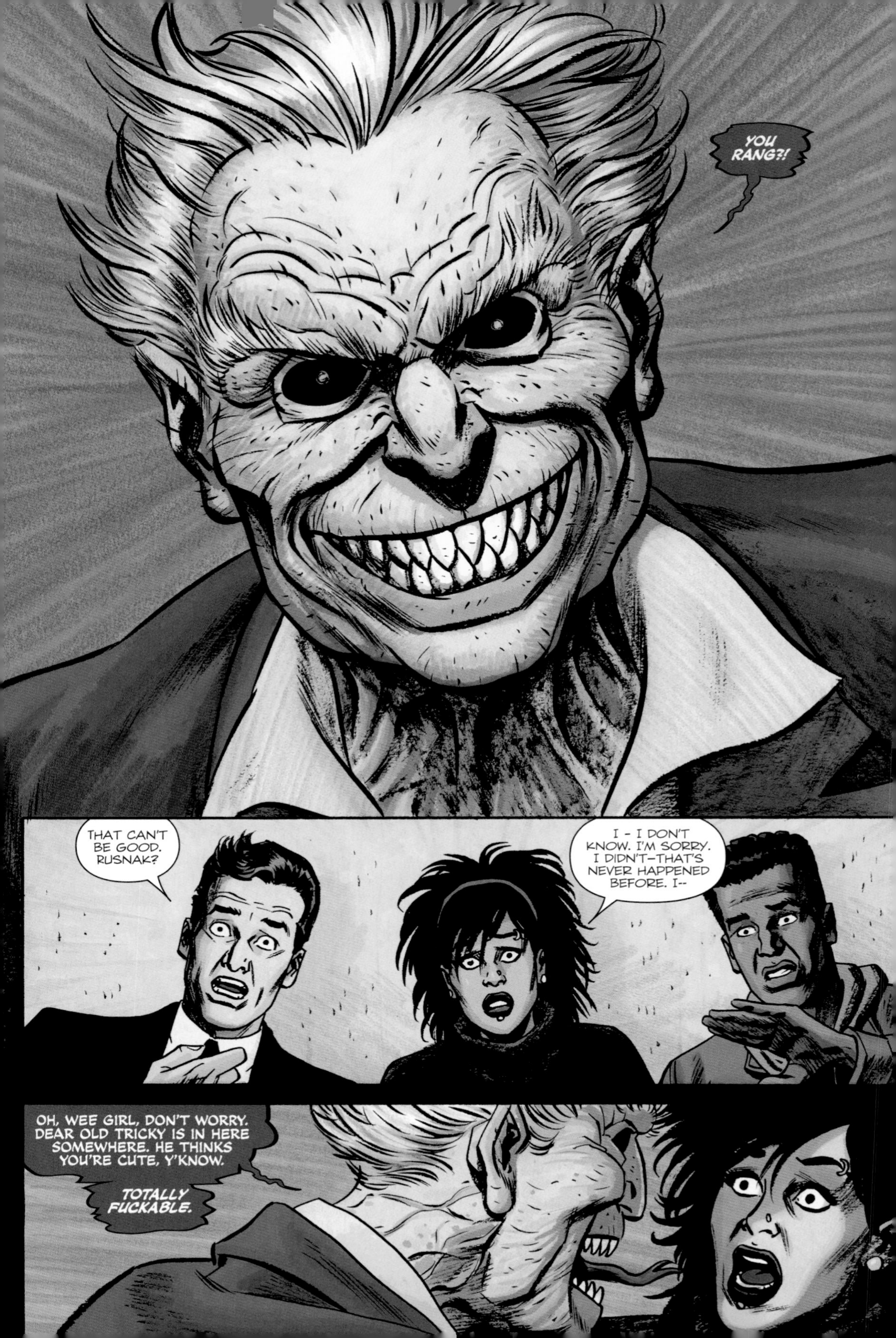
YOU RANG?!
THAT CAN'T BE GOOD. RUSNAK?
I - I DON'T KNOW. I'M SORRY. I DIDN'T—THAT'S NEVER HAPPENED BEFORE. I--
OH, WEE GIRL, DON'T WORRY. DEAR OLD TRICKY IS IN HERE SOMEWHERE. HE THINKS YOU'RE CUTE, Y'KNOW.
TOTALLY FUCKABLE.

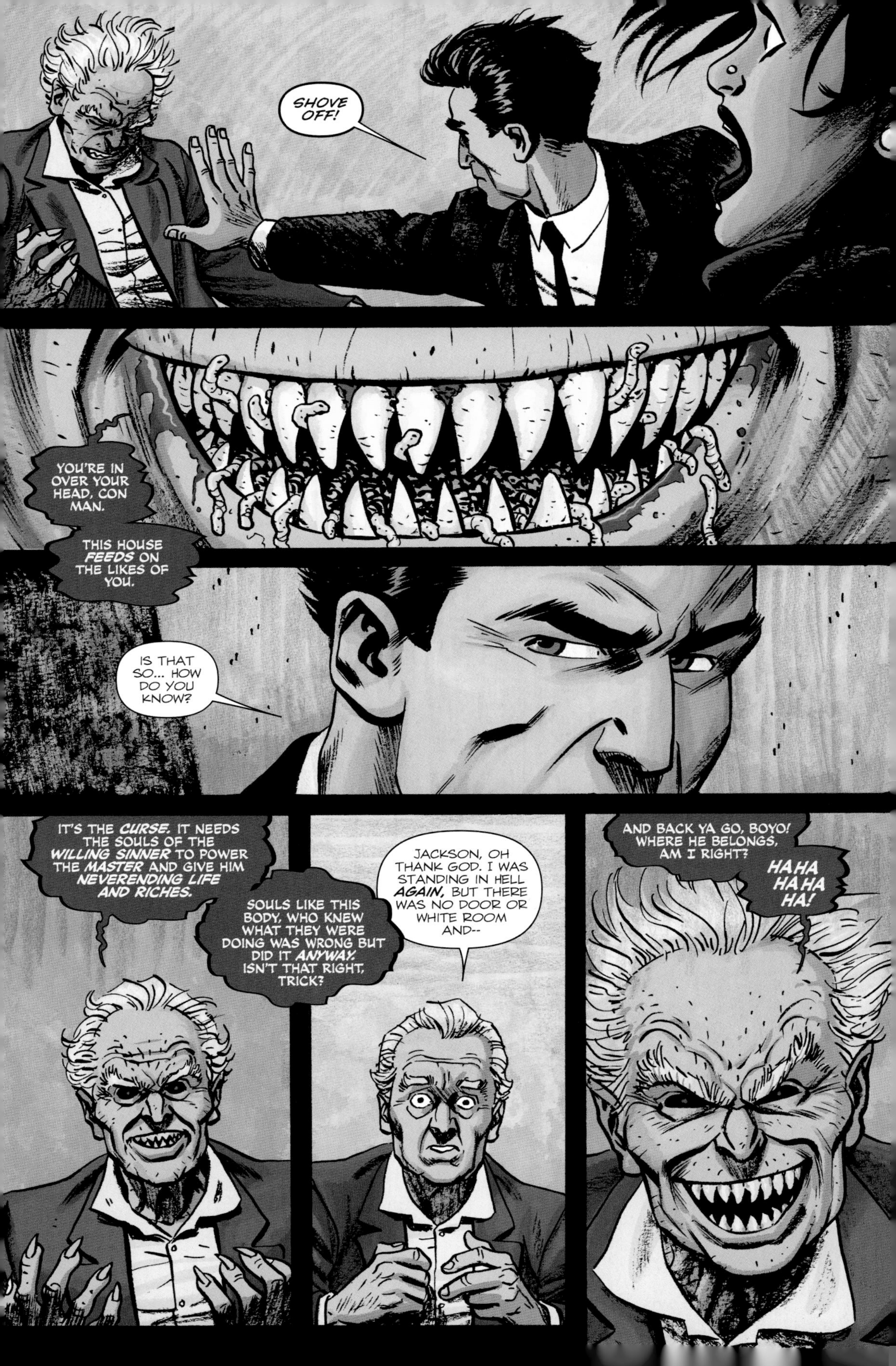
SHOVE OFF!
YOU'RE IN OVER YOUR HEAD, CON MAN.
THIS HOUSE FEEDS ON THE LIKES OF YOU.
IS THAT SO... HOW DO YOU KNOW?
IT'S THE CURSE. IT NEEDS THE SOULS OF THE WILLING SINNER TO POWER THE MASTER AND GIVE HIM NEVERENDING LIFE AND RICHES.
SOULS LIKE THIS BODY, WHO KNEW WHAT THEY WERE DOING WAS WRONG BUT DID IT ANYWAY. ISN'T THAT RIGHT, TRICK?
JACKSON, OH THANK GOD. I WAS STANDING IN HELL AGAIN, BUT THERE WAS NO DOOR OR WHITE ROOM AND--
AND BACK YA GO, BOYO! WHERE HE BELONGS, AM I RIGHT?
HAHA HAHA HA!

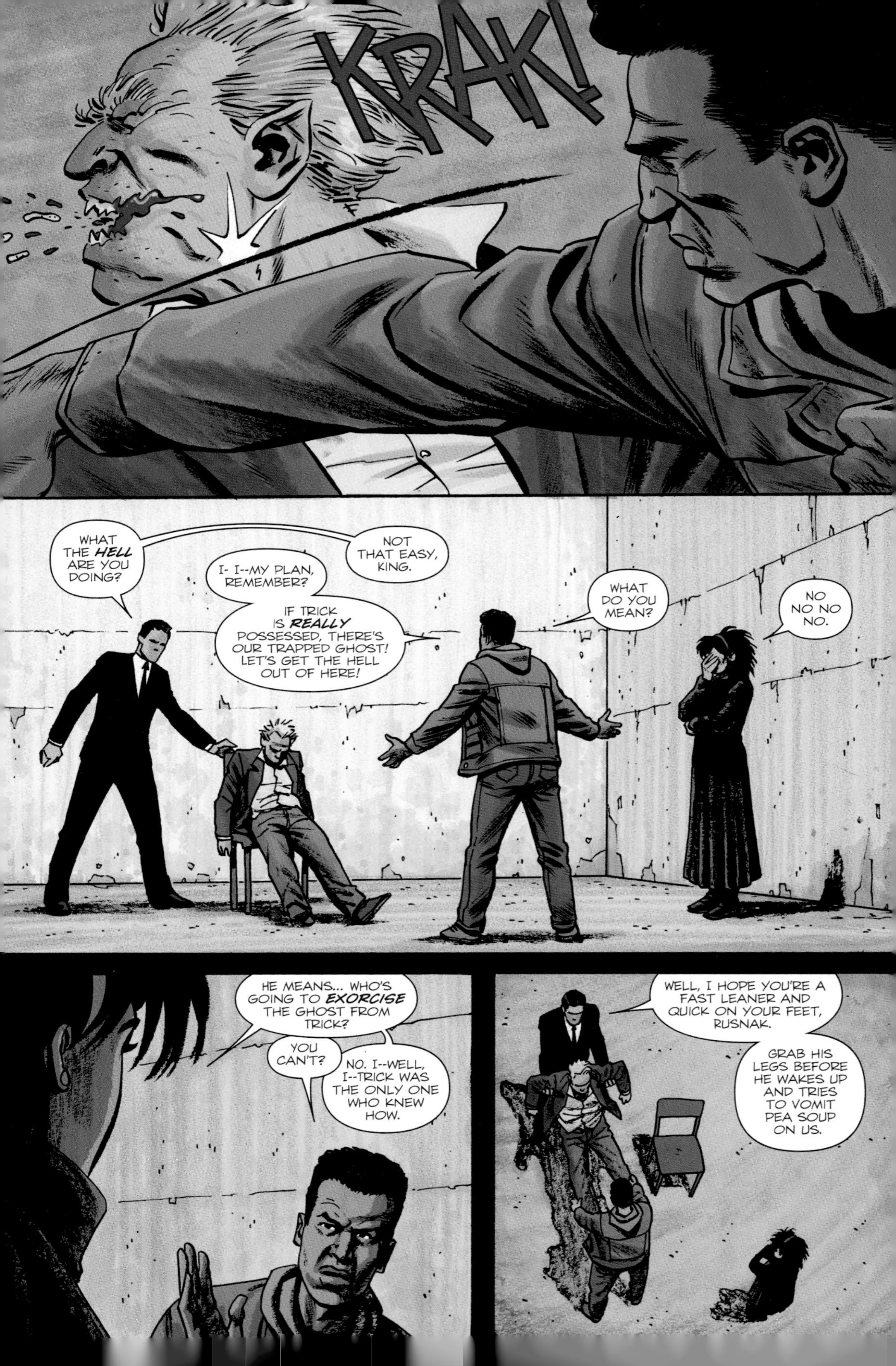
KRAK!
WHAT THE HELL ARE YOU DOING?
NOT THAT EASY, KING.
I- I--MY PLAN, REMEMBER?
IF TRICK IS REALLY POSSESSED, THERE'S OUR TRAPPED GHOST! LET'S GET THE HELL OUT OF HERE!
WHAT DO YOU MEAN?
NO NO NO NO.
HE MEANS... WHO'S GOING TO EXORCISE THE GHOST FROM TRICK?
YOU CAN'T?
NO. I--WELL, I--TRICK WAS THE ONLY ONE WHO KNEW HOW.
WELL, I HOPE YOU'RE A FAST LEANER AND QUICK ON YOUR FEET, RUSNAK.
GRAB HIS LEGS BEFORE HE WAKES UP AND TRIES TO VOMIT PEA SOUP ON US.

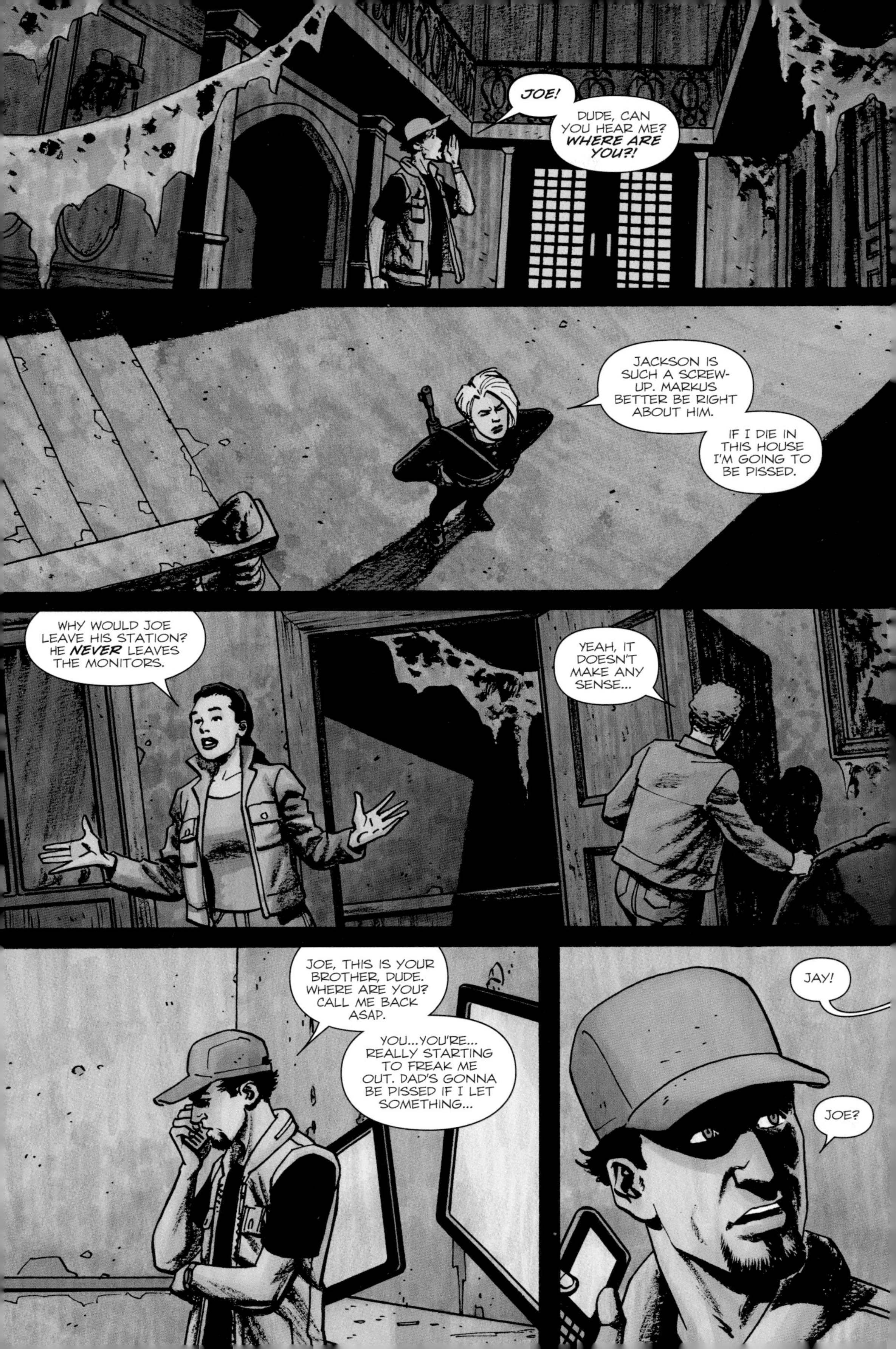
JOE!
DUDE, CAN YOU HEAR ME? WHERE ARE YOU?!
JACKSON IS SUCH A SCREW-UP. MARKUS BETTER BE RIGHT ABOUT HIM.
IF I DIE IN THIS HOUSE I'M GOING TO BE PISSED.
WHY WOULD JOE LEAVE HIS STATION? HE NEVER LEAVES THE MONITORS.
YEAH, IT DOESN'T MAKE ANY SENSE...
JOE, THIS IS YOUR BROTHER, DUDE. WHERE ARE YOU? CALL ME BACK ASAP.
YOU...YOU'RE... REALLY STARTING TO FREAK ME OUT. DAD'S GONNA BE PISSED IF I LET SOMETHING...
JAY!
JOE?

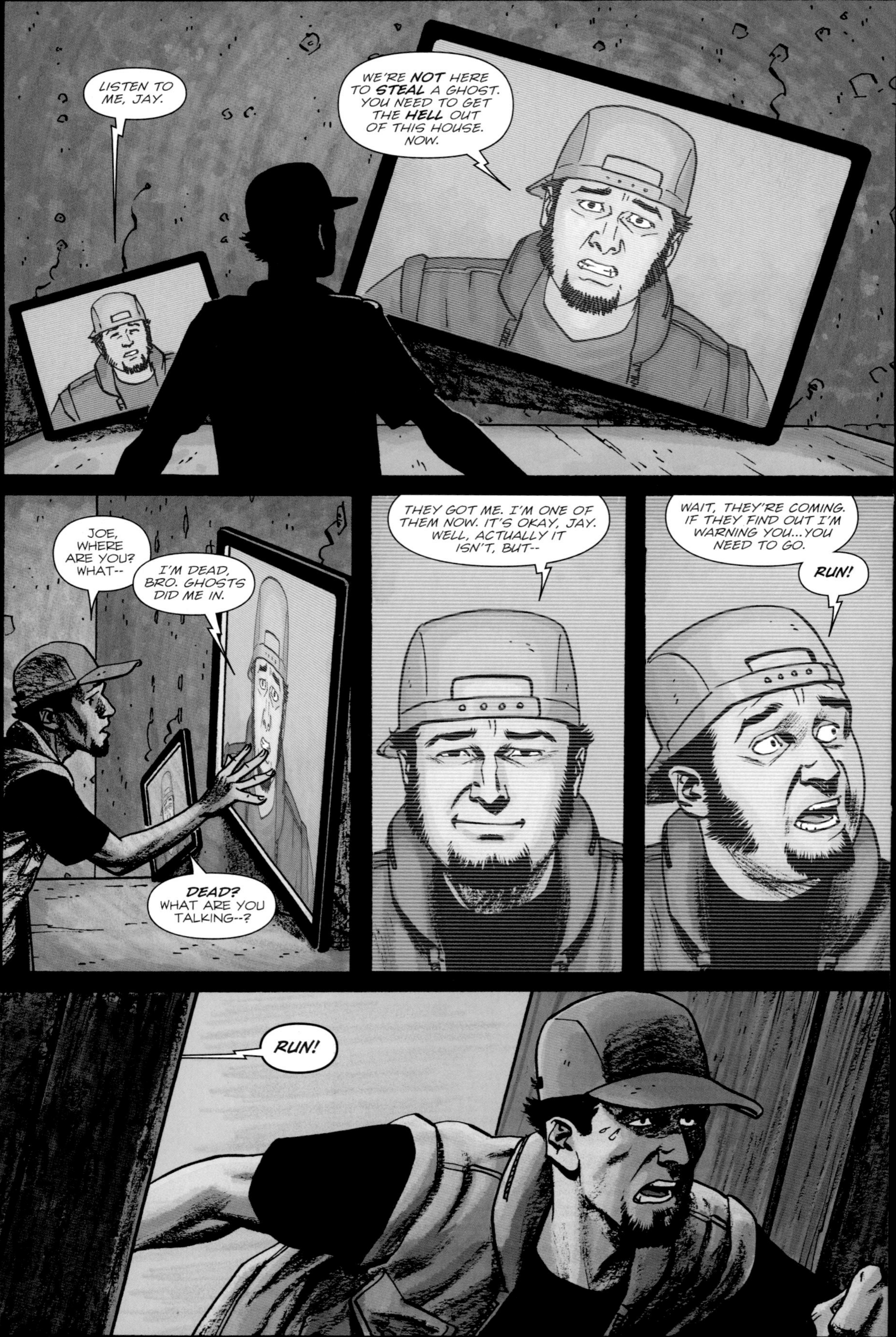
LISTEN TO ME, JAY.
WE'RE **NOT** HERE TO **STEAL** A GHOST. YOU NEED TO GET THE **HELL** OUT OF THIS HOUSE. NOW.
JOE, WHERE ARE YOU? WHAT--
I'M DEAD, BRO. GHOSTS DID ME IN.
DEAD? WHAT ARE YOU TALKING--?
THEY GOT ME. I'M ONE OF THEM NOW. IT'S OKAY, JAY. WELL, ACTUALLY IT ISN'T, BUT--
WAIT, THEY'RE COMING. IF THEY FIND OUT I'M WARNING YOU...YOU NEED TO GO.
RUN!
RUN!

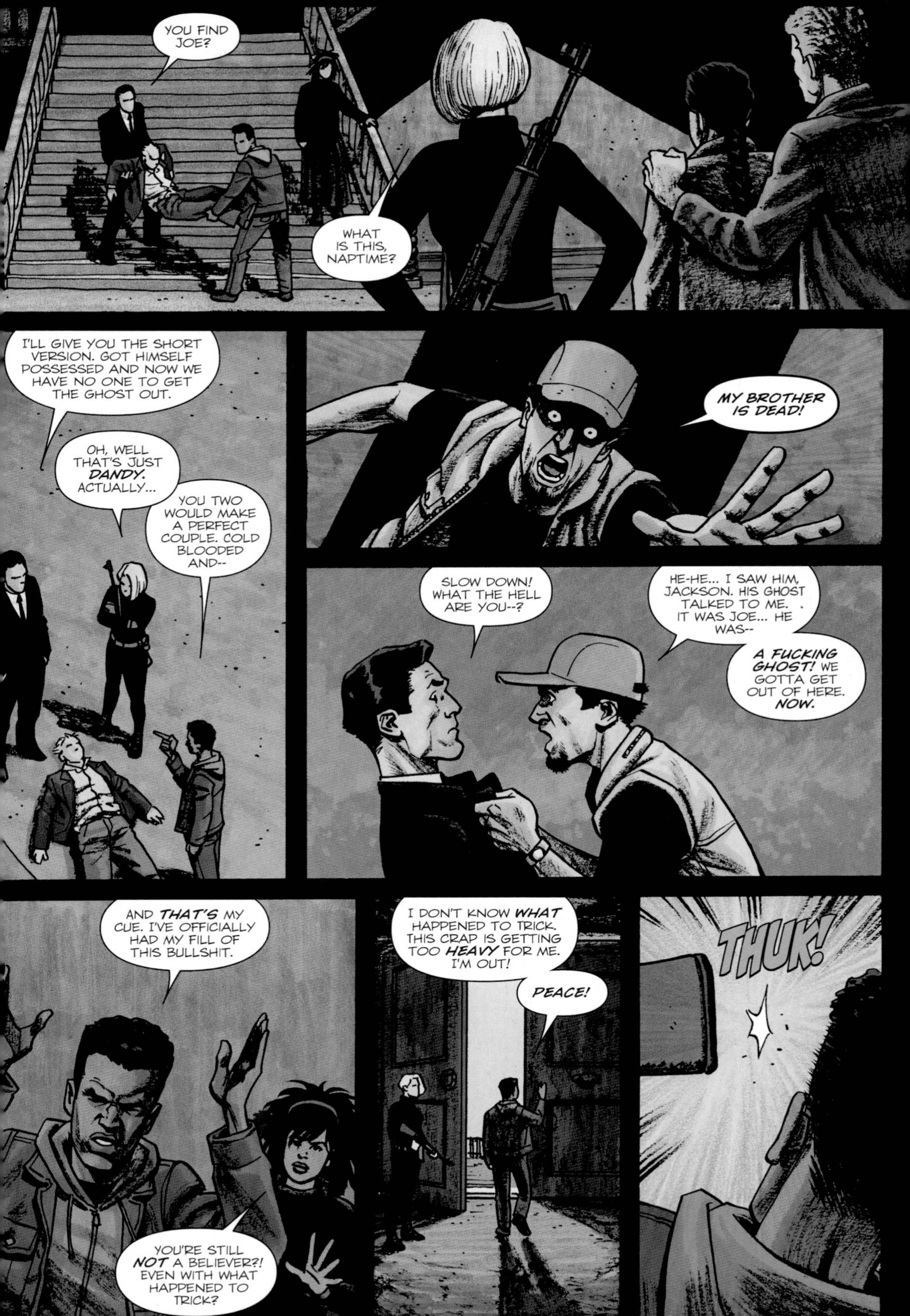

YOU FIND JOE?
WHAT IS THIS, NAPTIME?
I'LL GIVE YOU THE SHORT VERSION. GOT HIMSELF POSSESSED AND NOW WE HAVE NO ONE TO GET THE GHOST OUT.
OH, WELL THAT'S JUST **DANDY.** ACTUALLY...
YOU TWO WOULD MAKE A PERFECT COUPLE. COLD BLOODED AND--
MY BROTHER IS DEAD!
SLOW DOWN! WHAT THE HELL ARE YOU--?
HE-HE... I SAW HIM, JACKSON. HIS GHOST TALKED TO ME. IT WAS JOE... HE WAS--
A FUCKING GHOST! WE GOTTA GET OUT OF HERE. ***NOW.***
AND ***THAT'S*** MY CUE. I'VE OFFICIALLY HAD MY FILL OF THIS BULLSHIT.
YOU'RE STILL ***NOT*** A BELIEVER?! EVEN WITH WHAT HAPPENED TO TRICK?
I DON'T KNOW ***WHAT*** HAPPENED TO TRICK. THIS CRAP IS GETTING TOO ***HEAVY*** FOR ME. I'M OUT!
PEACE!
THUK!

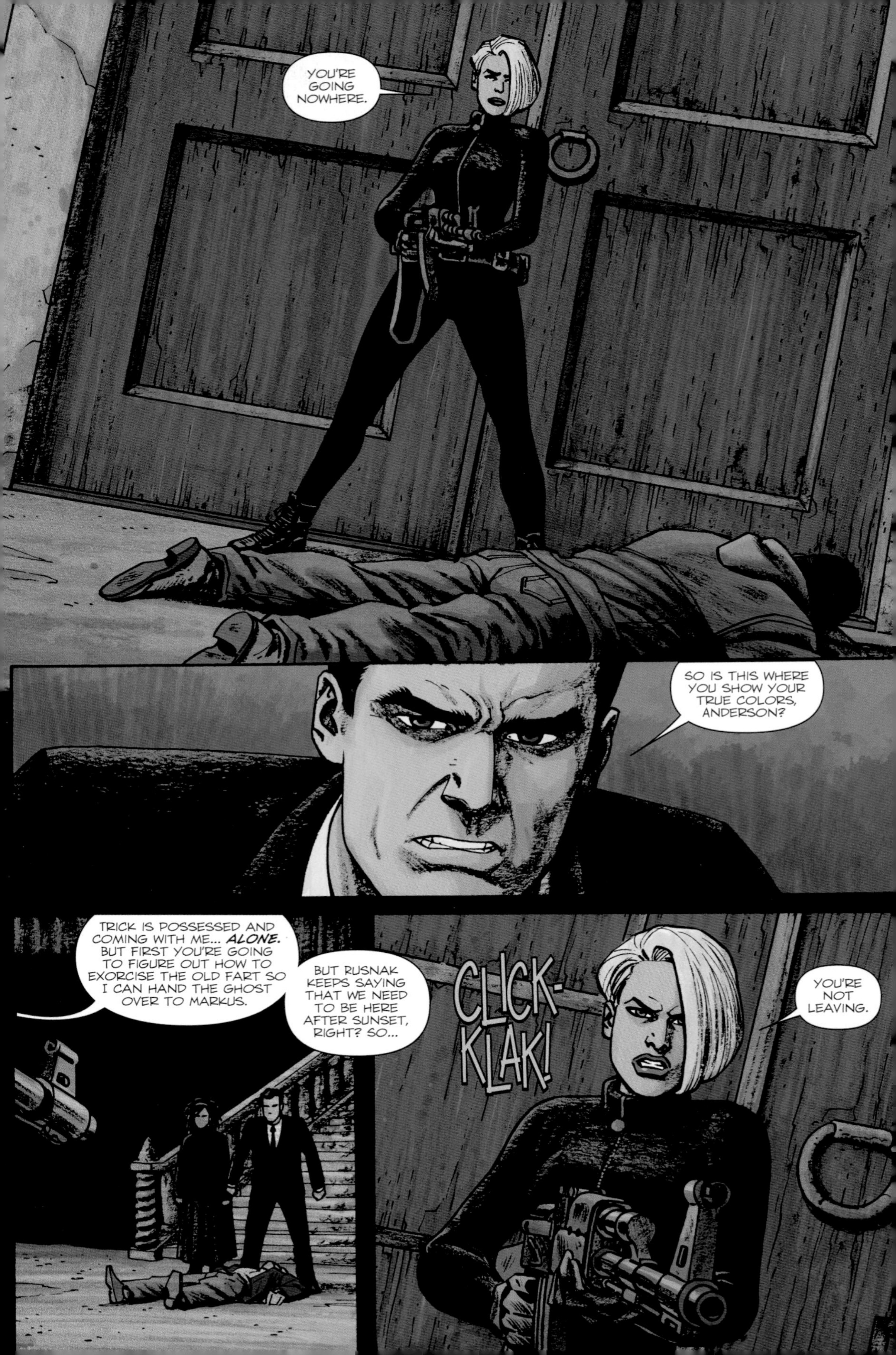
YOU'RE GOING NOWHERE.
SO IS THIS WHERE YOU SHOW YOUR TRUE COLORS, ANDERSON?
TRICK IS POSSESSED AND COMING WITH ME... *ALONE.* BUT FIRST YOU'RE GOING TO FIGURE OUT HOW TO EXORCISE THE OLD FART SO I CAN HAND THE GHOST OVER TO MARKUS.
BUT RUSNAK KEEPS SAYING THAT WE NEED TO BE HERE AFTER SUNSET, RIGHT? SO...
CLICK-KLAK!
YOU'RE NOT LEAVING.

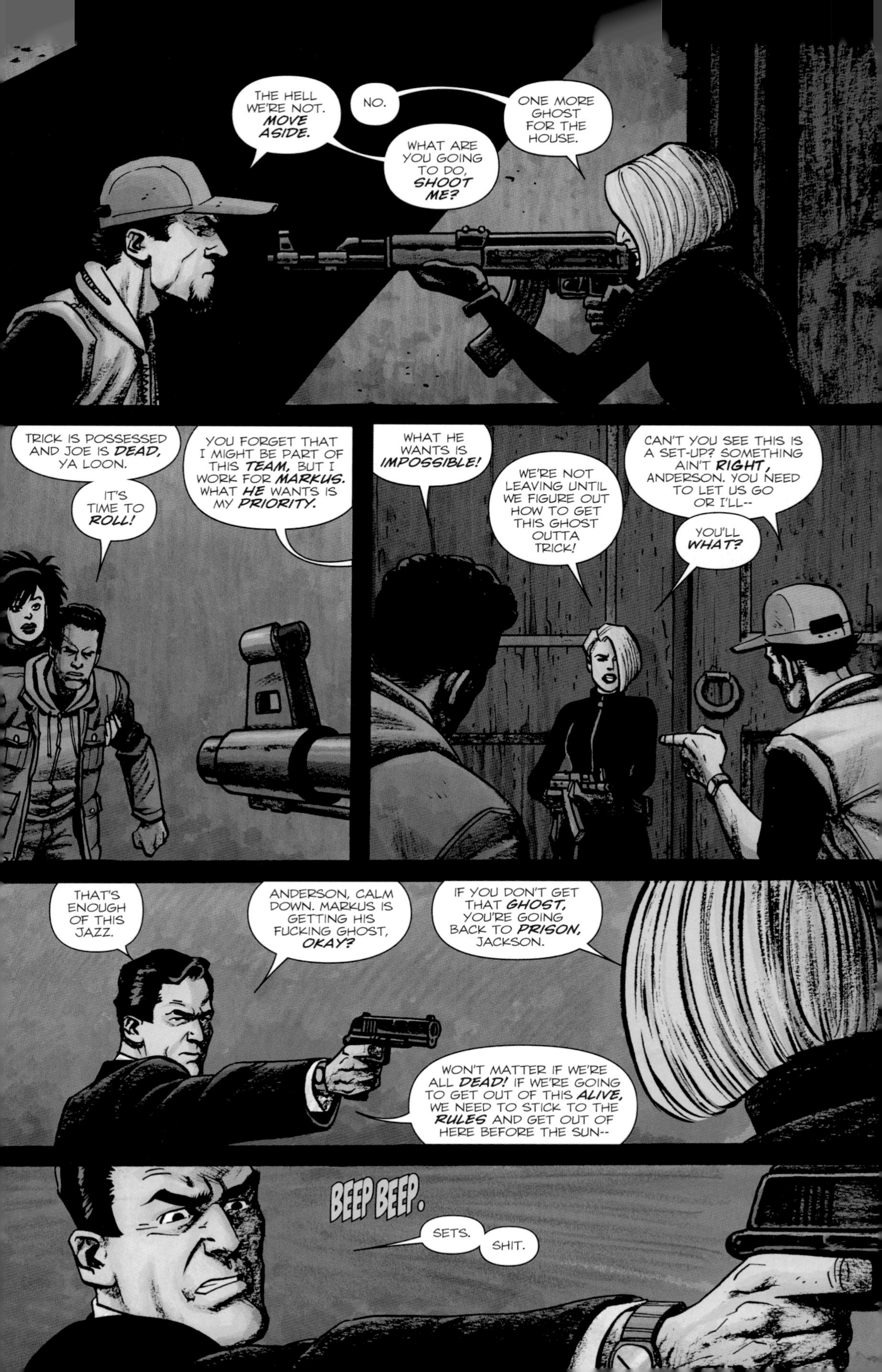
THE HELL WE'RE NOT. MOVE ASIDE.
NO.
WHAT ARE YOU GOING TO DO, SHOOT ME?
ONE MORE GHOST FOR THE HOUSE.
TRICK IS POSSESSED AND JOE IS DEAD, YA LOON.
IT'S TIME TO ROLL!
YOU FORGET THAT I MIGHT BE PART OF THIS TEAM, BUT I WORK FOR MARKUS. WHAT HE WANTS IS MY PRIORITY.
WHAT HE WANTS IS IMPOSSIBLE!
WE'RE NOT LEAVING UNTIL WE FIGURE OUT HOW TO GET THIS GHOST OUTTA TRICK!
CAN'T YOU SEE THIS IS A SET-UP? SOMETHING AIN'T RIGHT, ANDERSON. YOU NEED TO LET US GO OR I'LL--
YOU'LL WHAT?
THAT'S ENOUGH OF THIS JAZZ.
ANDERSON, CALM DOWN. MARKUS IS GETTING HIS FUCKING GHOST, OKAY?
IF YOU DON'T GET THAT GHOST, YOU'RE GOING BACK TO PRISON, JACKSON.
WON'T MATTER IF WE'RE ALL DEAD! IF WE'RE GOING TO GET OUT OF THIS ALIVE, WE NEED TO STICK TO THE RULES AND GET OUT OF HERE BEFORE THE SUN--
BEEP BEEP.
SETS.
SHIT.

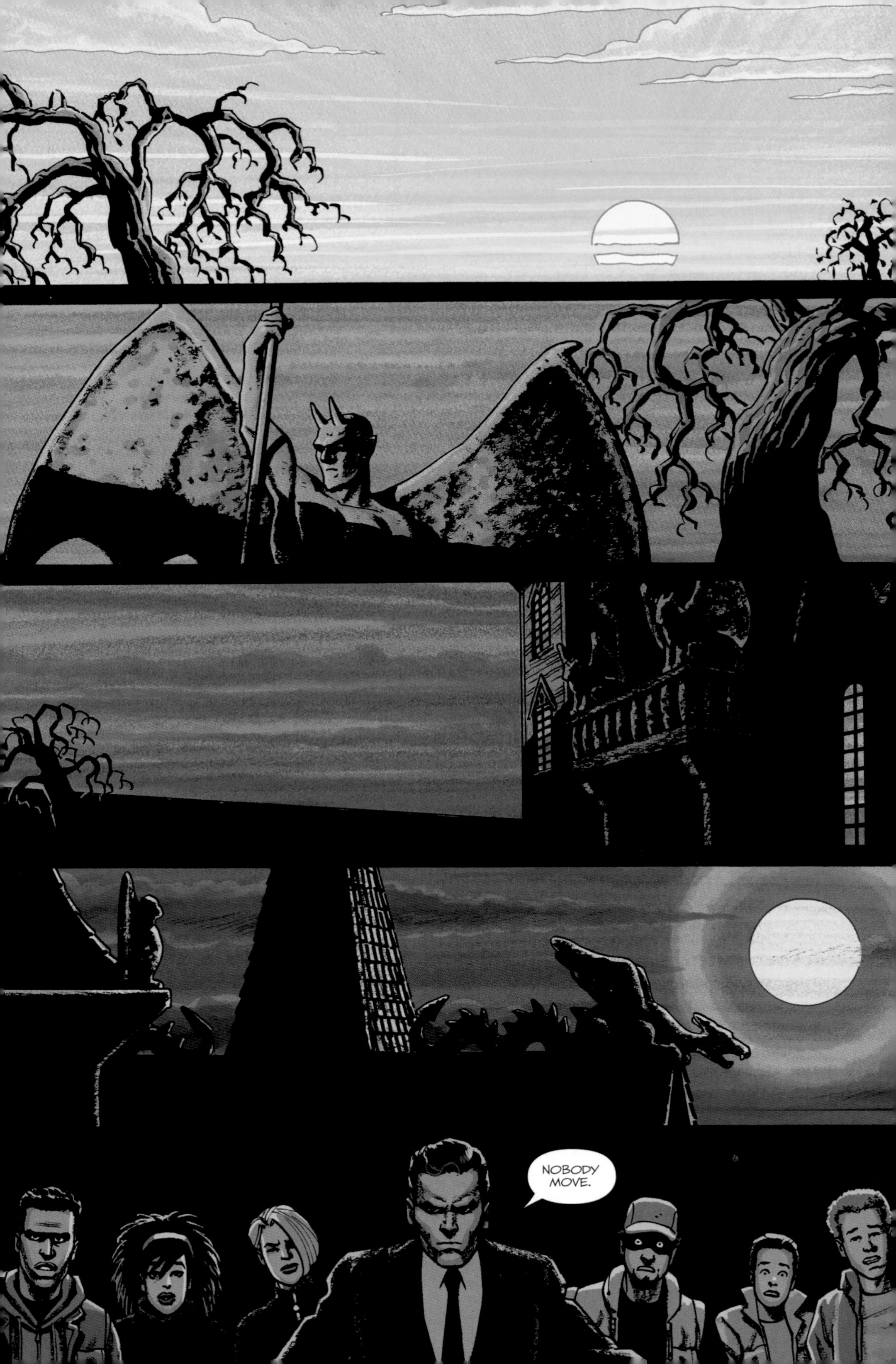
NOBODY MOVE.

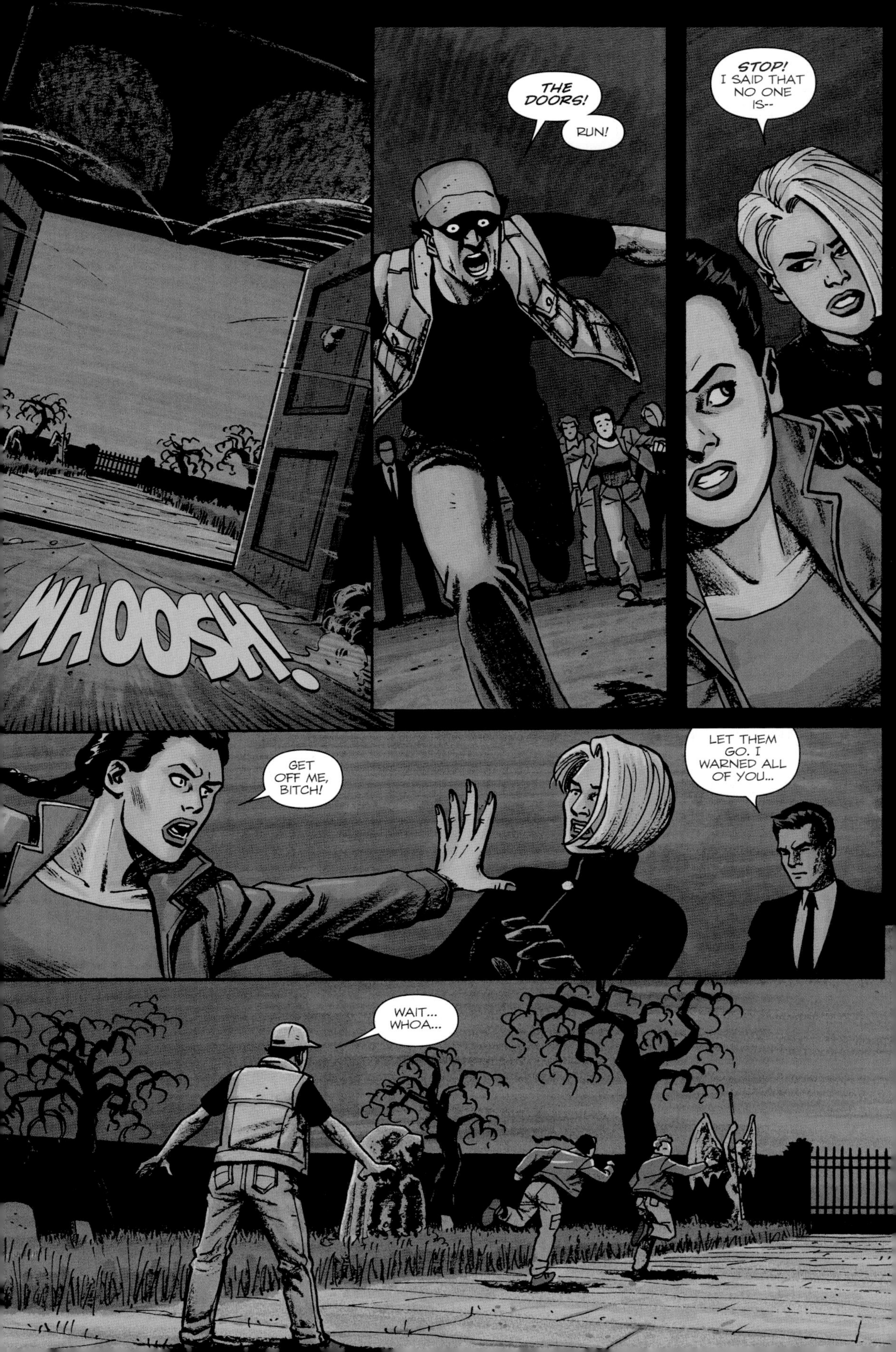
WHOOSH!
THE DOORS!
RUN!
STOP! I SAID THAT NO ONE IS--
GET OFF ME, BITCH!
LET THEM GO. I WARNED ALL OF YOU...
WAIT... WHOA...

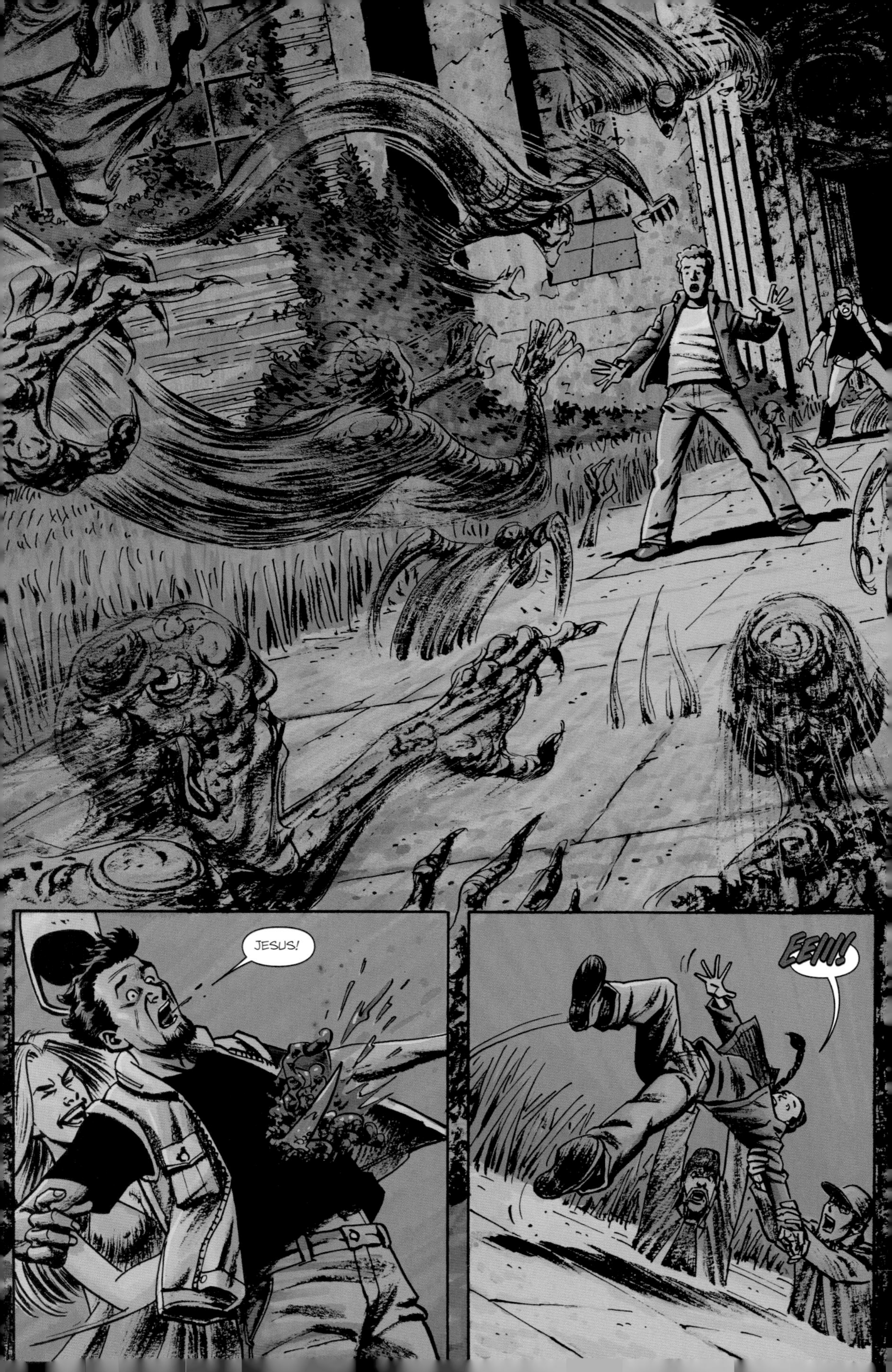
JESUS!
EEIII!

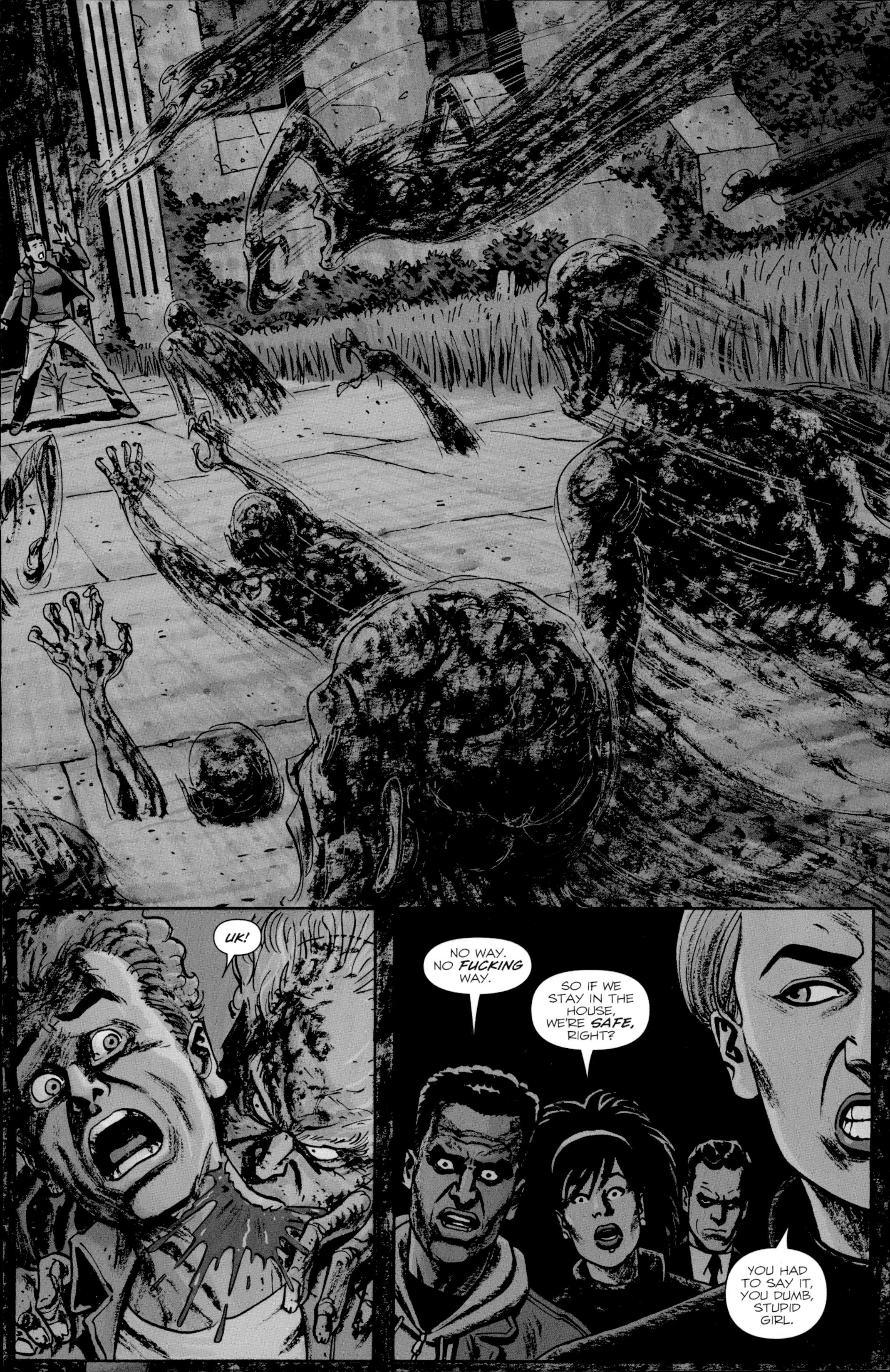
UK!
NO WAY. NO FUCKING WAY.
SO IF WE STAY IN THE HOUSE, WE'RE SAFE, RIGHT?
YOU HAD TO SAY IT, YOU DUMB, STUPID GIRL.

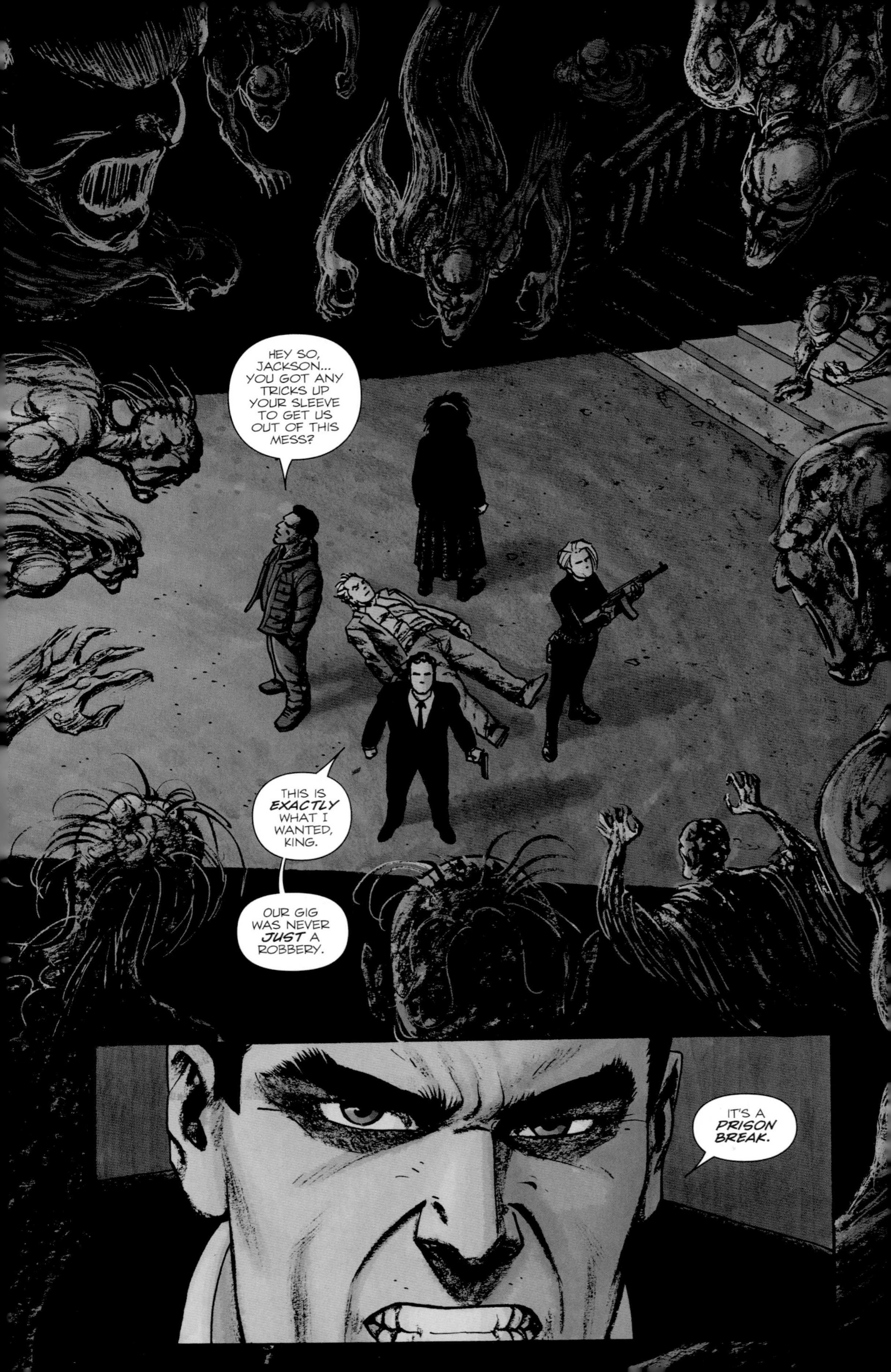
HEY SO, JACKSON... YOU GOT ANY TRICKS UP YOUR SLEEVE TO GET US OUT OF THIS MESS?
THIS IS EXACTLY WHAT I WANTED, KING.
OUR GIG WAS NEVER JUST A ROBBERY.
IT'S A PRISON BREAK.

CHAPTER FIVE

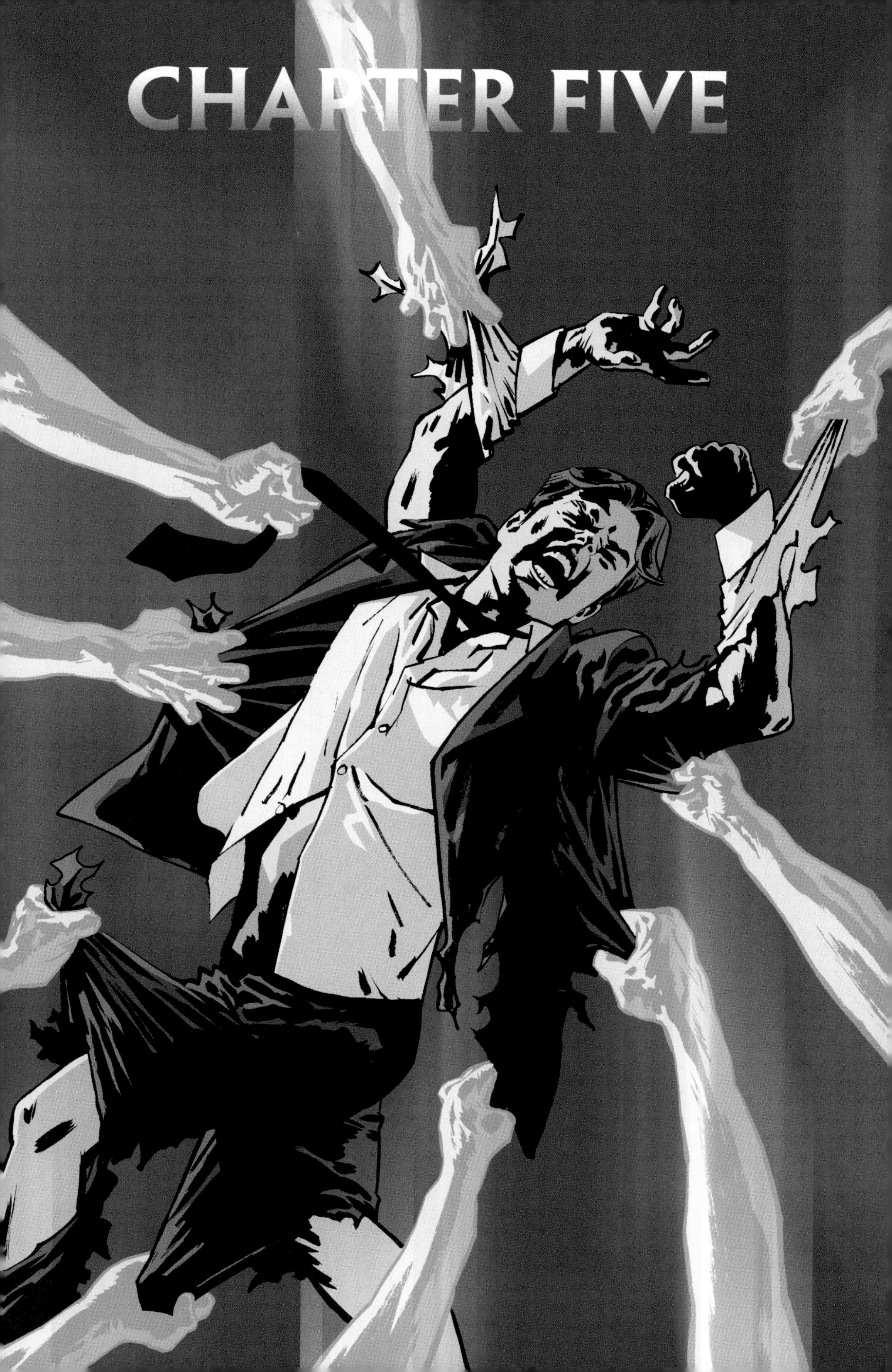

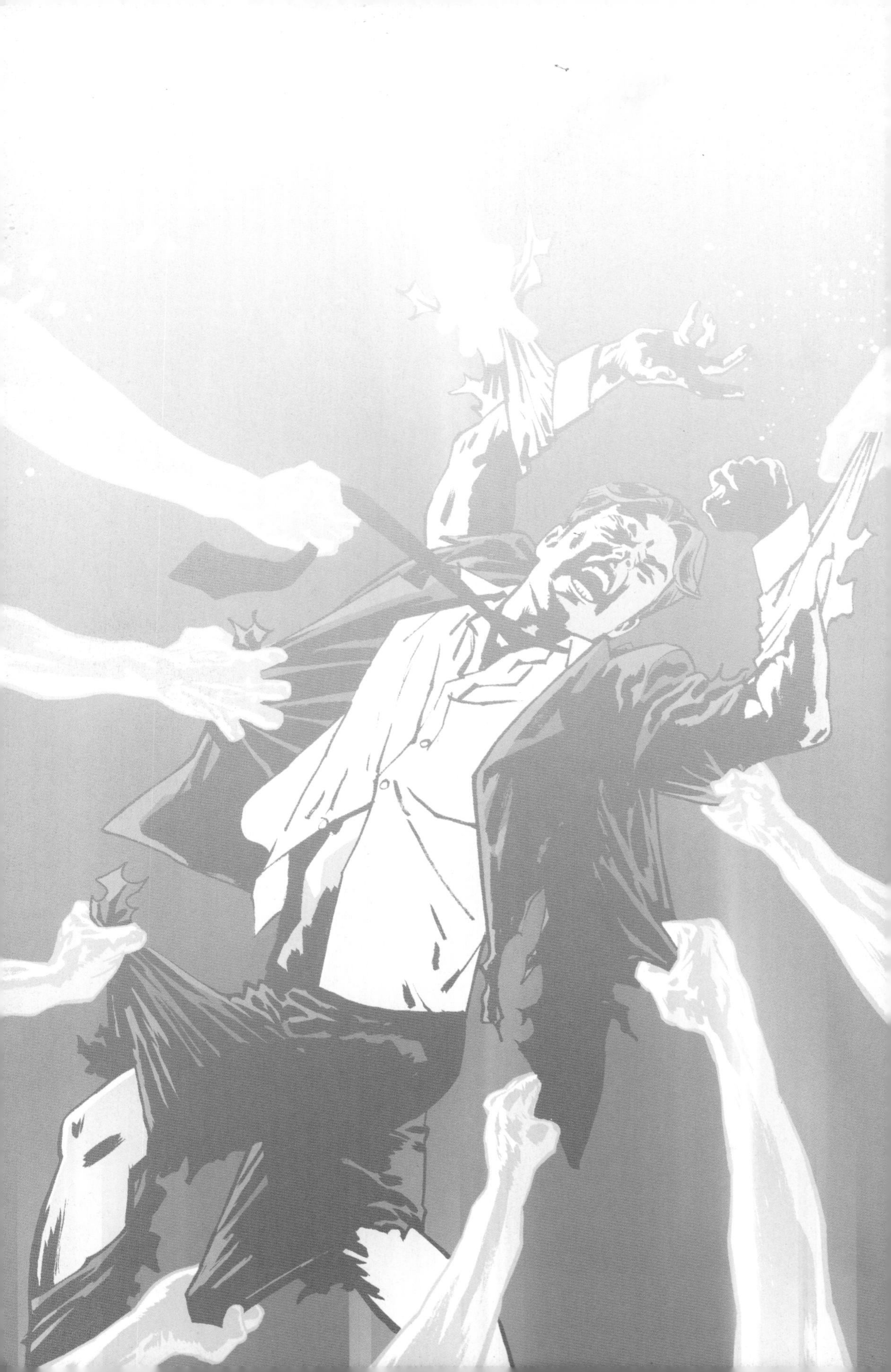

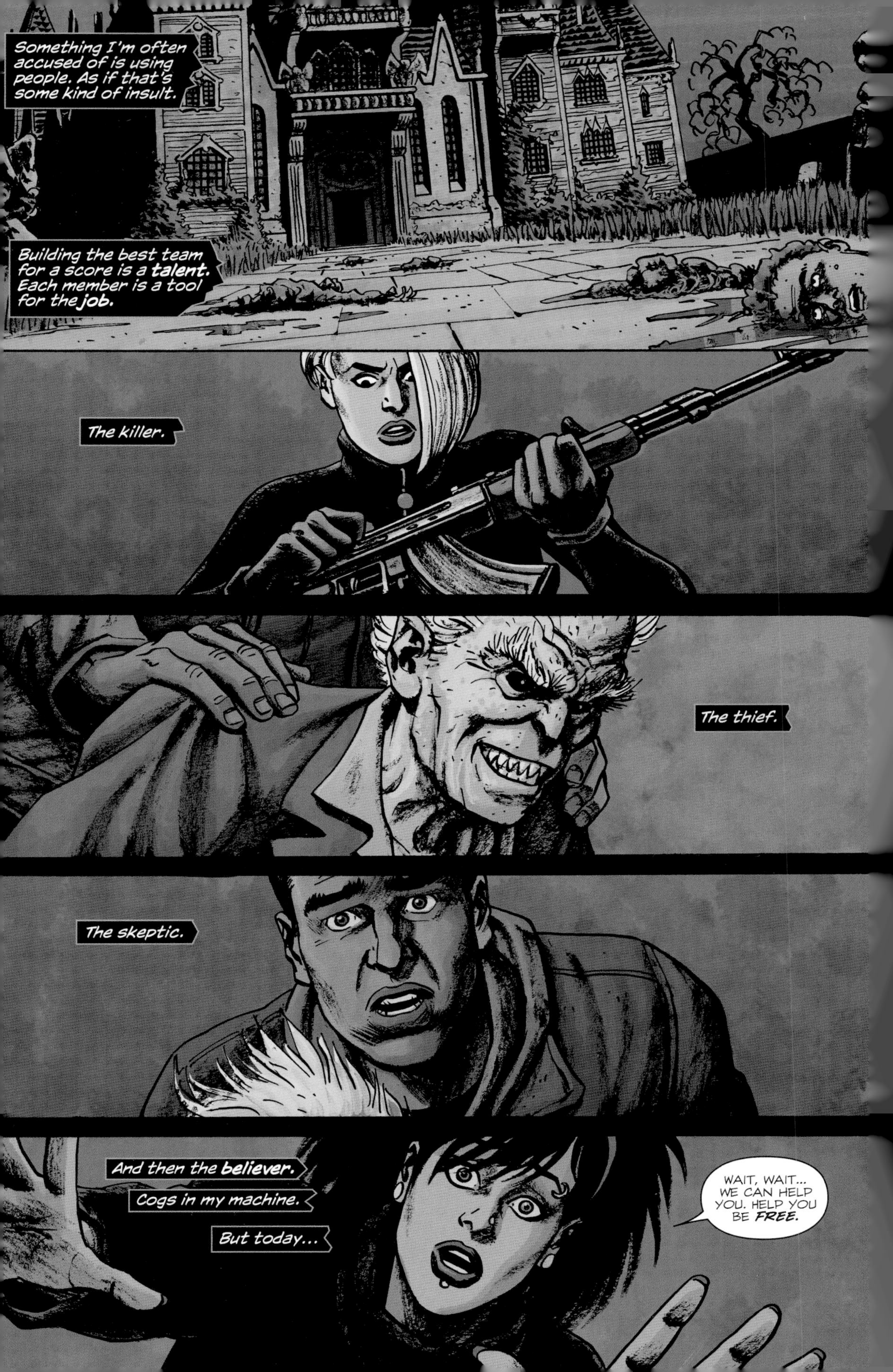

Something I'm often accused of is using people. As if that's some kind of insult.
Building the best team for a score is a talent. Each member is a tool for the job.
The killer.
The thief.
The skeptic.
And then the believer.
Cogs in my machine.
But today...
WAIT, WAIT... WE CAN HELP YOU. HELP YOU BE FREE.

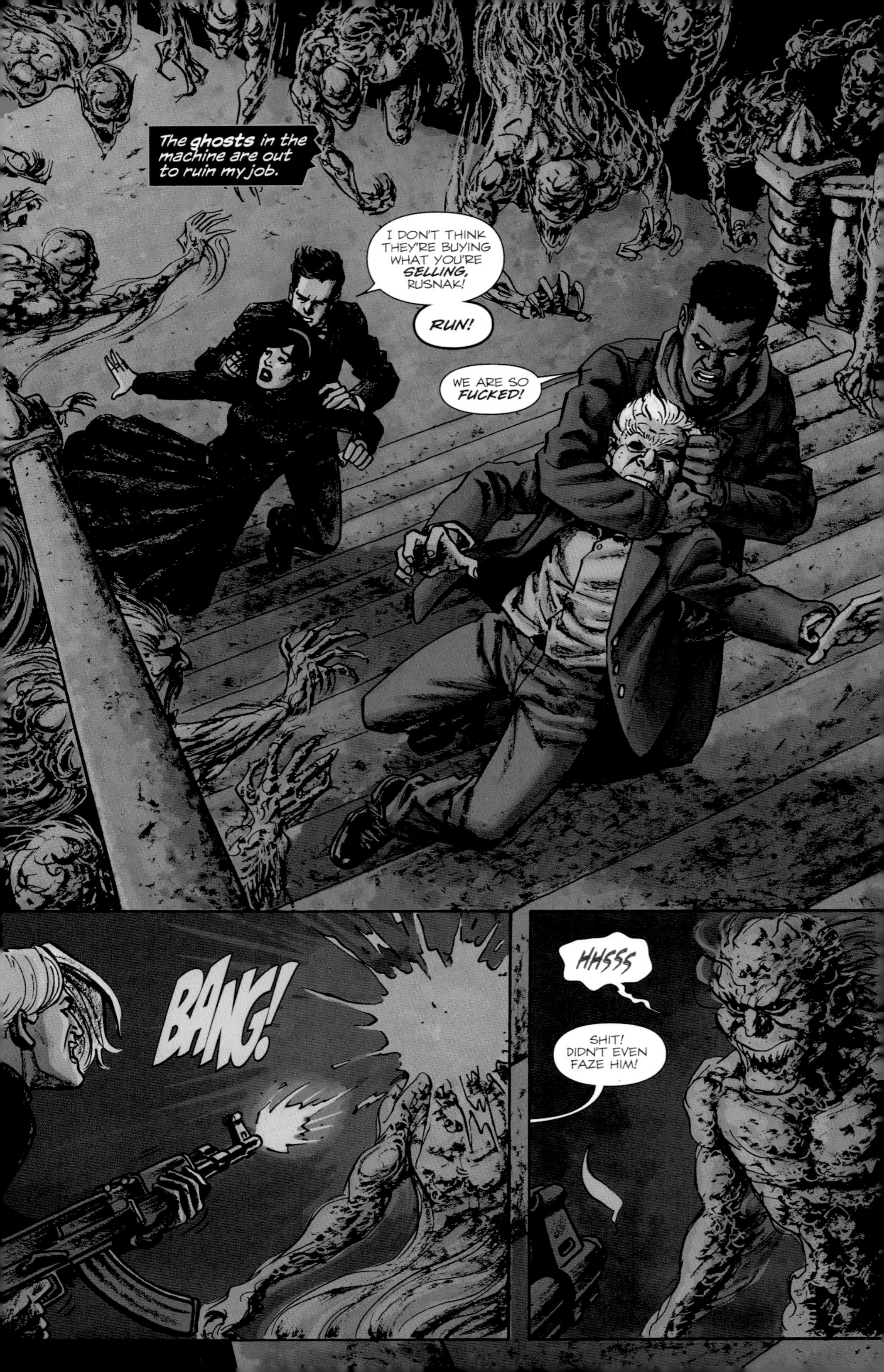
The ghosts in the machine are out to ruin my job.
I DON'T THINK THEY'RE BUYING WHAT YOU'RE SELLING, RUSNAK!
RUN!
WE ARE SO FUCKED!
BANG!
HHSSS
SHIT! DIDN'T EVEN FAZE HIM!

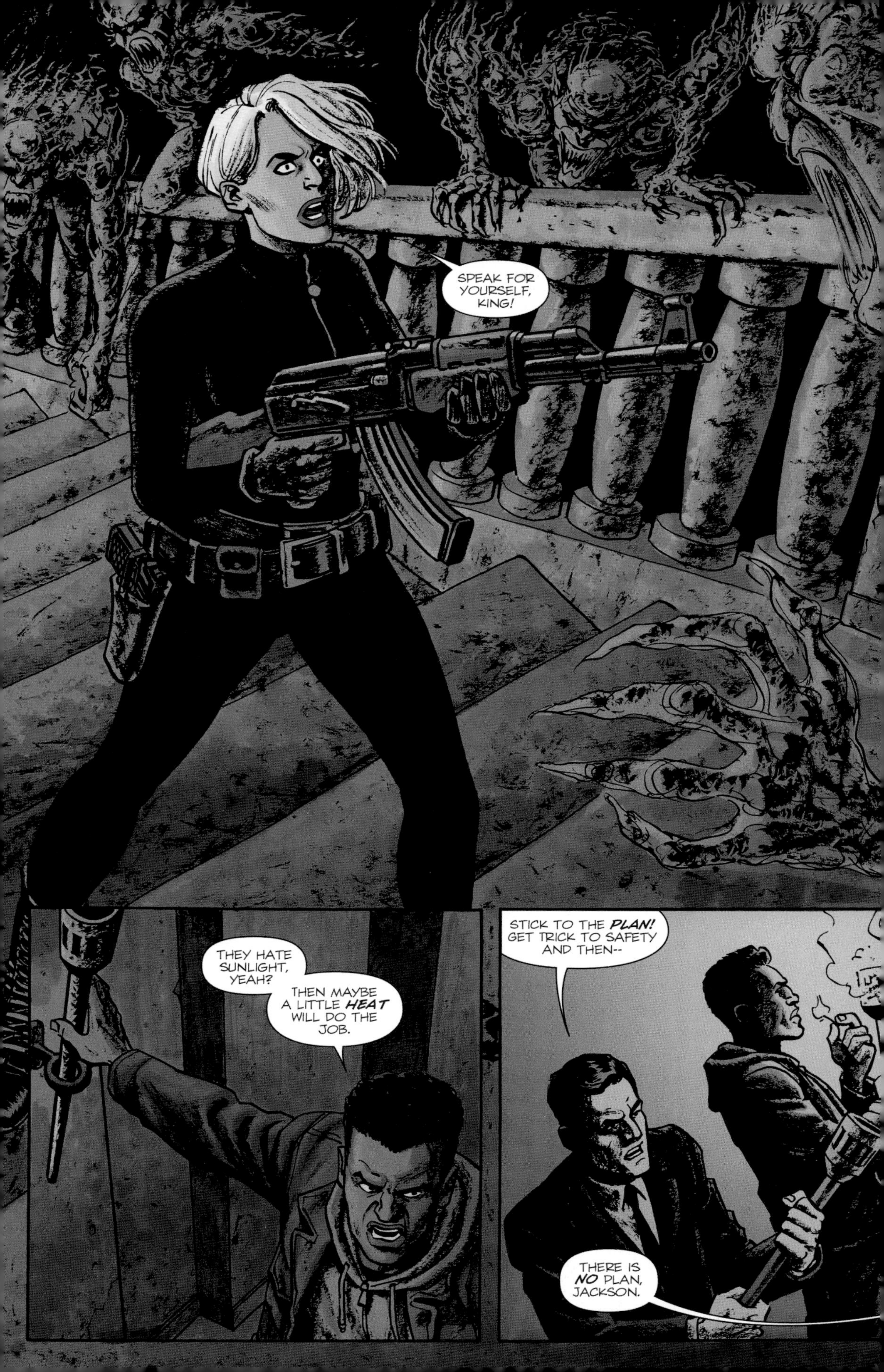
SPEAK FOR YOURSELF, KING!
THEY HATE SUNLIGHT, YEAH?
THEN MAYBE A LITTLE HEAT WILL DO THE JOB.
STICK TO THE PLAN! GET TRICK TO SAFETY AND THEN--
THERE IS NO PLAN, JACKSON.

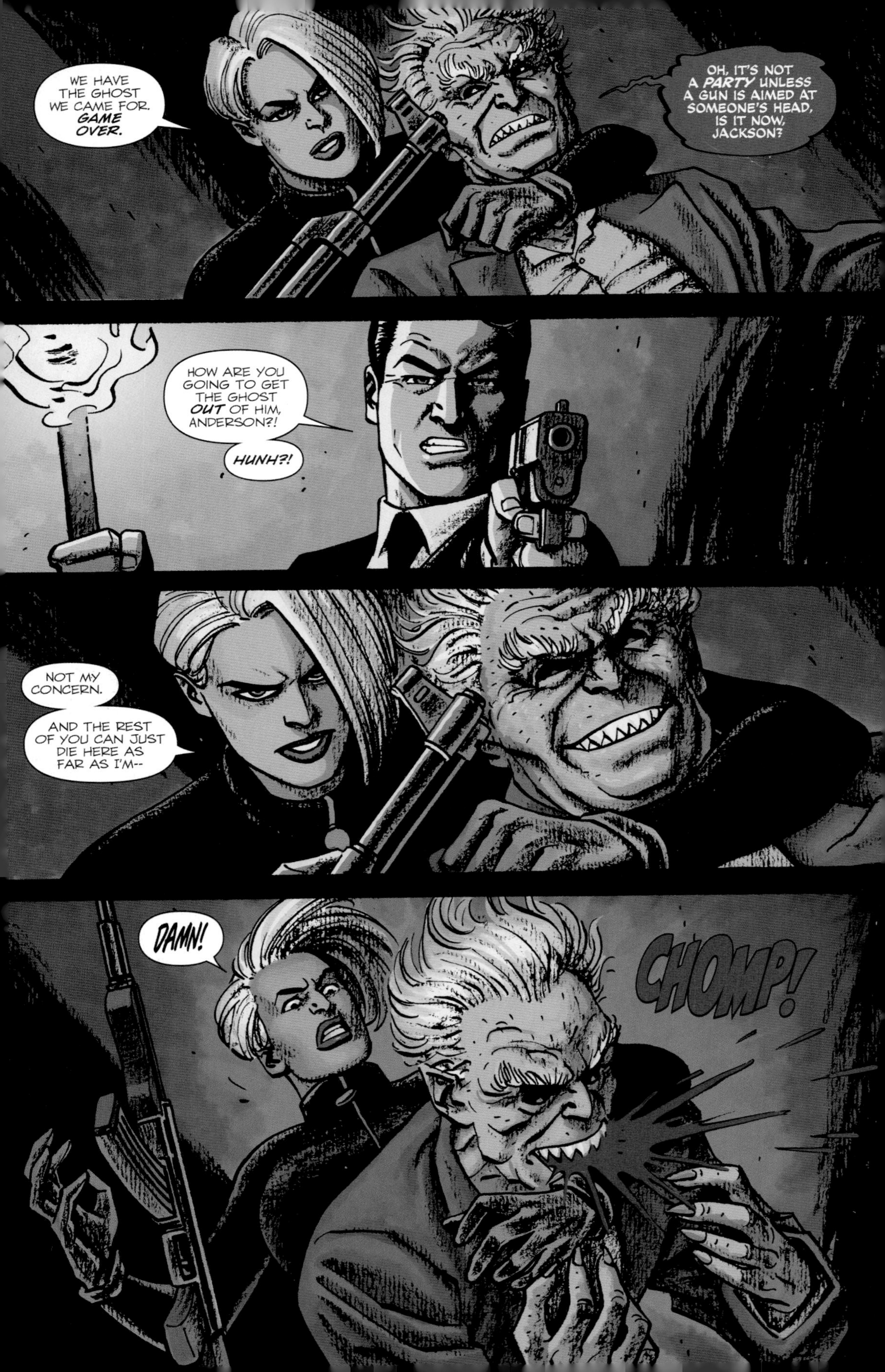
WE HAVE THE GHOST WE CAME FOR. GAME OVER.
OH, IT'S NOT A PARTY UNLESS A GUN IS AIMED AT SOMEONE'S HEAD, IS IT NOW, JACKSON?
HOW ARE YOU GOING TO GET THE GHOST OUT OF HIM, ANDERSON?!
HUNH?!
NOT MY CONCERN.
AND THE REST OF YOU CAN JUST DIE HERE AS FAR AS I'M--
DAMN!
CHOMP!

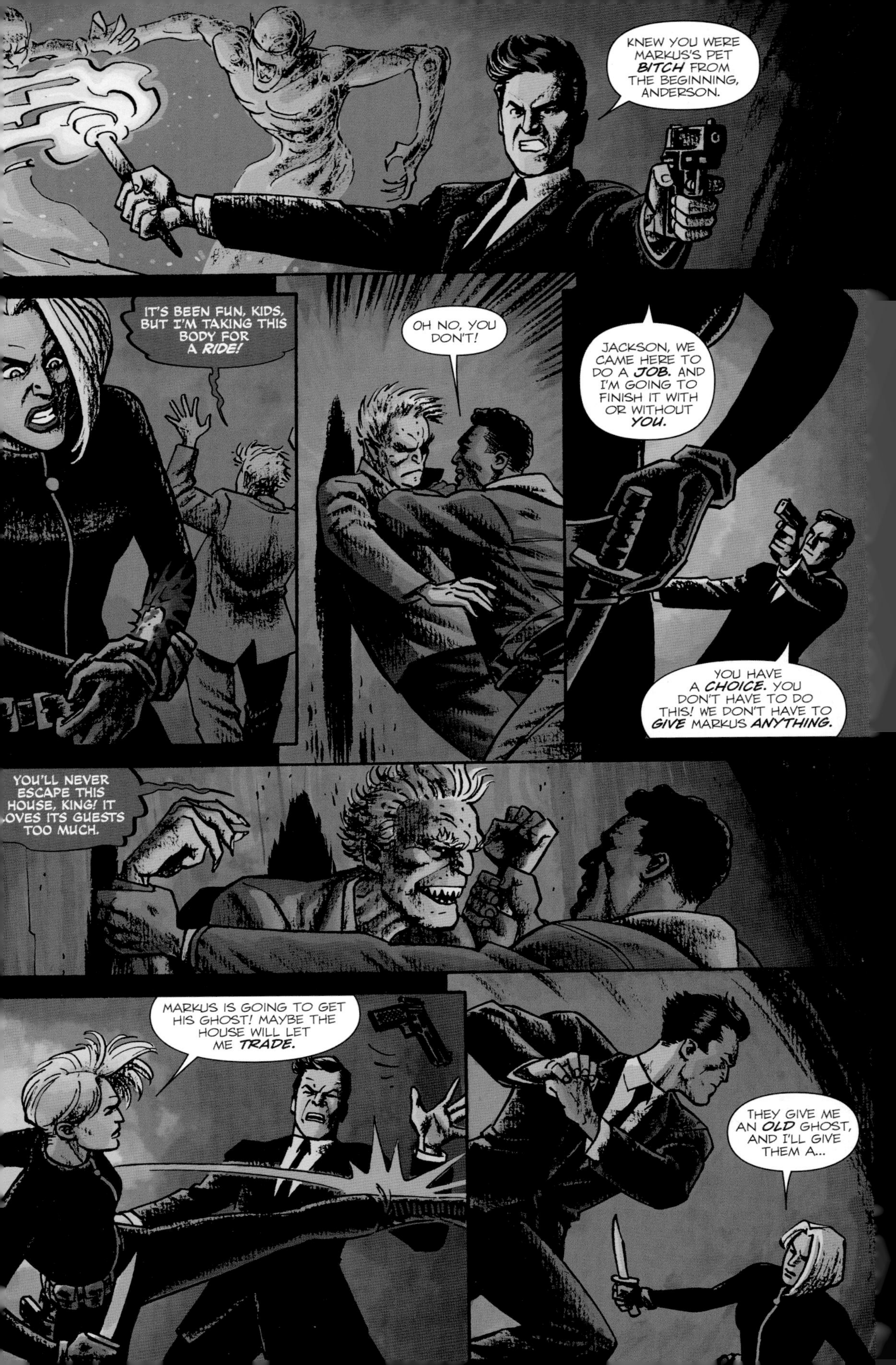
KNEW YOU WERE MARKUS'S PET BITCH FROM THE BEGINNING, ANDERSON.
IT'S BEEN FUN, KIDS, BUT I'M TAKING THIS BODY FOR A RIDE!
OH NO, YOU DON'T!
JACKSON, WE CAME HERE TO DO A JOB. AND I'M GOING TO FINISH IT WITH OR WITHOUT YOU.
YOU HAVE A CHOICE. YOU DON'T HAVE TO DO THIS! WE DON'T HAVE TO GIVE MARKUS ANYTHING.
YOU'LL NEVER ESCAPE THIS HOUSE, KING! IT LOVES ITS GUESTS TOO MUCH.
MARKUS IS GOING TO GET HIS GHOST! MAYBE THE HOUSE WILL LET ME TRADE.
THEY GIVE ME AN OLD GHOST, AND I'LL GIVE THEM A...

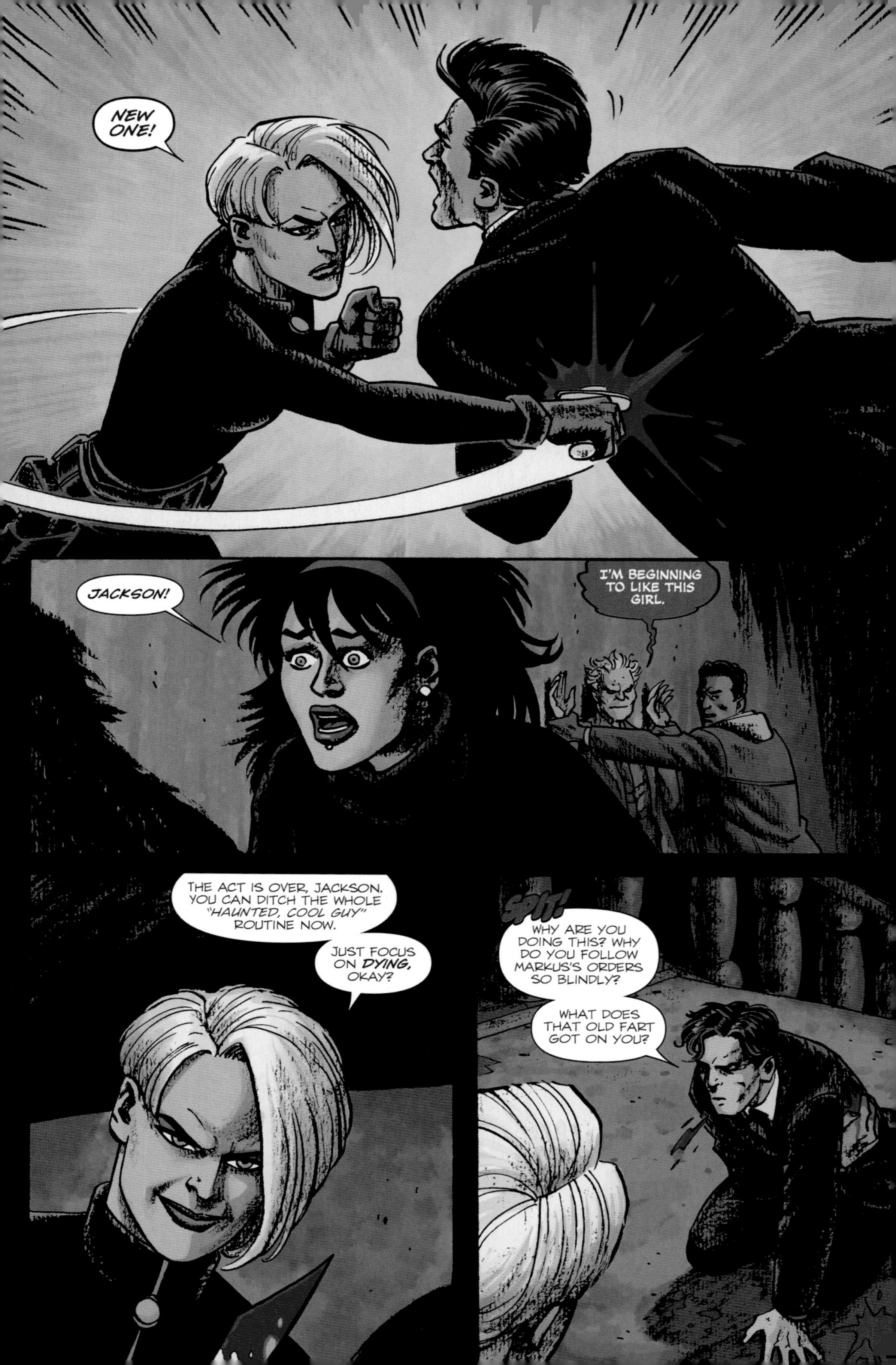
NEW ONE!
JACKSON!
I'M BEGINNING TO LIKE THIS GIRL.
THE ACT IS OVER, JACKSON. YOU CAN DITCH THE WHOLE "HAUNTED, COOL GUY" ROUTINE NOW.
JUST FOCUS ON DYING, OKAY?
SPIT!
WHY ARE YOU DOING THIS? WHY DO YOU FOLLOW MARKUS'S ORDERS SO BLINDLY?
WHAT DOES THAT OLD FART GOT ON YOU?

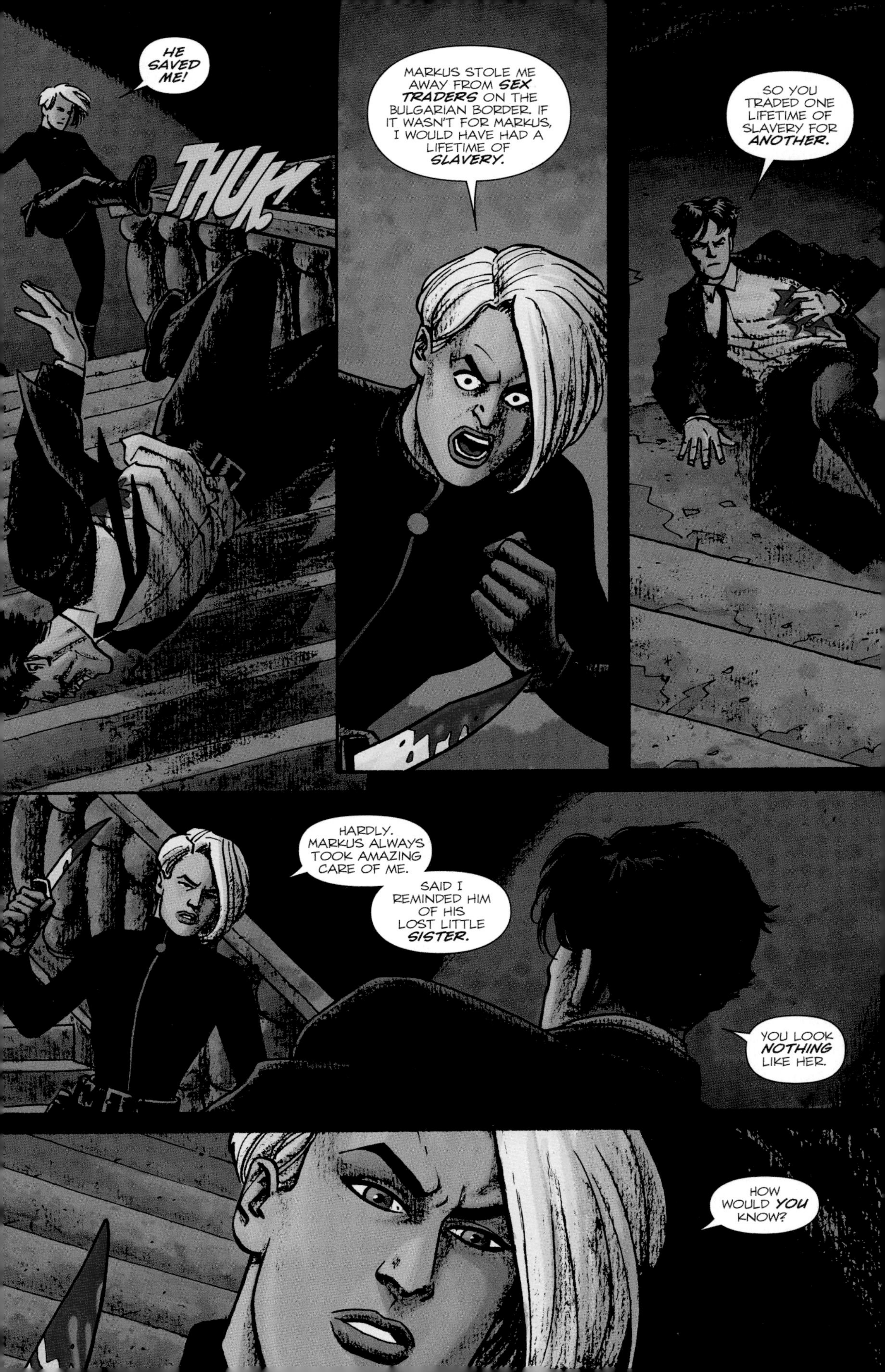
HE SAVED ME!
THUK!
MARKUS STOLE ME AWAY FROM SEX TRADERS ON THE BULGARIAN BORDER. IF IT WASN'T FOR MARKUS, I WOULD HAVE HAD A LIFETIME OF SLAVERY.
SO YOU TRADED ONE LIFETIME OF SLAVERY FOR ANOTHER.
HARDLY. MARKUS ALWAYS TOOK AMAZING CARE OF ME.
SAID I REMINDED HIM OF HIS LOST LITTLE SISTER.
YOU LOOK NOTHING LIKE HER.
HOW WOULD YOU KNOW?

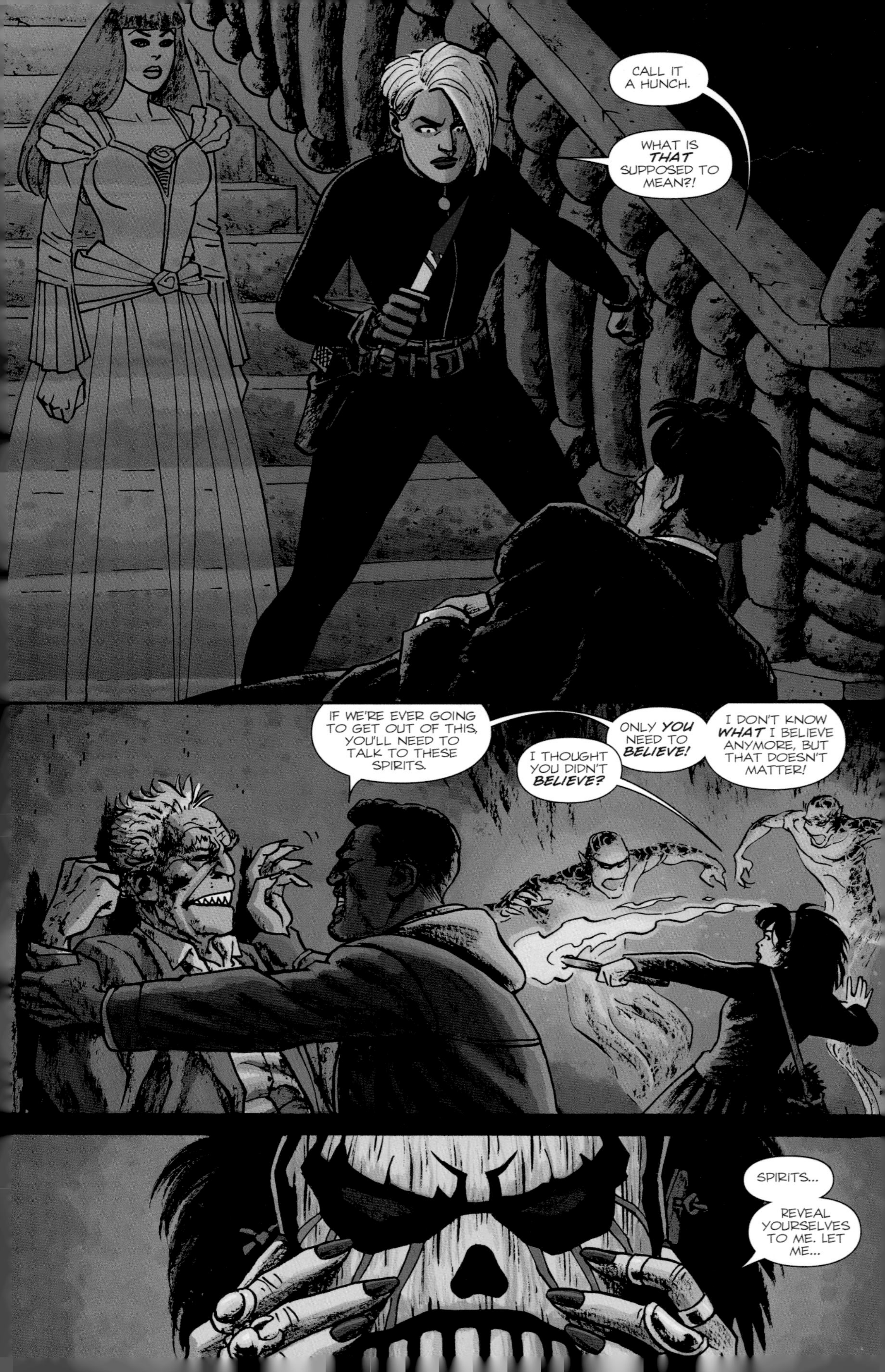
CALL IT A HUNCH.
WHAT IS THAT SUPPOSED TO MEAN?!
IF WE'RE EVER GOING TO GET OUT OF THIS, YOU'LL NEED TO TALK TO THESE SPIRITS.
I THOUGHT YOU DIDN'T BELIEVE?
ONLY YOU NEED TO BELIEVE!
I DON'T KNOW WHAT I BELIEVE ANYMORE, BUT THAT DOESN'T MATTER!
SPIRITS...
REVEAL YOURSELVES TO ME. LET ME...

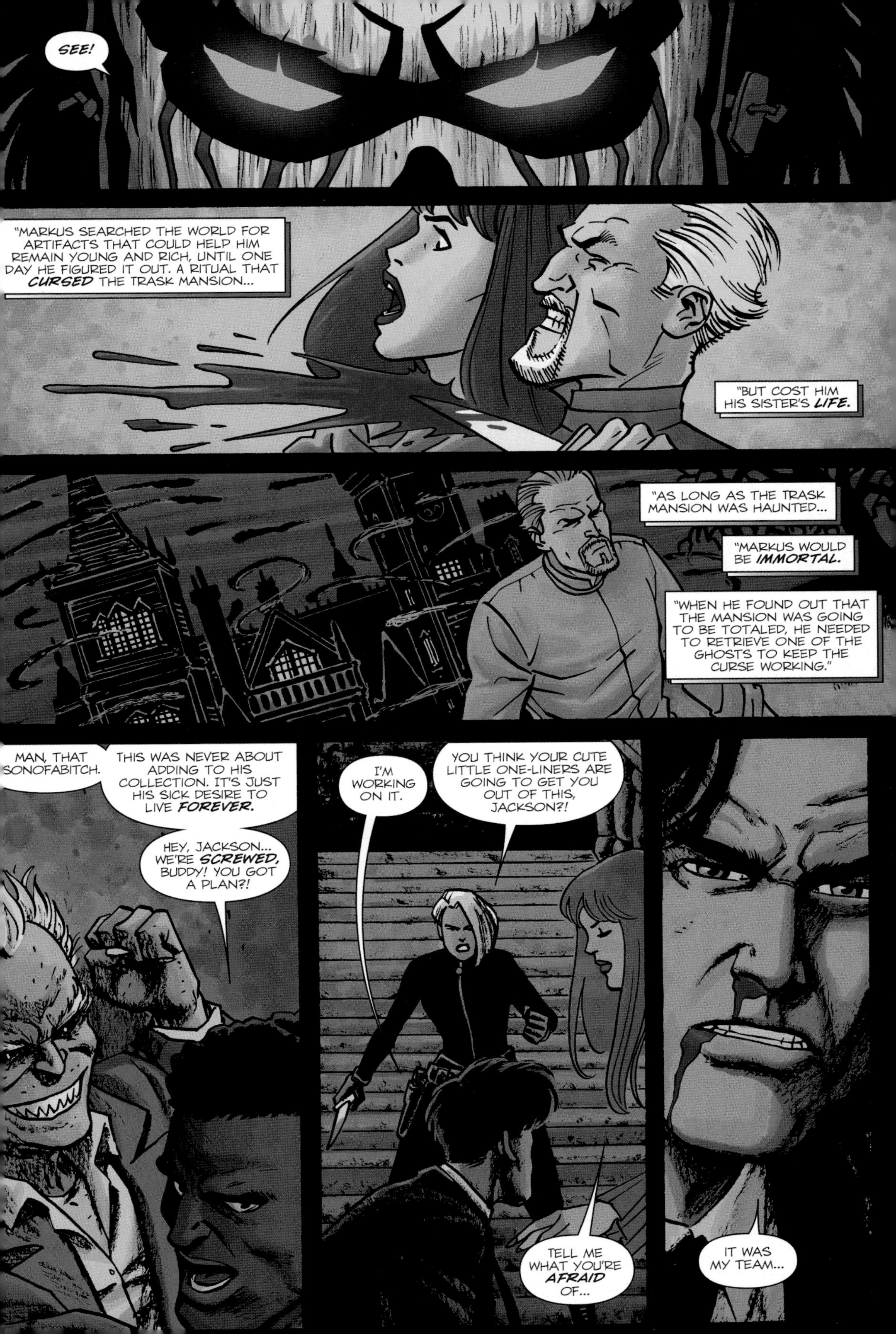
SEE!
"MARKUS SEARCHED THE WORLD FOR ARTIFACTS THAT COULD HELP HIM REMAIN YOUNG AND RICH, UNTIL ONE DAY HE FIGURED IT OUT. A RITUAL THAT CURSED THE TRASK MANSION...
"BUT COST HIM HIS SISTER'S LIFE.
"AS LONG AS THE TRASK MANSION WAS HAUNTED...
"MARKUS WOULD BE IMMORTAL.
"WHEN HE FOUND OUT THAT THE MANSION WAS GOING TO BE TOTALED, HE NEEDED TO RETRIEVE ONE OF THE GHOSTS TO KEEP THE CURSE WORKING."
MAN, THAT SONOFABITCH.
THIS WAS NEVER ABOUT ADDING TO HIS COLLECTION. IT'S JUST HIS SICK DESIRE TO LIVE FOREVER.
HEY, JACKSON... WE'RE SCREWED, BUDDY! YOU GOT A PLAN?!
I'M WORKING ON IT.
YOU THINK YOUR CUTE LITTLE ONE-LINERS ARE GOING TO GET YOU OUT OF THIS, JACKSON?!
TELL ME WHAT YOU'RE AFRAID OF...
IT WAS MY TEAM...

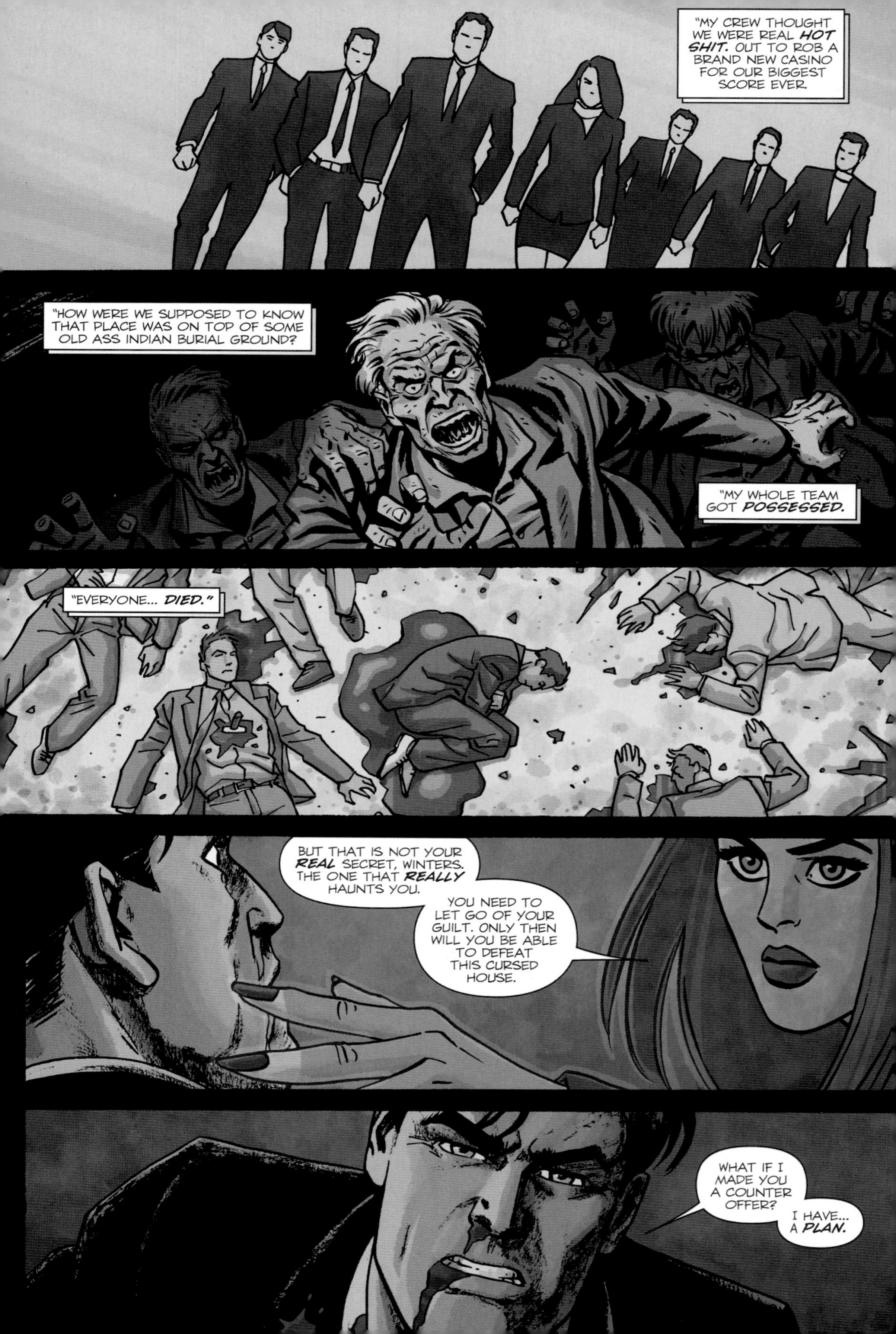
"MY CREW THOUGHT WE WERE REAL HOT SHIT. OUT TO ROB A BRAND NEW CASINO FOR OUR BIGGEST SCORE EVER.
"HOW WERE WE SUPPOSED TO KNOW THAT PLACE WAS ON TOP OF SOME OLD ASS INDIAN BURIAL GROUND?
"MY WHOLE TEAM GOT POSSESSED.
"EVERYONE... DIED."
BUT THAT IS NOT YOUR REAL SECRET, WINTERS. THE ONE THAT REALLY HAUNTS YOU.
YOU NEED TO LET GO OF YOUR GUILT. ONLY THEN WILL YOU BE ABLE TO DEFEAT THIS CURSED HOUSE.
WHAT IF I MADE YOU A COUNTER OFFER?
I HAVE... A PLAN.

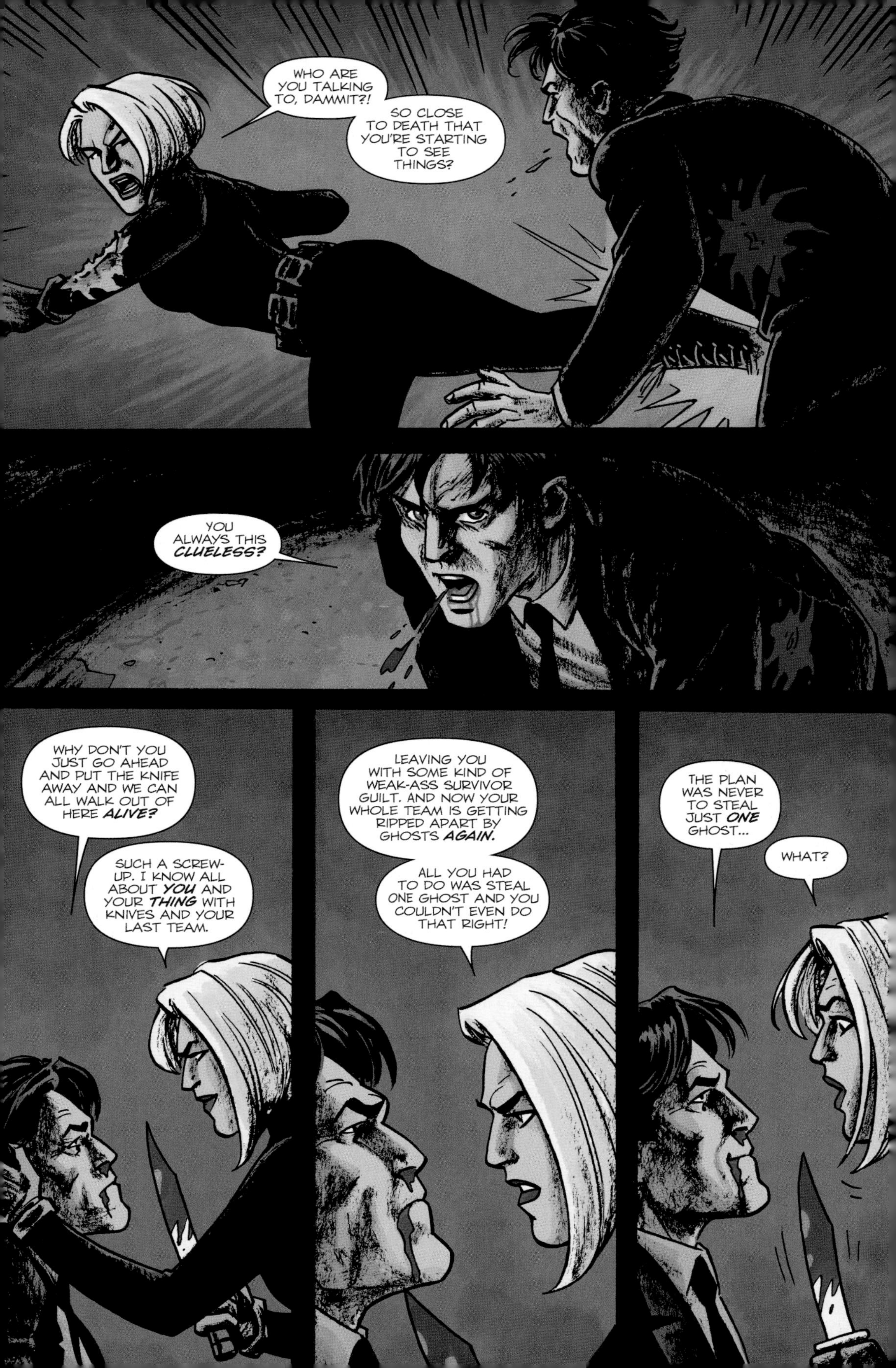
WHO ARE YOU TALKING TO, DAMMIT?!
SO CLOSE TO DEATH THAT YOU'RE STARTING TO SEE THINGS?
YOU ALWAYS THIS *CLUELESS?*
WHY DON'T YOU JUST GO AHEAD AND PUT THE KNIFE AWAY AND WE CAN ALL WALK OUT OF HERE *ALIVE?*
SUCH A SCREW-UP. I KNOW ALL ABOUT *YOU* AND YOUR *THING* WITH KNIVES AND YOUR LAST TEAM.
LEAVING YOU WITH SOME KIND OF WEAK-ASS SURVIVOR GUILT. AND NOW YOUR WHOLE TEAM IS GETTING RIPPED APART BY GHOSTS *AGAIN.*
ALL YOU HAD TO DO WAS STEAL ONE GHOST AND YOU COULDN'T EVEN DO THAT RIGHT!
THE PLAN WAS NEVER TO STEAL JUST *ONE* GHOST...
WHAT?

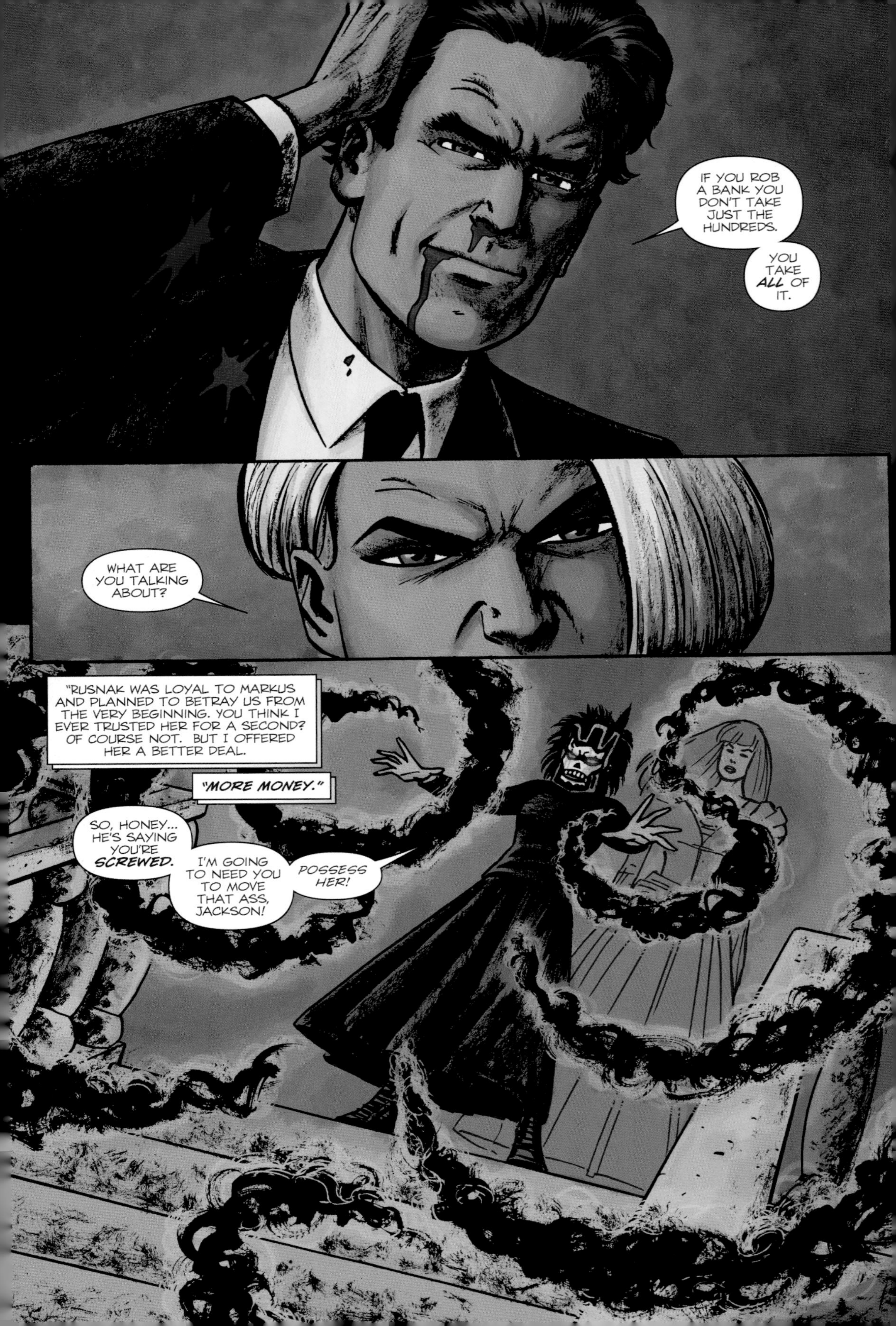
IF YOU ROB A BANK YOU DON'T TAKE JUST THE HUNDREDS.
YOU TAKE *ALL* OF IT.
WHAT ARE YOU TALKING ABOUT?
"RUSNAK WAS LOYAL TO MARKUS AND PLANNED TO BETRAY US FROM THE VERY BEGINNING. YOU THINK I EVER TRUSTED HER FOR A SECOND? OF COURSE NOT. BUT I OFFERED HER A BETTER DEAL.
"MORE MONEY."
SO, HONEY... HE'S SAYING YOU'RE ***SCREWED.***
I'M GOING TO NEED YOU TO MOVE THAT ASS, JACKSON!
POSSESS HER!

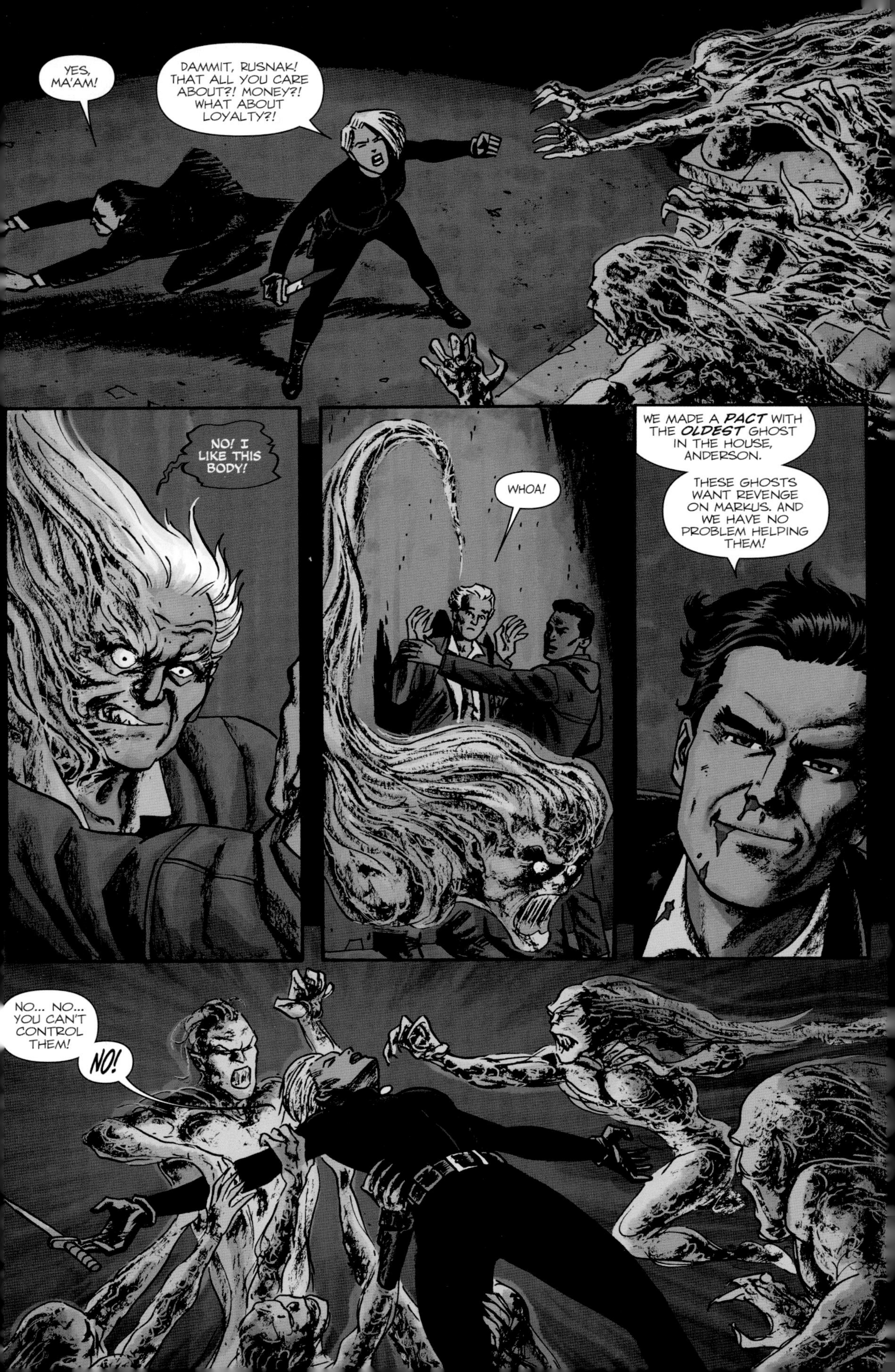
YES, MA'AM!
DAMMIT, RUSNAK! THAT ALL YOU CARE ABOUT?! MONEY?! WHAT ABOUT LOYALTY?!
NO! I LIKE THIS BODY!
WHOA!
WE MADE A PACT WITH THE OLDEST GHOST IN THE HOUSE, ANDERSON.
THESE GHOSTS WANT REVENGE ON MARKUS. AND WE HAVE NO PROBLEM HELPING THEM!
NO... NO... YOU CAN'T CONTROL THEM!
NO!

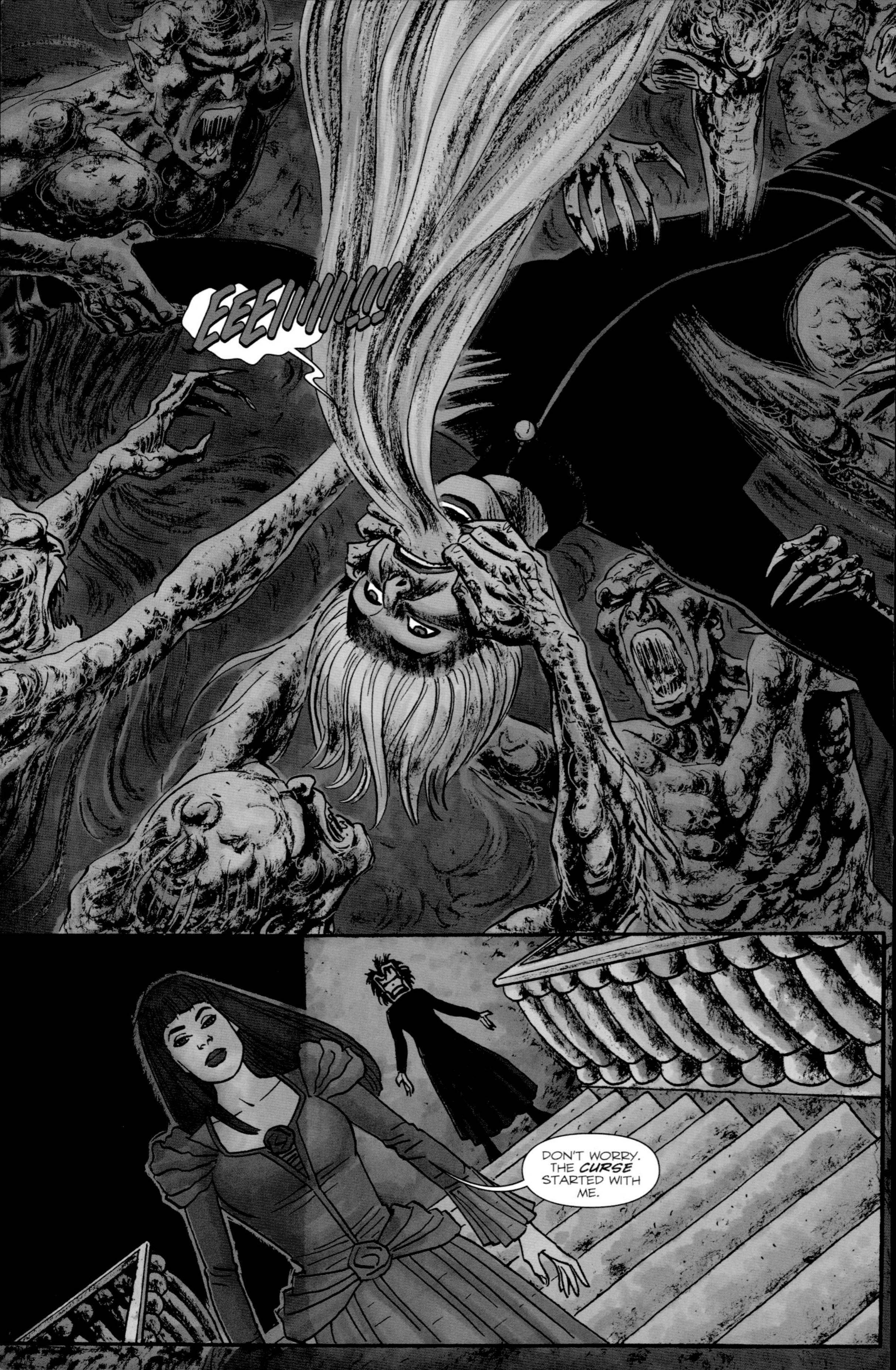

EEEIIIIIII!!!!
DON'T WORRY. THE CURSE STARTED WITH ME.

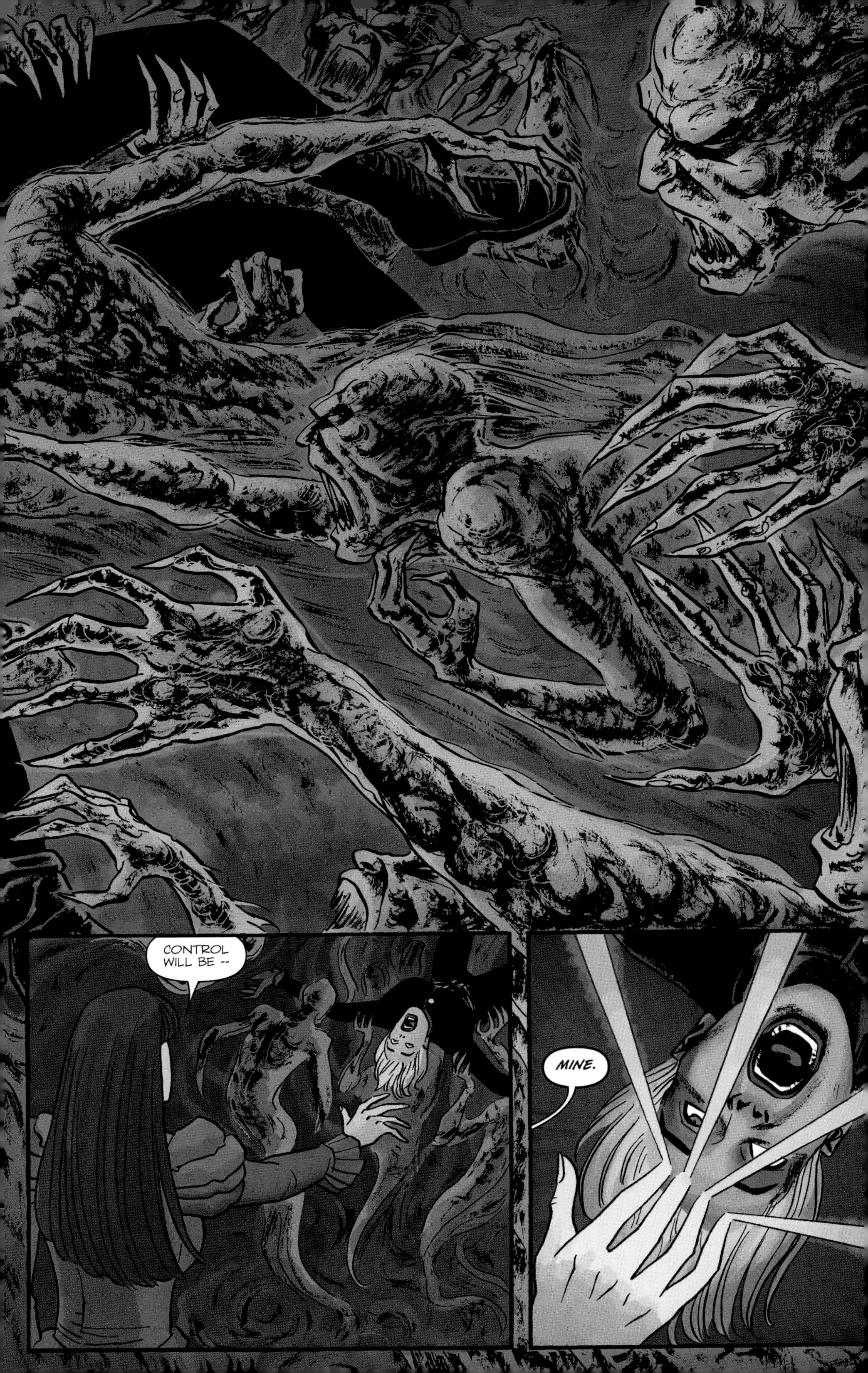
CONTROL WILL BE --
MINE.

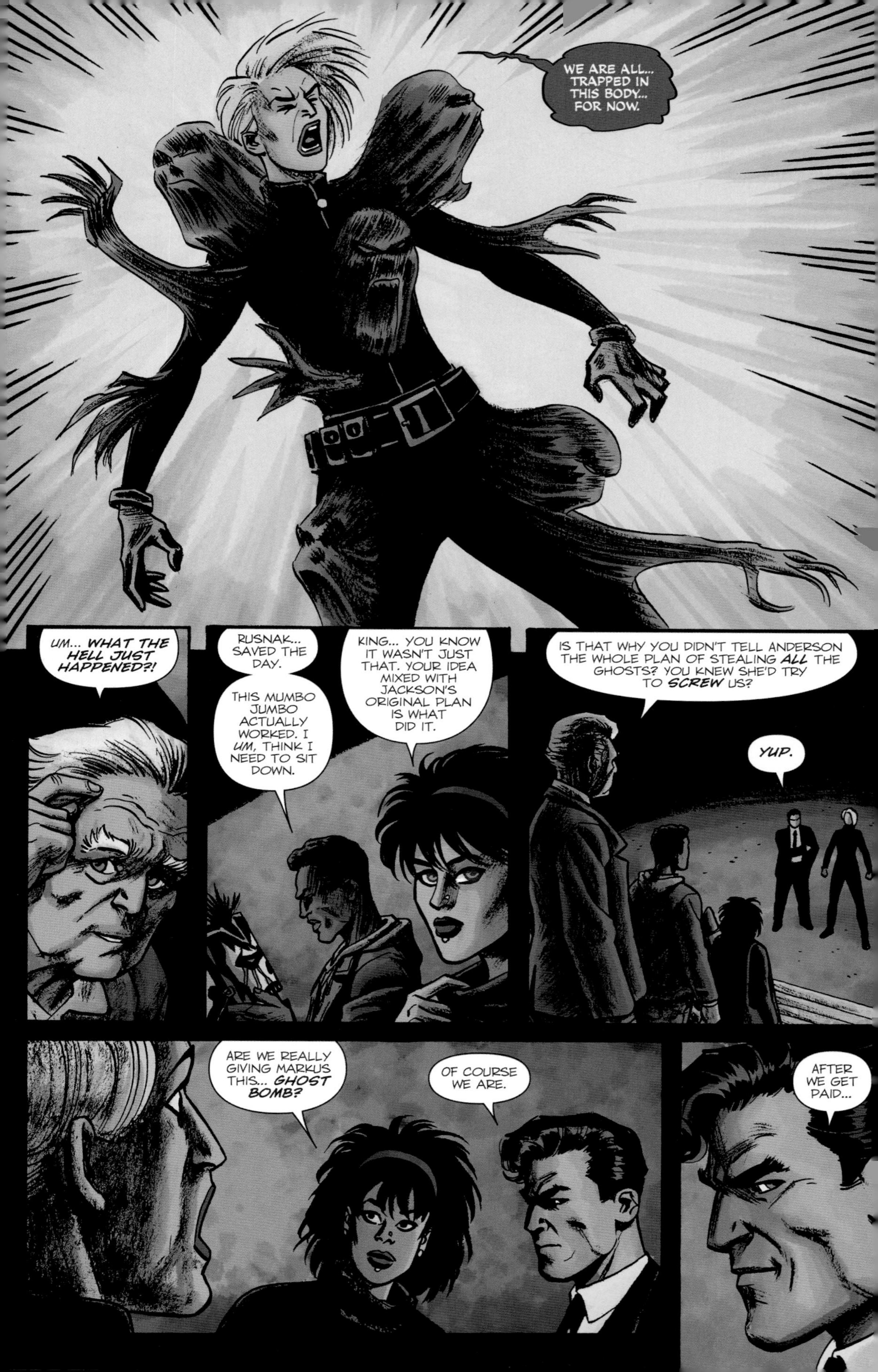
WE ARE ALL... TRAPPED IN THIS BODY... FOR NOW.
UM... WHAT THE HELL JUST HAPPENED?!
RUSNAK... SAVED THE DAY.
THIS MUMBO JUMBO ACTUALLY WORKED. I UM, THINK I NEED TO SIT DOWN.
KING... YOU KNOW IT WASN'T JUST THAT. YOUR IDEA MIXED WITH JACKSON'S ORIGINAL PLAN IS WHAT DID IT.
IS THAT WHY YOU DIDN'T TELL ANDERSON THE WHOLE PLAN OF STEALING ALL THE GHOSTS? YOU KNEW SHE'D TRY TO SCREW US?
YUP.
ARE WE REALLY GIVING MARKUS THIS... GHOST BOMB?
OF COURSE WE ARE.
AFTER WE GET PAID...

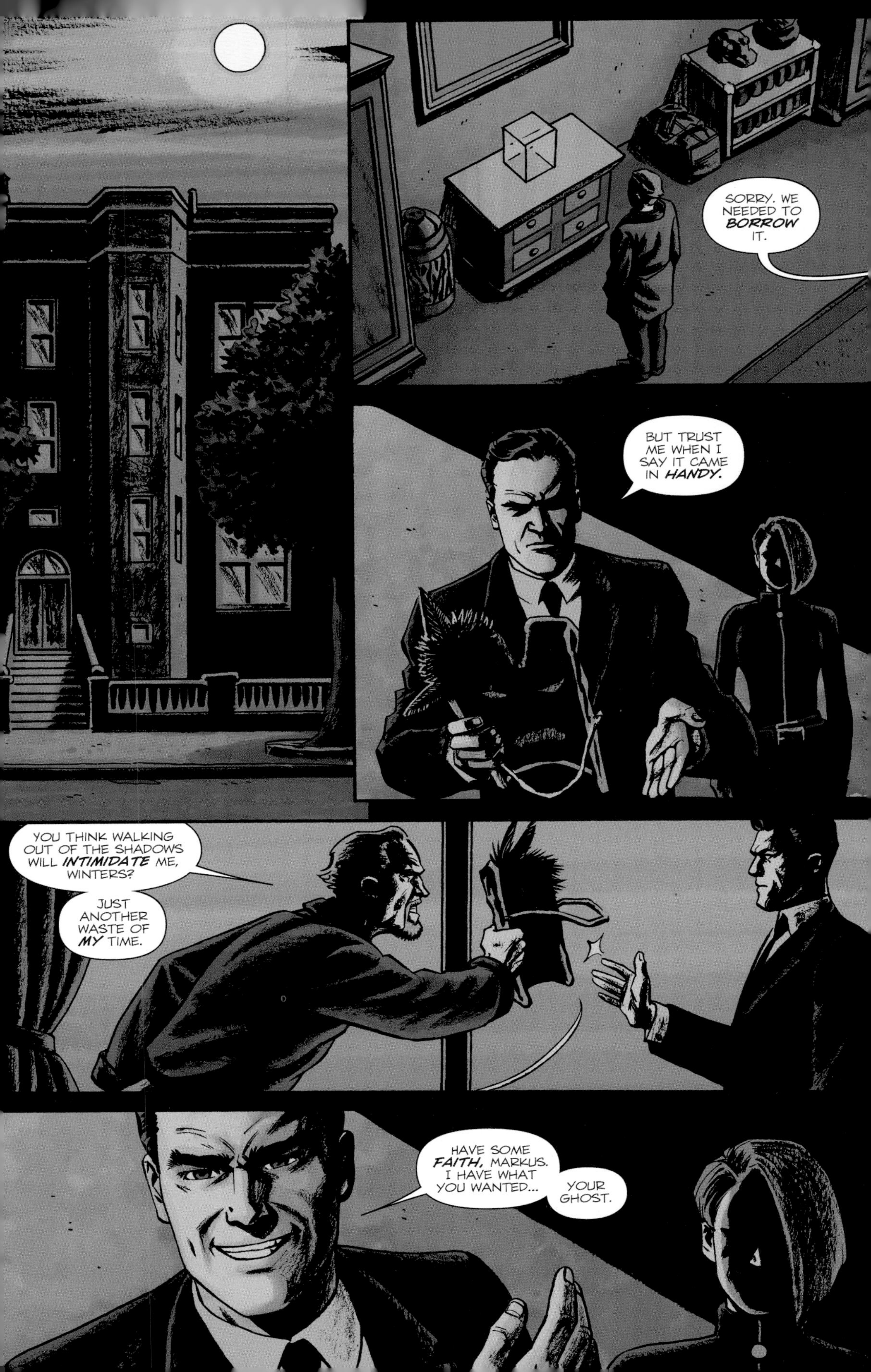
SORRY. WE NEEDED TO BORROW IT.
BUT TRUST ME WHEN I SAY IT CAME IN HANDY.
YOU THINK WALKING OUT OF THE SHADOWS WILL INTIMIDATE ME, WINTERS?
JUST ANOTHER WASTE OF MY TIME.
HAVE SOME FAITH, MARKUS. I HAVE WHAT YOU WANTED...
YOUR GHOST.

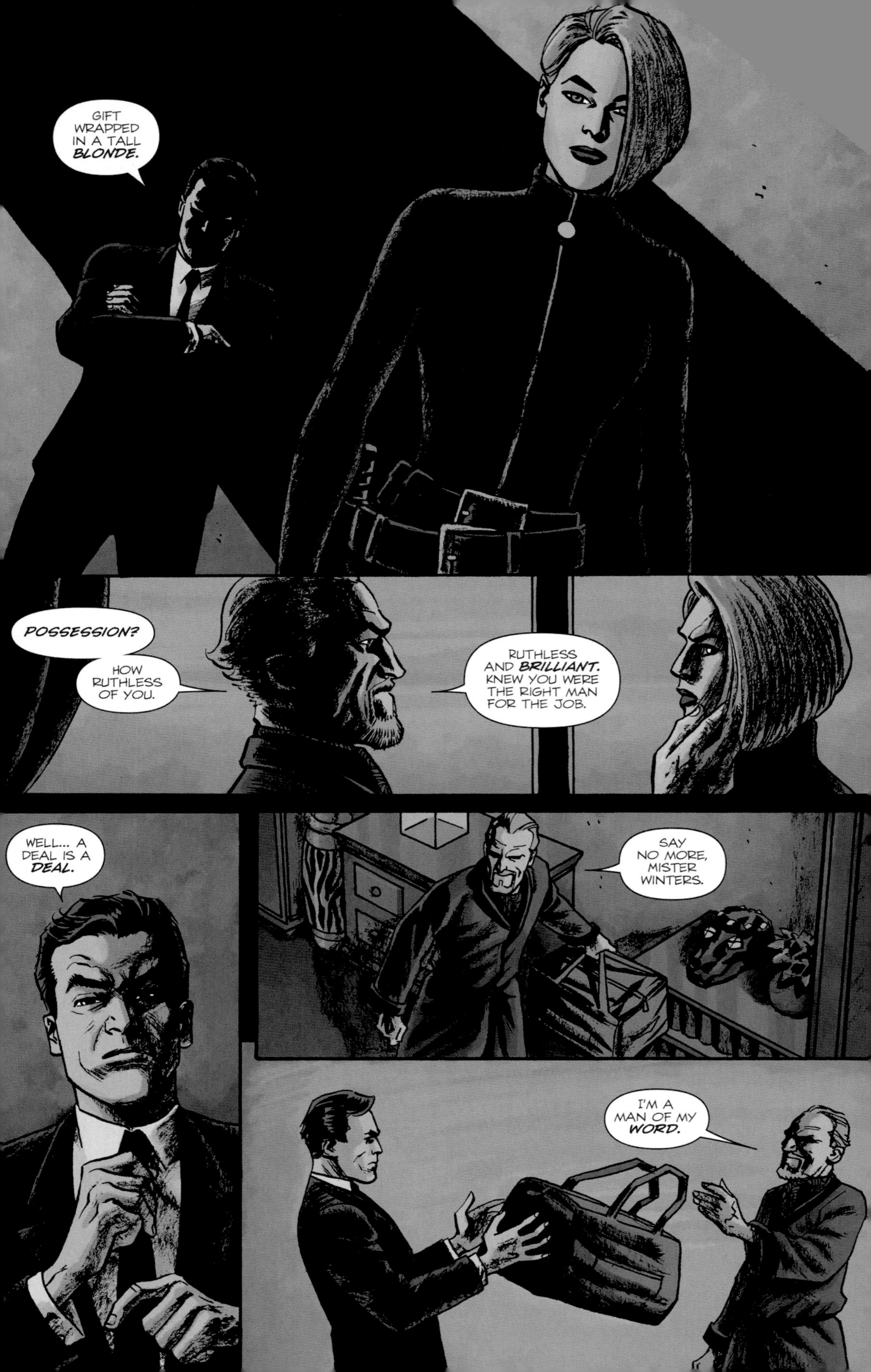
GIFT WRAPPED IN A TALL BLONDE.
POSSESSION?
HOW RUTHLESS OF YOU.
RUTHLESS AND BRILLIANT. KNEW YOU WERE THE RIGHT MAN FOR THE JOB.
WELL... A DEAL IS A DEAL.
SAY NO MORE, MISTER WINTERS.
I'M A MAN OF MY WORD.

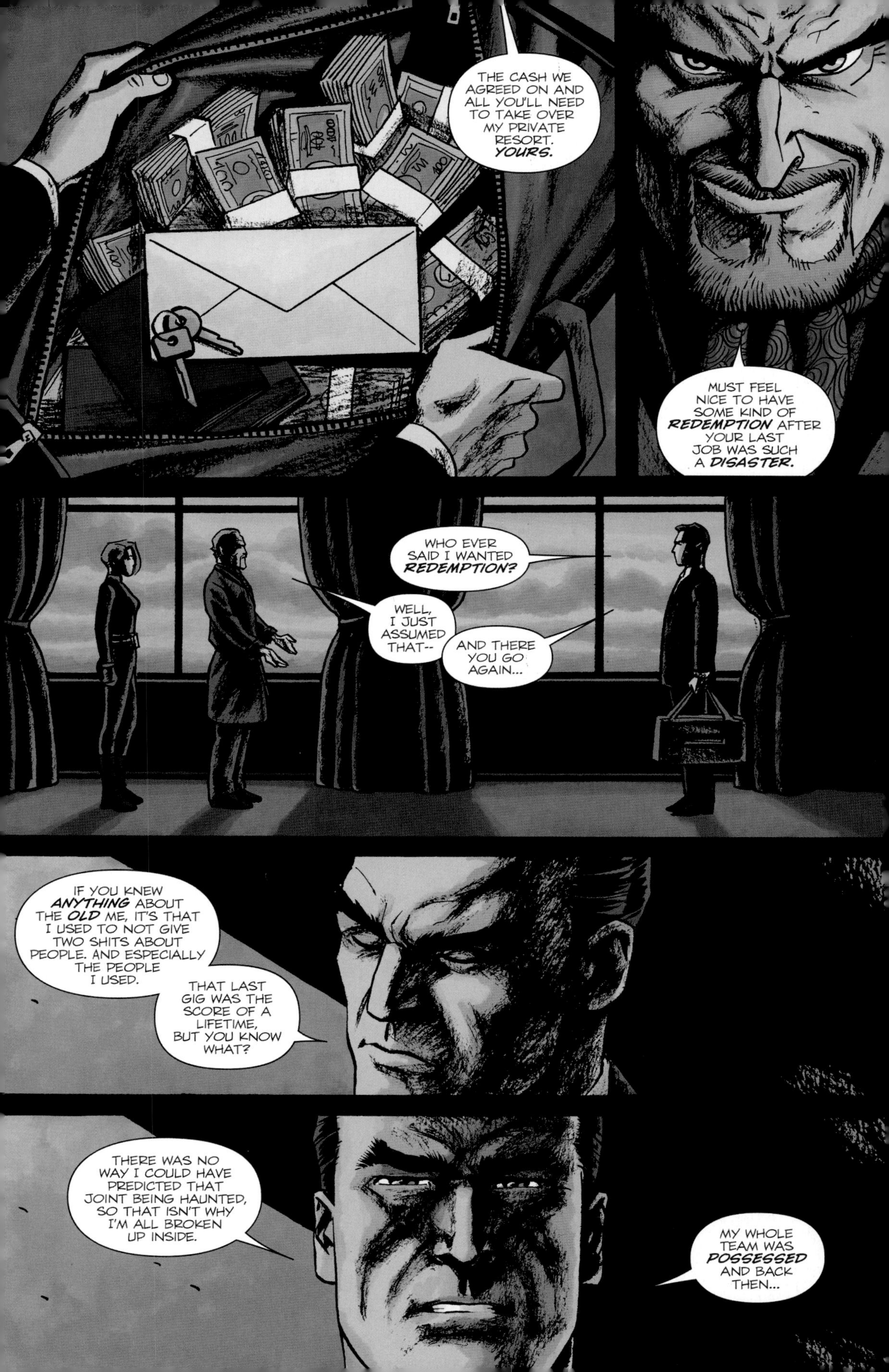
THE CASH WE AGREED ON AND ALL YOU'LL NEED TO TAKE OVER MY PRIVATE RESORT. YOURS.
MUST FEEL NICE TO HAVE SOME KIND OF REDEMPTION AFTER YOUR LAST JOB WAS SUCH A DISASTER.
WHO EVER SAID I WANTED REDEMPTION?
WELL, I JUST ASSUMED THAT--
AND THERE YOU GO AGAIN...
IF YOU KNEW ANYTHING ABOUT THE OLD ME, IT'S THAT I USED TO NOT GIVE TWO SHITS ABOUT PEOPLE. AND ESPECIALLY THE PEOPLE I USED.
THAT LAST GIG WAS THE SCORE OF A LIFETIME, BUT YOU KNOW WHAT?
THERE WAS NO WAY I COULD HAVE PREDICTED THAT JOINT BEING HAUNTED, SO THAT ISN'T WHY I'M ALL BROKEN UP INSIDE.
MY WHOLE TEAM WAS POSSESSED AND BACK THEN...

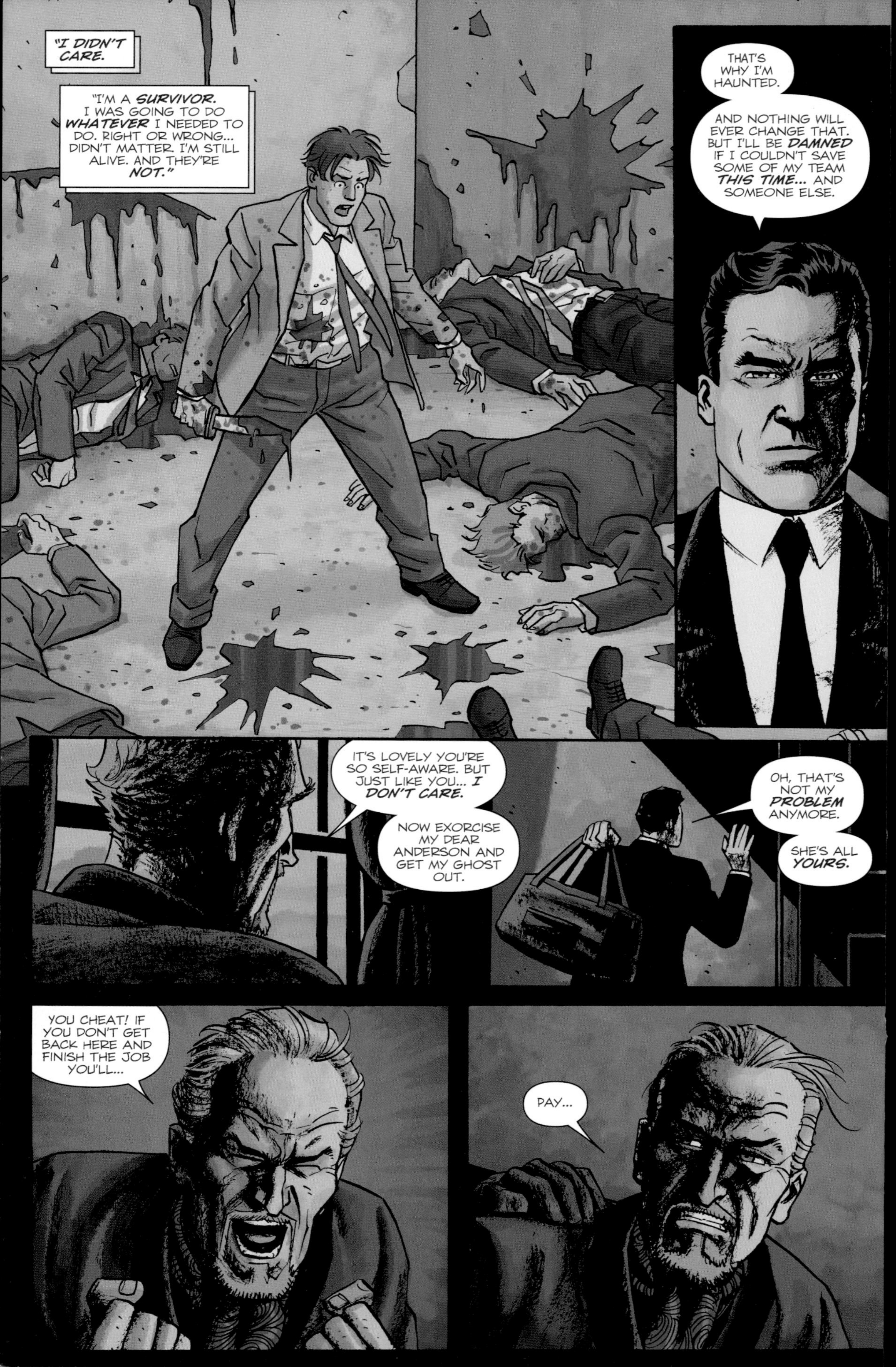
"I DIDN'T CARE.
"I'M A SURVIVOR. I WAS GOING TO DO WHATEVER I NEEDED TO DO. RIGHT OR WRONG... DIDN'T MATTER. I'M STILL ALIVE. AND THEY'RE NOT."
THAT'S WHY I'M HAUNTED.
AND NOTHING WILL EVER CHANGE THAT. BUT I'LL BE DAMNED IF I COULDN'T SAVE SOME OF MY TEAM THIS TIME... AND SOMEONE ELSE.
IT'S LOVELY YOU'RE SO SELF-AWARE. BUT JUST LIKE YOU... I DON'T CARE.
NOW EXORCISE MY DEAR ANDERSON AND GET MY GHOST OUT.
OH, THAT'S NOT MY PROBLEM ANYMORE.
SHE'S ALL YOURS.
YOU CHEAT! IF YOU DON'T GET BACK HERE AND FINISH THE JOB YOU'LL...
PAY...

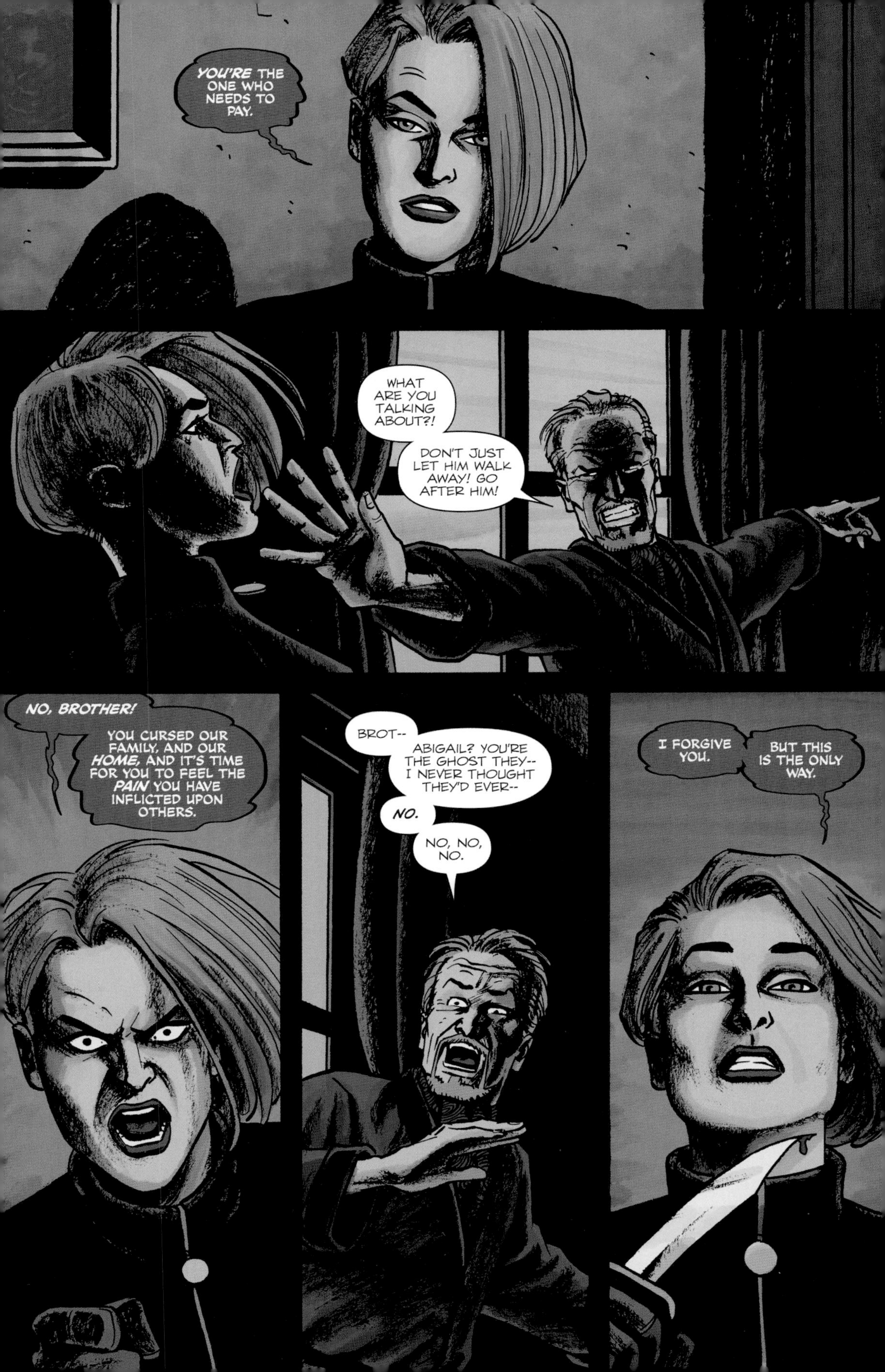
YOU'RE THE ONE WHO NEEDS TO PAY.
WHAT ARE YOU TALKING ABOUT?!
DON'T JUST LET HIM WALK AWAY! GO AFTER HIM!
NO, BROTHER!
YOU CURSED OUR FAMILY, AND OUR HOME, AND IT'S TIME FOR YOU TO FEEL THE PAIN YOU HAVE INFLICTED UPON OTHERS.
BROT--
ABIGAIL? YOU'RE THE GHOST THEY-- I NEVER THOUGHT THEY'D EVER--
NO.
NO, NO, NO.
I FORGIVE YOU.
BUT THIS IS THE ONLY WAY.

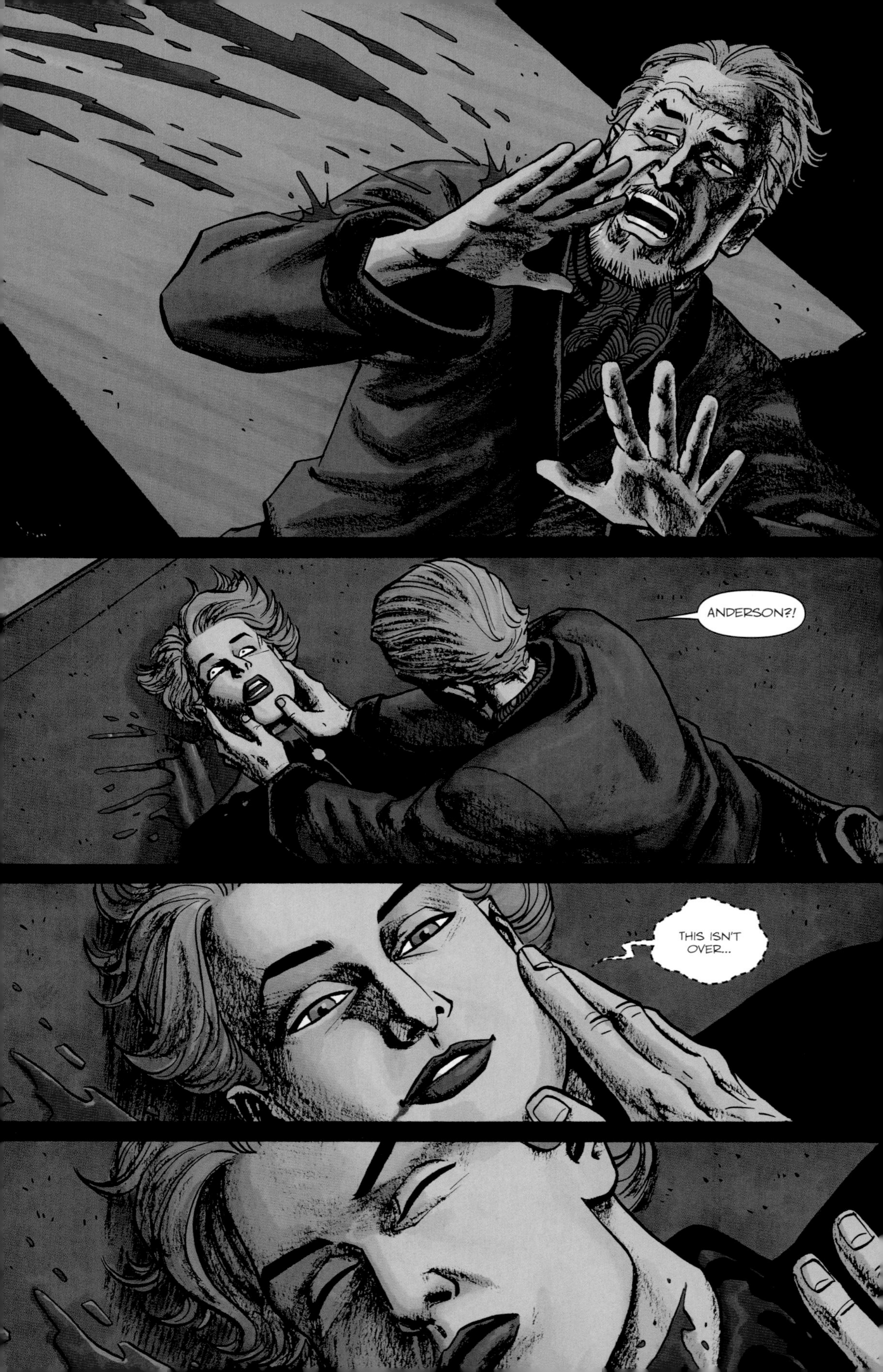
ANDERSON?!
THIS ISN'T OVER...

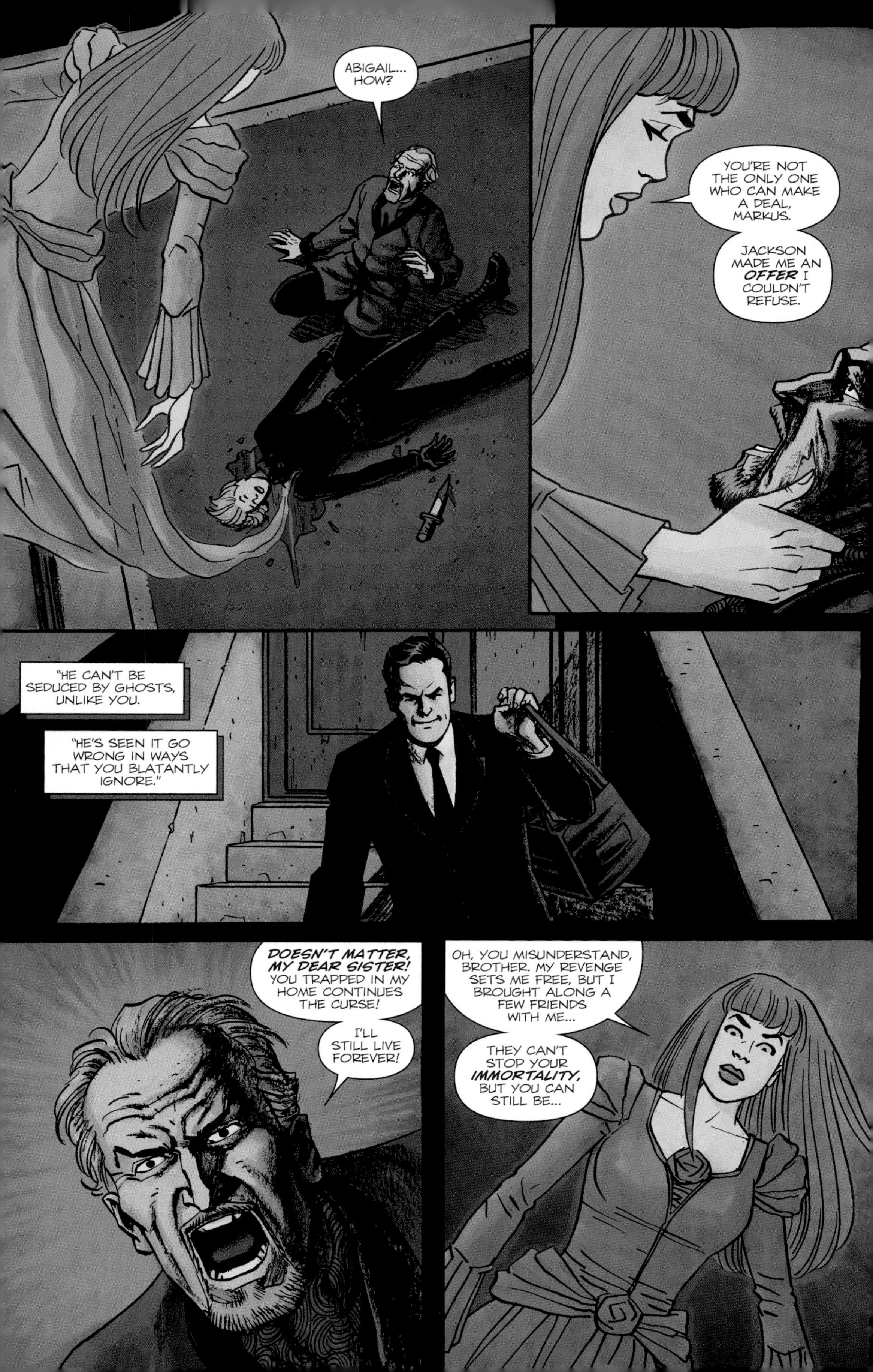
ABIGAIL... HOW?
YOU'RE NOT THE ONLY ONE WHO CAN MAKE A DEAL, MARKUS.
JACKSON MADE ME AN OFFER I COULDN'T REFUSE.
"HE CAN'T BE SEDUCED BY GHOSTS, UNLIKE YOU.
"HE'S SEEN IT GO WRONG IN WAYS THAT YOU BLATANTLY IGNORE."
DOESN'T MATTER, MY DEAR SISTER! YOU TRAPPED IN MY HOME CONTINUES THE CURSE!
I'LL STILL LIVE FOREVER!
OH, YOU MISUNDERSTAND, BROTHER. MY REVENGE SETS ME FREE, BUT I BROUGHT ALONG A FEW FRIENDS WITH ME...
THEY CAN'T STOP YOUR IMMORTALITY, BUT YOU CAN STILL BE...

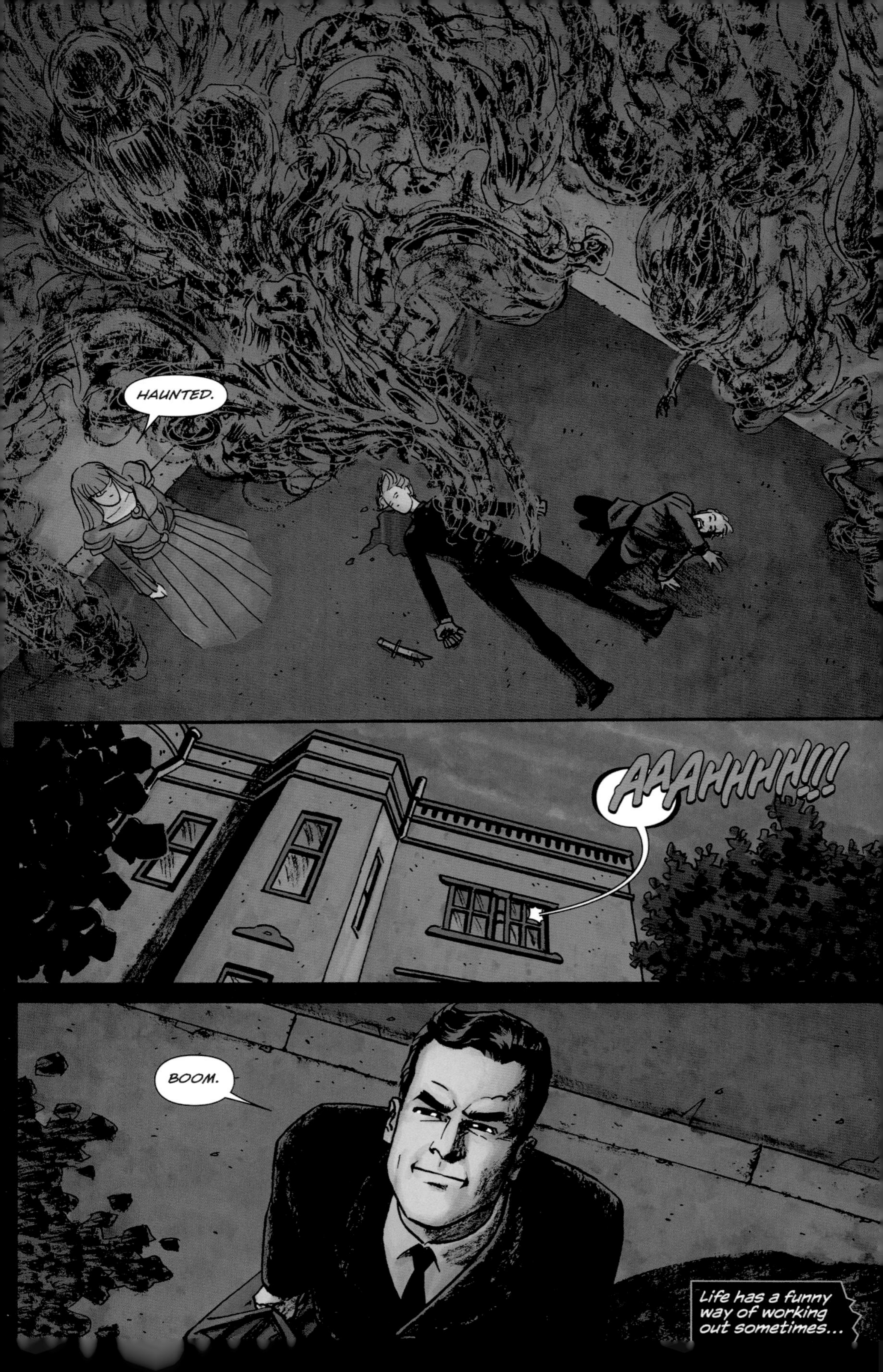
HAUNTED.
AAAHHHH!!!
BOOM.
Life has a funny way of working out sometimes...

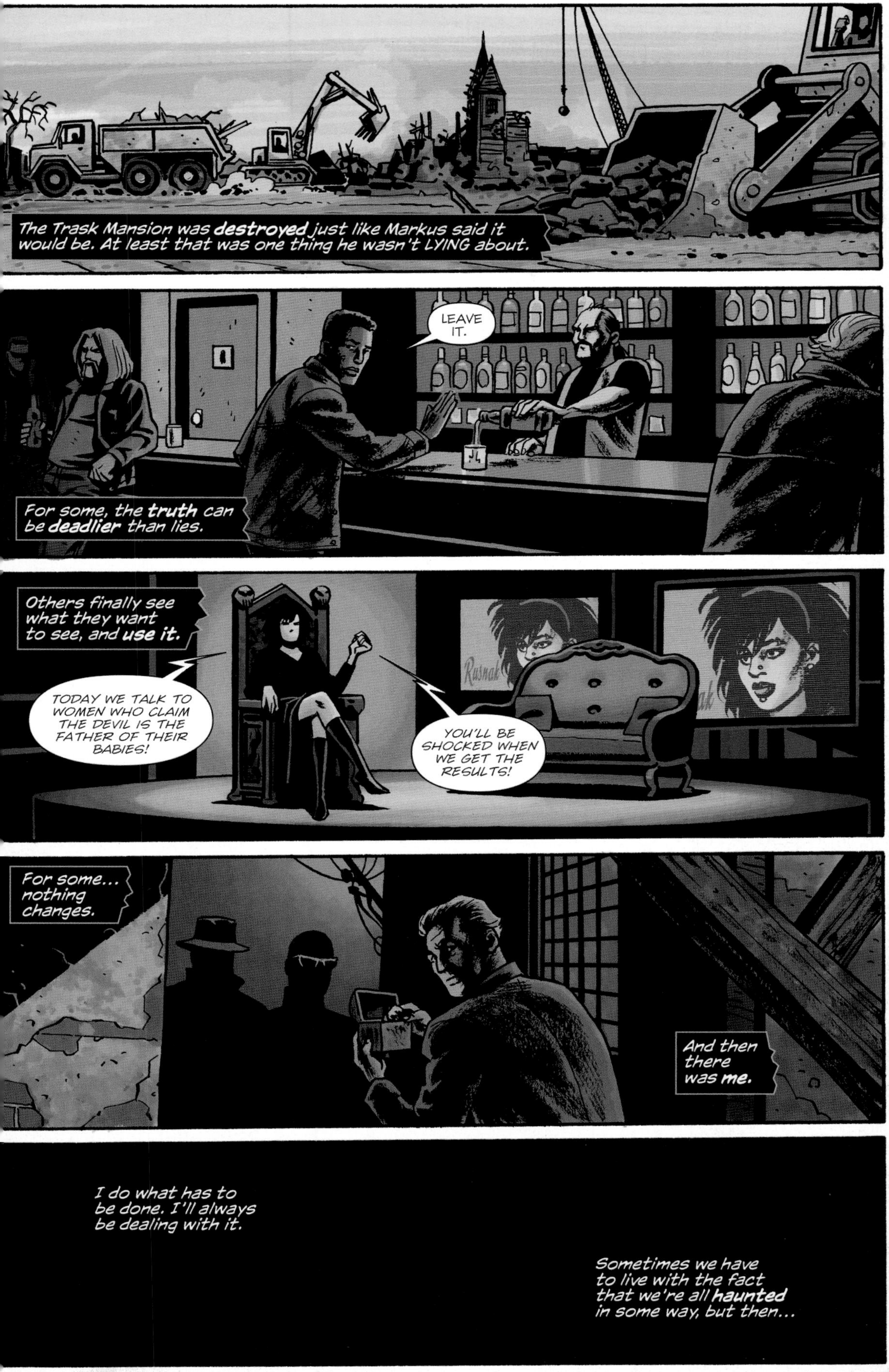
The Trask Mansion was destroyed just like Markus said it would be. At least that was one thing he wasn't LYING about.
LEAVE IT.
For some, the truth can be deadlier than lies.
Others finally see what they want to see, and use it.
TODAY WE TALK TO WOMEN WHO CLAIM THE DEVIL IS THE FATHER OF THEIR BABIES!
YOU'LL BE SHOCKED WHEN WE GET THE RESULTS!
Rusnak
For some... nothing changes.
And then there was me.
I do what has to be done. I'll always be dealing with it.
Sometimes we have to live with the fact that we're all haunted in some way, but then...

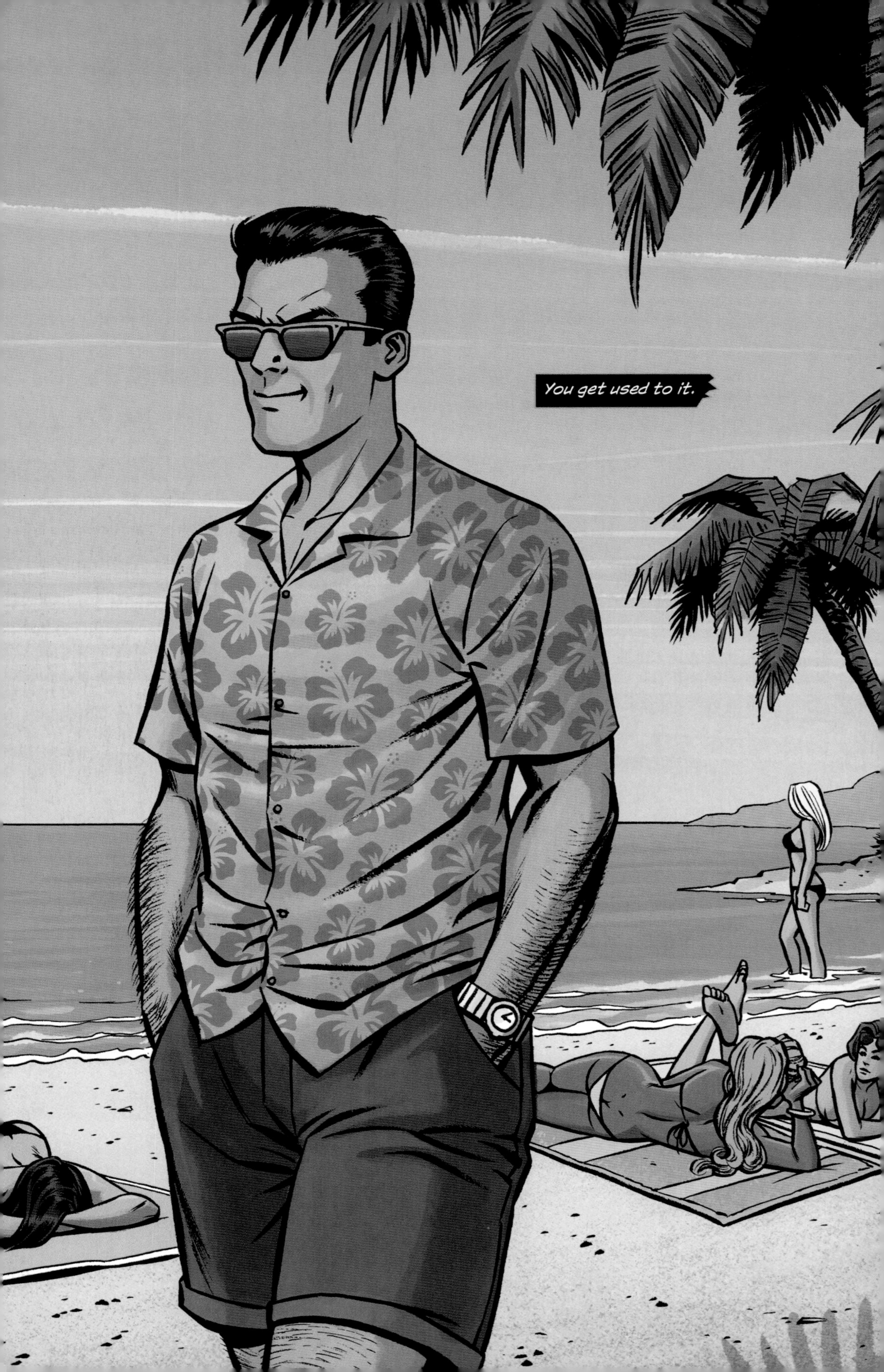
You get used to it.

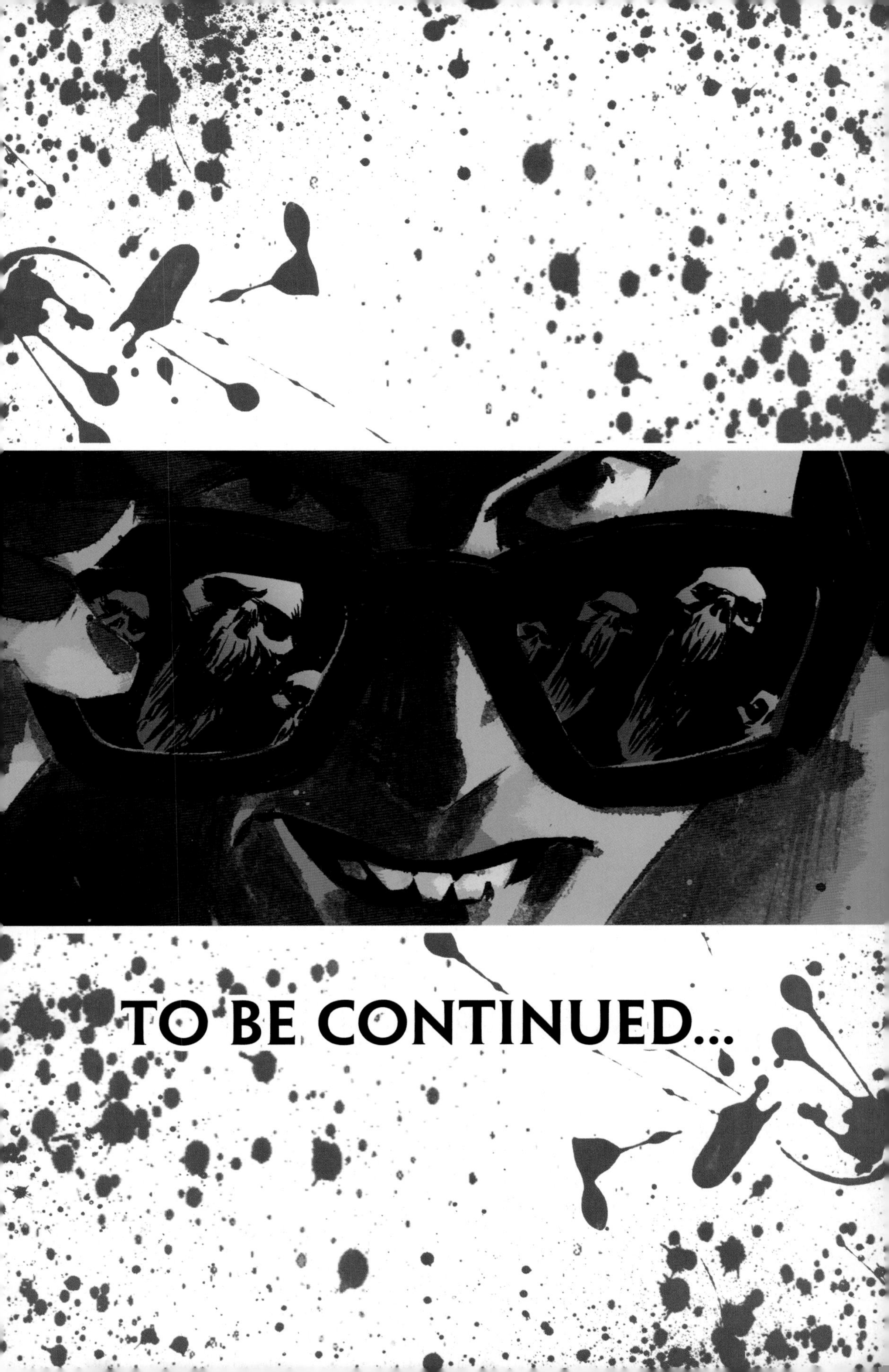
TO BE CONTINUED...

MORE BOOKS FROM
ROBERT KIRKMAN
AND SKYBOUND!

TO FIND YOUR NEAREST COMIC BOOK STORE, CALL:
1-888-COMIC-BOOK

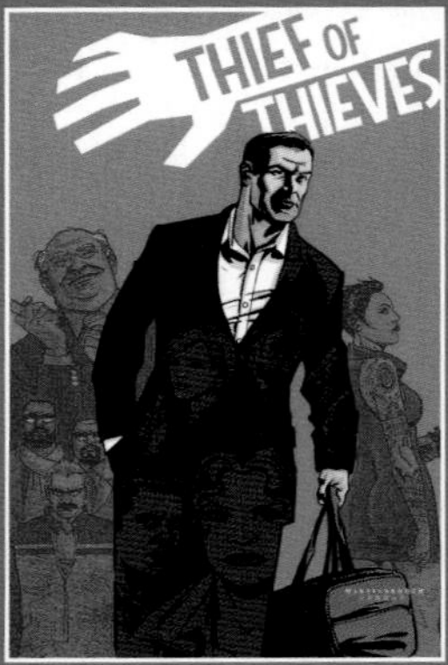
THIEF OF THIEVES

THIEF OF THIEVES
VOL. 1: "I QUIT."
ISBN: 978-1-60706-592-0
$14.99
VOL. 2: "HELP ME."
ISBN: 978-1-60706-676-7
$14.99

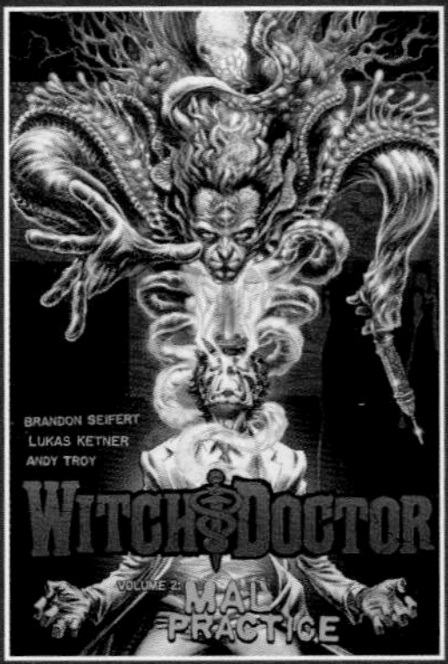
BRANDON SEIFERT
LUKAS KETNER
ANDY TROY
WITCH DOCTOR
VOLUME 2: MAL PRACTICE

WITCH DOCTOR
VOL. 1: UNDER THE KNIFE TP
ISBN: 978-1-60706-441-1
$12.99
VOL. 2: MAL PRACTICE TP
ISBN: 978-1-60706-693-4
$14.99

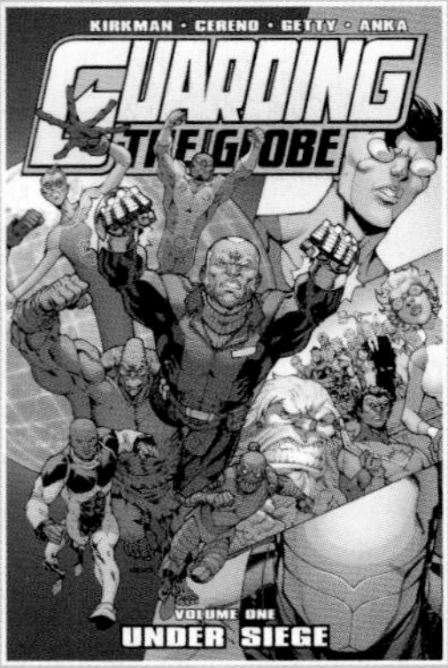
KIRKMAN · CERENO · GETTY · ANKA
GUARDING THE GLOBE
VOLUME ONE
UNDER SIEGE

GUARDING THE GLOBE
VOL. 1: UNDER SIEGE TP
ISBN: 978-1-60706-356-8
$16.99
VOL. 2: HARD TO KILL TP
ISBN: 978-1-60706-673-6
$16.99

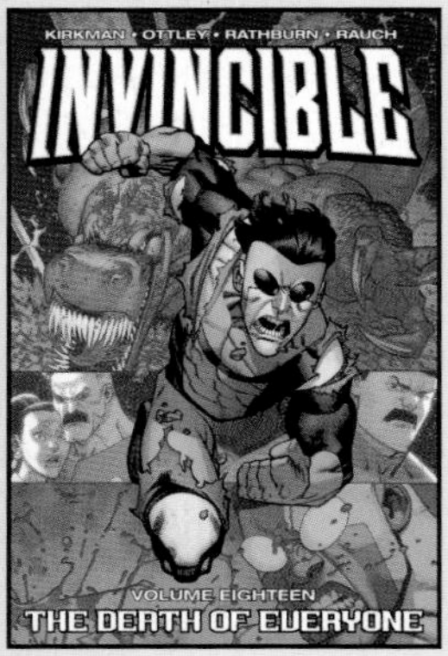
KIRKMAN · OTTLEY · RATHBURN · RAUCH
INVINCIBLE
VOLUME EIGHTEEN
THE DEATH OF EVERYONE

INVINCIBLE
VOL. 1: FAMILY MATTERS TP
ISBN: 978-1-58240-711-1
$12.99
VOL. 2: EIGHT IS ENOUGH TP
ISBN: 978-1-58240-347-2
$12.99
VOL. 3: PERFECT STRANGERS TP
ISBN: 978-1-58240-793-7
$12.99
VOL. 4: HEAD OF THE CLASS TP
ISBN: 978-1-58240-440-2
$14.95
VOL. 5: THE FACTS OF LIFE TP
ISBN: 978-1-58240-554-4
$14.99
VOL. 6: A DIFFERENT WORLD TP
ISBN: 978-1-58240-579-7
$14.99
VOL. 7: THREE'S COMPANY TP
ISBN: 978-1-58240-656-5
$14.99
VOL. 8: MY FAVORITE MARTIAN TP
ISBN: 978-1-58240-683-1
$14.99
VOL. 9: OUT OF THIS WORLD TP
ISBN: 978-1-58240-827-9
$14.99
VOL. 10: WHO'S THE BOSS TP
ISBN: 978-1-60706-013-0
$16.99
VOL. 11: HAPPY DAYS TP
ISBN: 978-1-60706-062-8
$16.99
VOL. 12: STILL STANDING TP
ISBN: 978-1-60706-166-3
$16.99
VOL. 13: GROWING PAINS TP
ISBN: 978-1-60706-251-6
$16.99
VOL. 14: THE VILTRUMITE WAR TP
ISBN: 978-1-60706-367-4
$19.99
VOL. 15: GET SMART TP
ISBN: 978-1-60706-498-5
$16.99
VOL. 16: FAMILY TIES TP
ISBN: 978-1-60706-579-1
$16.99
VOL. 17: WHAT'S HAPPENING TP
ISBN: 978-1-60706-662-0
$16.99
VOL. 18: DEATH OF EVERYONE TP
ISBN: 978-1-60706-762-7
$16.99
ULTIMATE COLLECTION, VOL. 1 HC
ISBN 978-1-58240-500-1
$34.95
ULTIMATE COLLECTION, VOL. 2 HC
ISBN: 978-1-58240-594-0
$34.99
ULTIMATE COLLECTION, VOL. 3 HC
ISBN: 978-1-58240-763-0
$34.99
ULTIMATE COLLECTION, VOL. 4 HC
ISBN: 978-1-58240-989-4
$34.99
ULTIMATE COLLECTION, VOL. 5 HC
ISBN: 978-1-60706-116-8
$34.99
ULTIMATE COLLECTION, VOL. 6 HC
ISBN: 978-1-60706-360-5
$34.99
ULTIMATE COLLECTION, VOL. 7 HC
ISBN: 978-1-60706-509-8
$39.99
ULTIMATE COLLECTION, VOL. 8 HC
ISBN: 978-1-60706-680-4
$39.99
COMPENDIUM VOL. 1
ISBN: 978-1-60706-411-4
$64.99
THE COMPLETE INVINCIBLE LIBRARY, VOL. 2 HC
ISBN: 978-1-60706-112-0
$125.00
THE COMPLETE INVINCIBLE LIBRARY, VOL. 3 HC
ISBN: 978-1-60706-421-3
$125.00
THE OFFICIAL HANDBOOK OF THE INVINCIBLE UNIVERSE TP
ISBN: 978-1-58240-831-6
$12.99
INVINCIBLE PRESENTS, VOL. 1: ATOM EVE & REX SPLODE TP
ISBN: 978-1-60706-255-4
$14.99

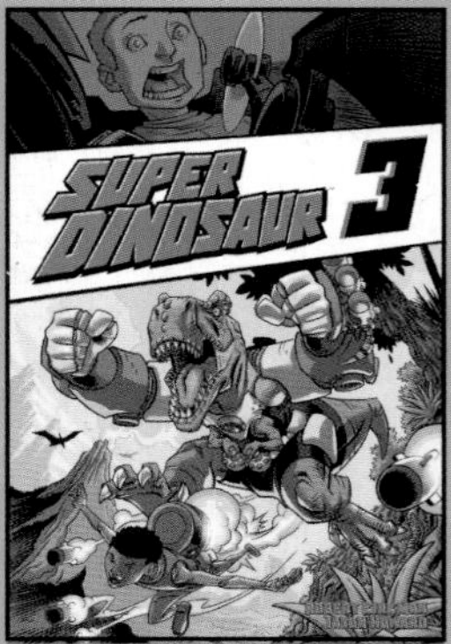
SUPER DINOSAUR 3

SUPER DINOSAUR
VOL. 1
ISBN: 978-1-60706-420-6
$9.99
VOL. 2
ISBN: 978-1-60706-568-5
$12.99
VOL. 3
ISBN: 978-1-60706-667-5
$12.99
DELUXE COLORING BOOK
ISBN: 978-1-60706-481-7
$4.99

THE ASTOUNDING WOLF-MAN
VOL. 1 TP
ISBN: 978-1-58240-862-0
$14.99
VOL. 2 TP
ISBN: 978-1-60706-007-9
$14.99
VOL. 3 TP
ISBN: 978-1-60706-111-3
$16.99
VOL. 4 TP
ISBN: 978-1-60706-249-3
$16.99

BATTLE POPE
VOL. 1: GENESIS TP
ISBN: 978-1-58240-572-8
$14.99
VOL. 2: MAYHEM TP
ISBN: 978-1-58240-529-2
$12.99
VOL. 3: PILLOW TALK TP
ISBN: 978-1-58240-677-0
$12.99
VOL. 4: WRATH OF GOD TP
ISBN: 978-1-58240-751-7
$9.99

BRIT
VOL. 1: OLD SOLDIER TP
ISBN: 978-1-58240-678-7
$14.99
VOL. 2: AWOL
ISBN: 978-1-58240-864-4
$14.99
VOL. 3: FUBAR
ISBN: 978-1-60706-061-1
$16.99

CAPES
VOL. 1: PUNCHING THE CLOCK TP
ISBN: 978-1-58240-756-2
$17.99

HAUNT
VOL. 1 TP
ISBN: 978-1-60706-154-0
$9.99
VOL. 2 TP
ISBN: 978-1-60706-229-5
$16.99
VOL. 3 TP
ISBN: 978-1-60706-552-4
$14.99
THE IMMORTAL EDITION, VOL. 1 HC
ISBN: 978-1-60706-241-7
$34.99

THE INFINITE
VOL. 1 TP
ISBN: 978-1-60706-475-6
$9.99

SUPERPATRIOT
AMERICA'S FIGHTING FORCE
ISBN: 978-1-58240-355-1
$14.99

TALES OF THE REALM
HARDCOVER
ISBN: 978-1-58240-426-0
$34.95
TRADE PAPERBACK
ISBN: 978-1-58240-394-6
$14.95

TECH JACKET
VOL. 1: THE BOY FROM EARTH TP
ISBN: 978-1-58240-771-5
$14.99

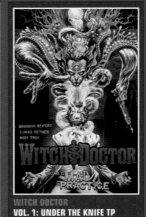